M000289337

NYSTCE
ATS-W SECONDARY ASSESSMENT OF TEACHING SKILLS - WRITTEN 91

By: Sharon Wynne, M.S.

XAMonline, INC.
Boston

To obtain permission(s) to use the material from this work for any purpose including workshops or seminars, please submit a written request to:

XAMonline, Inc.
25 First Street, Suite 106
Cambridge, MA 02141
Toll Free 1-800-509-4128
Email: info@xamonline.com
Web: www.xamonline.com
Fax: 1-617-583-5552

Library of Congress Cataloging-in-Publication Data

Wynne, Sharon A.
    NYSTCE ATS-W Secondary Assessment of Teaching Skills - Written 91 / Sharon A. Wynne. 2nd ed
    ISBN 978-1-60787-155-2
    1. NYSTCE ATS-W Secondary Assessment of Teaching Skills - Written 91
    2. Study Guides
    3. NYSTCE
    4. Teachers' Certification & Licensure
    5. Careers

Disclaimer:

The opinions expressed in this publication are the sole works of XAMonline and were created independently from the National Education Association, Educational Testing Service, or any State Department of Education, National Evaluation Systems or other testing affiliates.

Between the time of publication and printing, state specific standards as well as testing formats and Web site information may change and therefore would not be included in part or in whole within this product. Sample test questions are developed by XAMonline and reflect content similar to that on real tests; however, they are not former test questions. XAMonline assembles content that aligns with state standards but makes no claims nor guarantees teacher candidates a passing score. Numerical scores are determined by testing companies such as NES or ETS and then are compared with individual state standards. A passing score varies from state to state.

Printed in the United States of America   œ-1

NYSTCE ATS-W Secondary Assessment of Teaching Skills - Written 91
ISBN: 978-1-60787-155-2

Table of Contents

COMPETENCY 3

UNDERSTAND HOW FACTORS IN THE HOME, SCHOOL, AND COMMUNITY MAY AFFECT STUDENTS' DEVELOPMENT AND READINESS TO LEARN; AND USE THIS UNDERSTANDING TO CREATE A CLASSROOM ENVIRONMENT WITHIN WHICH ALL STUDENTS CAN DEVELOP AND LEARN

COMPETENCY 4

UNDERSTAND LANGUAGE AND LITERACY DEVELOPMENT, AND USE THIS KNOWLEDGE IN ALL CONTENT AREAS TO DEVELOP THE LISTENING, SPEAKING, READING, AND WRITING SKILLS OF STUDENTS, INCLUDING STUDENTS FOR WHOM ENGLISH IS NOT THEIR PRIMARY LANGUAGE

COMPETENCY 8

UNDERSTAND CURRICULUM DEVELOPMENT, AND APPLY KNOWLEDGE OF FACTORS AND PROCESSES IN CURRICULAR DECISION MAKING 81

COMPETENCY 9

UNDERSTAND THE INTERRELATIONSHIP BETWEEN ASSESSMENT AND INSTRUCTION AND HOW TO USE FORMAL AND INFORMAL ASSESSMENT TO LEARN ABOUT STUDENTS, PLAN INSTRUCTION, MONITOR STUDENT UNDERSTANDING IN THE CONTEXT OF INSTRUCTION, AND MAKE EFFECTIVE INSTRUCTIONAL MODIFICATIONS 87

COMPETENCY 10

UNDERSTAND INSTRUCTIONAL PLANNING AND APPLY KNOWLEDGE OF PLANNING PROCESSES TO DESIGN EFFECTIVE INSTRUCTION THAT PROMOTES THE LEARNING OF ALL STUDENTS 100

COMPETENCY 11

COMPETENCY 12

COMPETENCY 13

COMPETENCY 14

UNDERSTAND COMMUNICATION PRACTICES THAT ARE EFFECTIVE IN PROMOTING STUDENT LEARNING AND CREATING A CLIMATE OF TRUST AND SUPPORT IN THE CLASSROOM, AND HOW TO USE A VARIETY OF COMMUNICATION MODES TO SUPPORT INSTRUCTION

COMPETENCY 15

UNDERSTAND USES OF TECHNOLOGY, INCLUDING INSTRUCTIONAL AND ASSISTIVE TECHNOLOGY, IN TEACHING AND LEARNING; AND APPLY THIS KNOWLEDGE TO USE TECHNOLOGY EFFECTIVELY AND TO TEACH STUDENTS HOW TO USE TECHNOLOGY TO ENHANCE THEIR LEARNING

COMPETENCY 19
UNDERSTAND RECIPROCAL RIGHTS AND RESPONSIBILITIES IN SITUATIONS INVOLVING INTERACTIONS BETWEEN TEACHERS AND STUDENTS, PARENTS, GUARDIANS, COMMUNITY MEMBERS, COLLEAGUES, SCHOOL ADMINISTRATORS, AND OTHER SCHOOL PERSONNEL

SAMPLE TEST

ASSESSMENT OF TEACHING SKILLS— PERFORMANCE (ATS-P)

BONUS SAMPLE TEST

NYSTCE

ATS-W SECONDARY ASSESSMENT OF TEACHING SKILLS - WRITTEN 91

SECTION 1
ABOUT XAMONLINE

XAMonline—A Specialty Teacher Certification Company

Created in 1996, XAMonline was the first company to publish study guides for state-specific teacher certification examinations. Founder Sharon Wynne found it frustrating that materials were not available for teacher certification preparation and decided to create the first single, state-specific guide. XAMonline has grown into a company of over 1,800 contributors and writers and offers over 300 titles for the entire PRAXIS series and every state examination. No matter what state you plan on teaching in, XAMonline has a unique teacher certification study guide just for you.

XAMonline—Value and Innovation

We are committed to providing value and innovation. Our print-on-demand technology allows us to be the first in the market to reflect changes in test standards and user feedback as they occur. Our guides are written by experienced teachers who are experts in their fields. And our content reflects the highest standards of quality. Comprehensive practice tests with varied levels of rigor means that your study experience will closely match the actual in-test experience.

To date, XAMonline has helped nearly 600,000 teachers pass their certification or licensing exams. Our commitment to preparation exceeds simply providing the proper material for study—it extends to helping teachers **gain mastery** of the subject matter, giving them the **tools** to become the most effective classroom leaders possible, and ushering today's students toward a **successful future**.

SECTION 2
ABOUT THIS STUDY GUIDE

Purpose of This Guide

Is there a little voice inside of you saying, "Am I ready?" Our goal is to replace that little voice and remove all doubt with a new voice that says, "I AM READY. **Bring it on!**" by offering the highest quality of teacher certification study guides.

Organization of Content

You will see that while every test may start with overlapping general topics, each is very unique in the skills they wish to test. Only XAMonline presents custom content that analyzes deeper than a title, a subarea, or an objective. Only XAMonline presents content and sample test assessments along with **focus statements**, the deepest-level rationale and interpretation of the skills that are unique to the exam.

Title and field number of test

→Each exam has its own name and number. XAMonline's guides are written to give you the content you need to know for the specific exam you are taking. You can be confident when you buy our guide that it contains the information you need to study for the specific test you are taking.

Subareas

→These are the major content categories found on the exam. XAMonline's guides are written to cover all of the subareas found in the test frameworks developed for the exam.

Objectives

→These are standards that are unique to the exam and represent the main subcategories of the subareas/content categories. XAMonline's guides are written to address every specific objective required to pass the exam.

Focus statements

→These are examples and interpretations of the objectives. You find them in parenthesis directly following the objective. They provide detailed examples of the range, type, and level of content that appear on the test questions. **Only XAMonline's guides drill down to this level.**

How do we compare with our competitors?

XAMonline—drills down to the focus statement level.
CliffsNotes and REA—organized at the objective level
Kaplan—provides only links to content
MoMedia—content not specific to the state test

Each subarea is divided into manageable sections that cover the specific skill areas. Explanations are easy to understand and thorough. You'll find that every test answer contains a rejoinder so if you need a refresher or further review after taking the test, you'll know exactly to which section you must return.

How to Use This Book

Our informal polls show that most people begin studying up to eight weeks prior to the test date, so start early. Then ask yourself some questions: How much do you really know? Are you coming to the test straight from your teacher-education program or are you having to review subjects you haven't considered in ten years? Either way, take a **diagnostic or assessment test** first. Also, spend time on sample tests so that you become accustomed to the way the actual test will appear.

This guide comes with an online diagnostic test of 30 questions found online at *www.XAMonline.com*. It is a little boot camp to get you up for the task and reveal things about your compendium of knowledge in general. Although this guide is structured to follow the order of the test, you are not required to study in that order. By finding a time-management and study plan that fits your life you will be more effective. The results of your diagnostic or self-assessment test can be a guide for how to manage your time and point you toward an area that needs more attention.

After taking the diagnostic exam, fill out the **Personalized Study Plan** page at the beginning of each chapter. Review the competencies and skills covered in that chapter and check the boxes that apply to your study needs. If there are sections you already know you can skip, check the "skip it" box. Taking this step will give you a study plan for each chapter.

Week	Activity
8 weeks prior to test	Take a diagnostic test found at www.XAMonline.com
7 weeks prior to test	Build your Personalized Study Plan for each chapter. Check the "skip it" box for sections you feel you are already strong in. ✗ **SKIP IT** ☐
6-3 weeks prior to test	For each of these four weeks, choose a content area to study. You don't have to go in the order of the book. It may be that you start with the content that needs the most review. Alternately, you may want to ease yourself into plan by starting with the most familiar material.
2 weeks prior to test	Take the sample test, score it, and create a review plan for the final week before the test.
1 week prior to test	Following your plan (which will likely be aligned with the areas that need the most review) go back and study the sections that align with the questions you may have gotten wrong. Then go back and study the sections related to the questions you answered correctly. If need be, create flashcards and drill yourself on any area that you makes you anxious.

SECTION 3
ABOUT THE NYSTCE SECONDARY ASSESSMENT OF TEACHING SKILLS 91 (ATS-W)

What Is the NYSTCE Secondary Assessment of Teaching Skills 91 (ATS-W)?

The NYSTCE Secondary Assessment of Teaching Skills 91 (ATS-W) is meant to assess mastery of the basic pedagogical knowledge and skills required to teach students in New York public schools. It is administered by Pearson Education on behalf of the New York Department of Education.

Often **your own state's requirements** determine whether or not you should take any particular test. The most reliable source of information regarding this is your state's Department of Education. This resource should have a complete list of testing centers and dates. Test dates vary by subject area and not all test dates necessarily include your particular test, so be sure to check carefully.

If you are in a teacher-education program, check with the Education Department or the Certification Officer for specific information for testing and testing timelines. The Certification Office should have most of the information you need.

If you choose an alternative route to certification you can either rely on our Web site at *www.XAMonline.com* or on the resources provided by an alternative certification program. Many states now have specific agencies devoted to alternative certification and there are some national organizations as well, for example:

National Association for Alternative Certification
http://www.alt-teachercert.org/index.asp

Interpreting Test Results

Contrary to what you may have heard, the results of the NYSTCE Secondary Assessment of Teaching Skills 91 (ATS-W) are not based on time. More accurately, you will be scored on the raw number of points you earn in relation to the raw number of points available. Each question is worth one raw point. It is likely to your benefit to complete as many questions in the time allotted, but it will not necessarily work to your advantage if you hurry through the test.

Follow the guidelines provided by Pearson for interpreting your score. The Web site offers a sample test score sheet and clearly explains how/whether the scores are scaled and what to expect if you have an essay portion on your test.

What's on the Test?

The NYSTCE Secondary Assessment of Teaching Skills 91 (ATS-W) consists of approximately 80 multiple-choice questions and 1 constructed-response essay. The breakdown of the questions is as follows:

Category	Question Type	Approximate Percentage of the Test
I: Student Development and Learning	Multiple choice	25%
II: Instruction and Assessment	Multiple choice	38%
III: The Professional Environment	Multiple choice	17%
IV: Instruction and Assessment	Constructed response	20%

Question Types

You're probably thinking, enough already, I want to study! Indulge us a little longer while we explain that there is actually more than one type of multiple-choice question. You can thank us later after you realize how well prepared you are for your exam.

1. Complete the Statement. The name says it all. In this question type you'll be asked to choose the correct completion of a given statement. For example:

> The Dolch Basic Sight Words consist of a relatively short list of words that children should be able to:
>
> A. Sound out
>
> B. Know the meaning of
>
> C. Recognize on sight
>
> D. Use in a sentence

The correct answer is A. In order to check your answer, test out the statement by adding the choices to the end of it.

2. **Which of the Following.** One way to test your answer choice for this type of question is to replace the phrase "which of the following" with your selection. Use this example:

> **Which of the following words is one of the twelve most frequently used in children's reading texts:**
>
> A. There
>
> B. This
>
> C. The
>
> D. An

Don't look! Test your answer. _____ is one of the twelve most frequently used in children's reading texts. Did you guess C? Then you guessed correctly.

3. **Roman Numeral Choices.** This question type is used when there is more than one possible correct answer. For example:

> **Which of the following two arguments accurately supports the use of cooperative learning as an effective method of instruction?**
> I.   Cooperative learning groups facilitate healthy competition between individuals in the group.
> II. Cooperative learning groups allow academic achievers to carry or cover for academic underachievers.
> III. Cooperative learning groups make each student in the group accountable for the success of the group.
> IV. Cooperative learning groups make it possible for students to reward other group members for achieving.
>
> A. I and II
>
> B. II and III
>
> C. I and III
>
> D. III and IV

Notice that the question states there are **two** possible answers. It's best to read all the possibilities first before looking at the answer choices. In this case, the correct answer is D.

4. **Negative Questions.** This type of question contains words such as "not," "least," and "except." Each correct answer will be the statement that does **not** fit the situation described in the question. Such as:

> **Multicultural education is not**
>
> A. An idea or concept
>
> B. A "tack-on" to the school curriculum
>
> C. An educational reform movement
>
> D. A process

Think to yourself that the statement could be anything but the correct answer. This question form is more open to interpretation than other types, so read carefully and don't forget that you're answering a negative statement.

5. **Questions that Include Graphs, Tables, or Reading Passages.** As always, read the question carefully. It likely asks for a very specific answer and not a broad interpretation of the visual. Here is a simple (though not statistically accurate) example of a graph question:

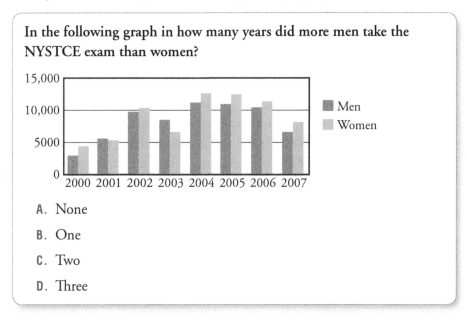

> **In the following graph in how many years did more men take the NYSTCE exam than women?**
>
> A. None
>
> B. One
>
> C. Two
>
> D. Three

It may help you to simply circle the two years that answer the question. Make sure you've read the question thoroughly and once you've made your determination, double check your work. The correct answer is C.

SECTION 4
HELPFUL HINTS

Study Tips

1. **You are what you eat.** Certain foods aid the learning process by releasing natural memory enhancers called CCKs (cholecystokinin) composed of tryptophan, choline, and phenylalanine. All of these chemicals enhance the neurotransmitters associated with memory and certain foods release memory enhancing chemicals. A light meal or snacks of one of the following foods fall into this category:

   - Milk
   - Rice
   - Eggs
   - Fish
   - Nuts and seeds
   - Oats
   - Turkey

   The better the connections, the more you comprehend!

2. **See the forest for the trees.** In other words, get the concept before you look at the details. One way to do this is to take notes as you read, paraphrasing or summarizing in your own words. Putting the concept in terms that are comfortable and familiar may increase retention.

3. **Question authority.** Ask why, why, why? Pull apart written material paragraph by paragraph and don't forget the captions under the illustrations. For example, if a heading reads *Stream Erosion* put it in the form of a question (Why do streams erode? What is stream erosion?) then find the answer within the material. If you train your mind to think in this manner you will learn more and prepare yourself for answering test questions.

4. **Play mind games.** Using your brain for reading or puzzles keeps it flexible. Even with a limited amount of time your brain can take in data (much like a computer) and store it for later use. In ten minutes you can: read two paragraphs (at least), quiz yourself with flash cards, or review notes. Even if you don't fully understand something on the first pass, your mind stores it for recall, which is why frequent reading or review increases chances of retention and comprehension.

5. **Get pointed in the right direction.** Use arrows to point to important passages or pieces of information. It's easier to read than a page full of yellow highlights. Highlighting can be used sparingly, but add an arrow to the margin to call attention to it.

6. The pen is mightier than the sword. Learn to take great notes. A by-product of our modern culture is that we have grown accustomed to getting our information in short doses. We've subconsciously trained ourselves to assimilate information into neat little packages. Messy notes fragment the flow of information. Your notes can be much clearer with proper formatting. *The Cornell Method* is one such format. This method was popularized in *How to Study in College*, Ninth Edition, by Walter Pauk. You can benefit from the method without purchasing an additional book by simply looking up the method online. Below is a sample of how *The Cornell Method* can be adapted for use with this guide.

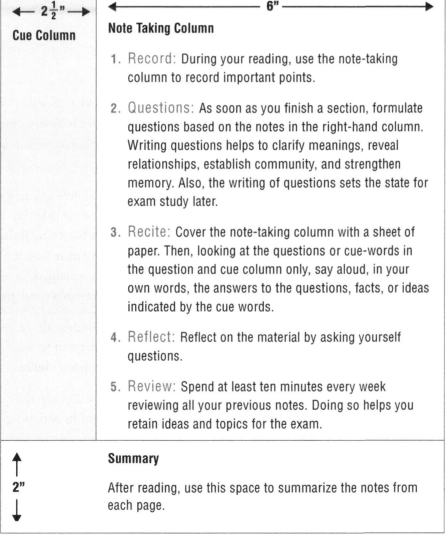

← 2½" → Cue Column	←————————— 6" —————————→ Note Taking Column
	1. Record: During your reading, use the note-taking column to record important points.
	2. Questions: As soon as you finish a section, formulate questions based on the notes in the right-hand column. Writing questions helps to clarify meanings, reveal relationships, establish community, and strengthen memory. Also, the writing of questions sets the state for exam study later.
	3. Recite: Cover the note-taking column with a sheet of paper. Then, looking at the questions or cue-words in the question and cue column only, say aloud, in your own words, the answers to the questions, facts, or ideas indicated by the cue words.
	4. Reflect: Reflect on the material by asking yourself questions.
	5. Review: Spend at least ten minutes every week reviewing all your previous notes. Doing so helps you retain ideas and topics for the exam.
↑ 2" ↓	**Summary** After reading, use this space to summarize the notes from each page.

Adapted from How to Study in College, Ninth Edition, by Walter Pauk, ©2008 Wadsworth

7. **Place yourself in exile and set the mood.** Set aside a particular place and time to study that best suits your personal needs and biorhythms. If you're a night person, burn the midnight oil. If you're a morning person set yourself up with some coffee and get to it. Make your study time and place as free from distraction as possible and surround yourself with what you need, be it silence or music. Studies have shown that music can aid in concentration, absorption, and retrieval of information. Not all music, though. Classical music is said to work best

The proctor will write the start time where it can be seen and then, later, provide the time remaining, typically fifteen minutes before the end of the test.

8. **Check your budget.** You should at least review all the content material before your test, but allocate the most amount of time to the areas that need the most refreshing. It sounds obvious, but it's easy to forget. You can use the study rubric above to balance your study budget.

Testing Tips

1. **Get smart, play dumb.** Sometimes a question is just a question. No one is out to trick you, so don't assume that the test writer is looking for something other than what was asked. Stick to the question as written and don't overanalyze.

2. **Do a double take.** Read test questions and answer choices at least twice because it's easy to miss something, to transpose a word or some letters. If you have no idea what the correct answer is, skip it and come back later if there's time. If you're still clueless, it's okay to guess. Remember, you're scored on the number of questions you answer correctly and you're not penalized for wrong answers. The worst case scenario is that you miss a point from a good guess.

3. **Turn it on its ear.** The syntax of a question can often provide a clue, so make things interesting and turn the question into a statement to see if it changes the meaning or relates better (or worse) to the answer choices.

4. **Get out your magnifying glass.** Look for hidden clues in the questions because it's difficult to write a multiple-choice question without giving away part of the answer in the options presented. In most questions you can readily eliminate one or two potential answers, increasing your chances of answering correctly to 50/50, which will help out if you've skipped a question and gone back to it (see tip #2).

5. **Call it intuition.** Often your first instinct is correct. If you've been studying the content you've likely absorbed something and have subconsciously retained the knowledge. On questions you're not sure about trust your instincts because a first impression is usually correct.

6. Graffiti. Sometimes it's a good idea to mark your answers directly on the test booklet and go back to fill in the optical scan sheet later. You don't get extra points for perfectly blackened ovals. If you choose to manage your test this way, be sure not to mismark your answers when you transcribe to the scan sheet.

7. Become a clock-watcher. You have a set amount of time to answer the questions. Don't get bogged down laboring over a question you're not sure about when there are ten others you could answer more readily. If you choose to follow the advice of tip #5, be sure you leave time near the end to go back and fill in the scan sheet.

Do the Drill

No matter how prepared you feel it's sometimes a good idea to apply Murphy's Law. So the following tips might seem silly, mundane, or obvious, but we're including them anyway.

1. Remember, you are what you eat, so bring a snack. Choose from the list of energizing foods that appear earlier in the introduction.

2. You're not too sexy for your test. Wear comfortable clothes. You'll be distracted if your belt is too tight or if you're too cold or too hot.

3. Lie to yourself. Even if you think you're a prompt person, pretend you're not and leave plenty of time to get to the testing center. Map it out ahead of time and do a dry run if you have to. There's no need to add road rage to your list of anxieties.

4. Bring sharp number 2 pencils. It may seem impossible to forget this need from your school days, but you might. And make sure the erasers are intact, too.

5. No ticket, no test. Bring your admission ticket as well as **two** forms of identification, including one with a picture and signature. You will not be admitted to the test without these things.

6. You can't take it with you. Leave any study aids, dictionaries, notebooks, computers, and the like at home. Certain tests **do** allow a scientific or four-function calculator, so check ahead of time to see if your test does.

7. Prepare for the desert. Any time spent on a bathroom break **cannot** be made up later, so use your judgment on the amount you eat or drink.

8. Quiet, Please! Keeping your own time is a good idea, but not with a timepiece that has a loud ticker. If you use a watch, take it off and place it nearby but not so that it distracts you. And **silence your cell phone**.

To the best of our ability, we have compiled the content you need to know in this book and in the accompanying online resources. The rest is up to you. You can use the study and testing tips or you can follow your own methods. Either way, you can be confident that there aren't any missing pieces of information and there shouldn't be any surprises in the content on the test.

If you have questions about test fees, registration, electronic testing, or other content verification issues please visit *www.nystce.nesinc.com*.

Good luck!

Sharon Wynne
Founder, XAMonline

DOMAIN I
STUDENT DEVELOPMENT AND LEARNING

PERSONALIZED STUDY PLAN

KNOWN MATERIAL/ SKIP IT

PAGE		COMPETENCY AND SKILL	KNOWN MATERIAL/ SKIP IT
5	**1:**	**Understand human development, including developmental processes and variations, and use this understanding to promote student development and learning**	☐
	1.1:	Demonstrates knowledge of adolescent human development	☑
	1.2:	Identifies physical, cognitive, linguistic, social, emotional, and moral development of students	☑
	1.3:	Recognizes development differences in students and the implications of this developmental variation	☑
	1.4:	Identifies how a student's development may affect learning	☐
	1.5:	Applies knowledge of developmental characteristics to evaluate instructional goals	☐
	1.6:	Selects appropriate instructional strategies to promote development and learning	☐
13	**2:**	**Understand learning processes, and use this understanding to promote student development and learning**	☐
	2.1:	Analyzes how development and learning processes interact	☐
	2.2:	Analyzes how students construct meaning and develop skills	☐
	2.3:	Demonstrates knowledge of learning strategies	☐
	2.4:	Analyzes factors that affect student learning	☐
	2.5:	Recognizes how teacher and student roles affect learning	☐
	2.6:	Recognizes strategies for promoting independent thinking and learning	☐
24	**3:**	**Understand how factors in the home, school, and community may affect students' development and readiness to learn; and use this understanding to create a classroom environment within which all students can develop and learn**	☐
	3.1:	Recognizes the impact of socio-cultural factors on learning	☐
	3.2:	Analyzes how students' personal health may affect their development and learning	☐
	3.3:	Recognizes how family life and home environment affect student development and learning	☐
	3.4:	Analyzes how school-wide structures and classroom factors may affect self-concept and learning	☐
	3.5:	Identifies classroom strategies that promote student development and learning	☐
	3.6:	Analyzes how peer interactions may promote or hinder a student's development	☐
	3.7:	Demonstrates knowledge of health, sexuality, and peer-related issues	☐

PERSONALIZED STUDY PLAN

KNOWN MATERIAL/ SKIP IT

PAGE	COMPETENCY AND SKILL	KNOWN MATERIAL/ SKIP IT
37	**4: Understand language and literacy development, and use this knowledge in all content areas to develop the listening, speaking, reading, and writing skills of students, including students for whom English is not their primary language**	☐
	4.1: Identifies factors that influence language acquisition	☐
	4.2: Identifies expected stages and patterns of second-language acquisition	☐
	4.3: Identifies approaches that are effective in promoting ELL development	☐
	4.4: Recognizes the role of oral language development in the development of English literacy	☐
	4.5: Identifies factors that influence literacy development	☐
	4.6: Recognizes similarities and differences between the English literacy development of native English speakers and ELLs	☐
	4.7: Uses knowledge of literacy development to select appropriate instructional strategies	☐
51	**5: Understand diverse student populations, and use knowledge of diversity within the school and the community to address the needs of all learners, to create a sense of community among students, and to promote students' appreciation of and respect for individuals and groups**	☐
	5.1: Recognizes strategies for teachers to understand students and promote community among diverse student groups	☐
	5.2: Applies strategies for working effectively with students from all cultures, socioeconomic circumstances, and home situations	☐
	5.3: Applies strategies for promoting diversity within the classroom and community	☐
	5.4: Analyzes how classroom environments that respect diversity promote positive student experiences	☐

PERSONALIZED STUDY PLAN

KNOWN MATERIAL/ SKIP IT

PAGE	COMPETENCY AND SKILL	
57	**6: Understand the characteristics and needs of students with disabilities, developmental delays, and exceptional abilities (including gifted and talented students); and use this knowledge to help students reach their highest levels of achievement and independence**	☐
	6.1: Demonstrates awareness of disabilities, delays, and abilities and their implications for learning	☐
	6.2: Applies criteria for evaluating, selecting, creating, and modifying materials and equipment to address individual special needs	☐
	6.3: Identifies teacher responsibilities and requirements associated with referring students for Individualized Education Plans (IEPs)	☐
	6.4: Demonstrates knowledge of basic service delivery models for students with special needs	☐
	6.5: Demonstrates knowledge of strategies to ensure that special needs students participate in all classroom activities	☐

COMPETENCY 1

UNDERSTAND HUMAN DEVELOPMENT, INCLUDING DEVELOPMENTAL PROCESSES AND VARIATIONS, AND USE THIS UNDERSTANDING TO PROMOTE STUDENT DEVELOPMENT AND LEARNING

> **SKILL 1.1** **Demonstrates knowledge of the major concepts, principles, and theories of human development** *(physical, cognitive, linguistic, social, emotional, and moral)* **as related to young adolescents and adolescents**

To be successful, a teacher must have a broad knowledge and thorough understanding of the development that typically occurs during the students' current period of life. More important, the teacher must understand how children learn best during each period of development. The most important premise of child development is that all domains of development (physical, social, and academic) are integrated. Development in each dimension is influenced by the other dimensions. Moreover, today's educator must also have knowledge of exceptionalities and how these exceptionalities affect all domains of a child's development.

Physical Development

It is important for the teacher to be aware of the physical stage of development and how the child's physical growth and development affect the child's cognitive learning. Factors determined by the physical stage of development include:

- Ability to sit and attend

- The need for activity

- The relationship between physical skills and self-esteem

- The degree to which physical involvement in an activity (as opposed to being able to understand an abstract concept) affects learning

Cognitive (Academic) Development

Children go through patterns of learning, beginning with preoperational thought processes, and they move to concrete operational thoughts. Eventually they begin to acquire the mental ability to think about and solve problems in their heads because they can manipulate objects symbolically. Children of most ages can use symbols such as words and numbers to represent objects and relations, but they need concrete reference points. To facilitate cognitive development, it is essential that children be encouraged to use and develop the thinking skills that they possess in solving problems that interest them. The content of the curriculum must be relevant, engaging, and meaningful to the students.

Social Development

Children progress through a variety of social stages. First, they begin with an awareness of their peers but have a lack of concern for the presence of these other children. Young children engage in "parallel" activities, playing alongside their peers without directly interacting with one another. Next, during the primary years, children develop an intense interest in peers. They establish productive, positive social and working relationships with one another. This stage of social growth continues throughout the child's formative period including the primary, middle, and high school years. It is necessary for teachers to recognize the importance of developing positive peer-group relationships and to provide opportunities and support for cooperative small group projects that not only develop cognitive ability but also promote peer interaction. The ability to work and relate effectively with peers is of major importance and contributes greatly to the child's sense of competence. In order to develop this sense of competence, children need to be successful in acquiring the knowledge and skills recognized by their culture as important; in the United States, among the most important are those skills that promote academic achievement.

> **SKILL 1.2** **Identifies sequences** *(milestones)* **and variations of physical, cognitive, linguistic, social, emotional, and moral development of students**

See also Skill 1.1

Students at the middle level are continually undergoing physical and emotional changes and development. No matter how well we might try to prepare them for this, they have no point of reference within their own life experiences. Everything that is occurring to them is new and unfamiliar to these students and often makes them uncomfortable about themselves and in the company of others. Often these physical, hormonal, and emotional changes will occur in spurts, moving some ahead of their peers, in general, and leaving some behind. In most cases, the individual feels different and often is treated as different by his or her peers. The

> *Students at the middle level are continually undergoing physical and emotional changes and development.*

student may feel socially awkward, and this may be reflected in schoolwork and especially in classroom participation. The teacher must be sensitive to the issues of a developing child and aware of the impact this may have on student learning, classroom decorum, and the cohesion among classmates that the teacher is trying to foster.

Adolescent Development

The teacher of students in later childhood and early adolescence should have a broad knowledge and understanding of the phases of development that typically occur during this stage of life. And the teacher must be aware of how receptive children are to specific methods of instruction and learning during each period of development. A significant premise in the study of child development holds that all domains of development (physical, social, and academic) are integrated; development in each dimension is influenced by the others. Equally important to the teacher's understanding of the process is the knowledge that developmental advances within the domains occur neither simultaneously nor parallel to one another, necessarily.

A significant premise in the study of child development holds that all domains of development (physical, social, and academic) are integrated; development in each dimension is influenced by the others.

Impact of physical changes

Early adolescence is characterized by dramatic physical changes moving the individual from childhood toward physical maturity. Early, prepubescent changes are noted with the appearance of secondary sexual characteristics. Girls experience a concurrent rapid growth in height that occurs between the ages of about 9.5 and 14.5 years, peaking somewhere around 12 years of age. Boys experience a concurrent rapid growth in height that occurs between the ages of about 10.5 to 11 and 16 to 18, peaking around age 14.

The sudden and rapid physical changes that young adolescents experience typically cause this period of development to be one of self-consciousness, sensitivity and concern over one's own body changes, and excruciating comparisons between oneself and peers. Because physical changes may not occur in a smooth, regular schedule, adolescents may go through stages of awkwardness, both in terms of appearance and physical mobility and coordination.

The sudden and rapid physical changes that young adolescents experience typically cause this period of development to be one of self-consciousness, sensitivity and concern over one's own body changes, and excruciating comparisons between oneself and peers.

The impact of these physical changes on individual students is to make them more self-aware, more self-conscious, and more self-absorbed. Constant comparison with peers developing at different rates will cause many individuals to feel inadequate or inferior, at least at times. While remaining sensitive to the genuine, emotional response of early adolescents to changes they cannot control and do not fully comprehend, the teacher will find it necessary to be more proactive in bringing students out of themselves and becoming interactive participants in the classroom learning experience.

SKILL 1.3 Recognizes the range of individual development differences in students within any given age group and the implications of this developmental variation for instructional decision making

Knowledge of age-appropriate expectations is fundamental to the teacher's positive relationship with students and being able to utilize effective instructional strategies. Equally important is the knowledge of what is individually appropriate for the specific children within a classroom. In this way, teachers are able to approach classroom groups and individual students with a respect for their emerging capabilities and meet the developmental needs of their students.

Differences in Development

Developmentalists recognize the fact that children progress through common patterns but may do so at different rates. These rates cannot typically be accelerated by adult pressure or input. Developmentally oriented teachers understand that variances in the school performance of different children often result from differences in their general developmental growth. With the establishment of inclusion classes throughout the schools, it is vital for all teachers to have a complete understanding of the characteristics of students' various disabilities and the possible implications on learning.

Selecting Learning Activities

The effective teacher selects learning activities based on specific learning objectives.

The effective teacher selects learning activities based on specific learning objectives. Ideally, teachers should not plan activities that fail to augment the specific objectives of the lesson. Learning activities should be planned with a learning objective in mind. Objective-driven learning activities tend to serve as a tool to reinforce the teacher's lesson presentation. Additionally, teacher-selected learning objectives should be aligned with state and district educational goals. State and district goals should focus on National Educational Goals (Goals 2000), and the specific strengths and weaknesses of individual students assigned to their class.

The effective teacher is cognizant of students' individual learning styles as well as human growth and development theory. He or she then applies these principles to the selection and implementation of appropriate classroom instructional activities.

Activities for younger students

Learning activities selected for younger students (below age eight) should focus on short time frames and be in a highly simplified form. The nature of the activity and the content in which the activity is presented affects the approach the students will use to process the information. Younger children tend to process information at a slower pace than children aged eight and older.

Activities for older students

On the other hand, when selecting and implementing learning activities for older children, teachers should focus on more complex ideas. Older students are capable of understanding more complex instructional activities. Moreover, effective teachers maintain a clear understanding of the developmental appropriateness of activities selected.

SKILL 1.4 **Identifies ways in which a student's development in one domain** *(physical, cognitive, linguistic, social, emotional, and moral)* **may affect learning and development in other domains**

Elementary-age children face many changes during their early school years, and these changes will impact how learning occurs in either a positive or negative manner. Some cognitive developments (i.e., learning to read) may broaden their areas of interest as students realize the amount of information (i.e., novels, magazines, nonfiction books) that is available. On the other hand, a young student's limited comprehension may inhibit some of their confidence (emotional) or conflict with values taught at home (moral). Joke telling (linguistic) becomes popular with children aged six or seven, and children may use this newly discovered "talent" to gain friends or social "stature" in their class (social). Learning within one domain often spills over into other areas for young students.

Learning and Adolescent Development

Likewise, learning continues to affect all domains as a child grows. Adolescence is a complex stage of life. While many people joke about the awkwardness of adolescence, it is particularly important to remember that this stage of life is the stage just before adulthood. While people do indeed develop further in adulthood, the changes are not as quick or significant as they are in adolescence.

Development within domains refers to the fact that different aspects of a human change as they mature. Some examples are:

1. Physical changes: Body growth, sexuality

2. Cognitive changes: Better ability to reason

3. Linguistic changes: A child's vocabulary develops further

4. Social changes: Figuring out identity

5. Emotional changes: Changes in ability to be concerned about other people

6. Moral changes: Testing limits

Interconnectedness of adolescent development

The important thing to remember about adolescent development within each of these domains is that they are not exclusive. For example, physical and emotional development are tied intricately, particularly when one feels awkward about his or her body, when emotional feelings are tied to sexuality, or when one feels that he or she does not look old enough (as rates of growth are obviously not similar). Moral and cognitive development often go hand-in-hand when an adolescent begins to identify reasons for behavior or searches for role models.

It is important, as an educator, to be sensitive to changes in adolescents. Just because a change in one area is not apparent does not mean there aren't changes in another area, hidden beneath the surface.

Problems not related to changes

Another area of extreme importance when dealing with adolescents is to realize that they may be deeply hurt over certain issues that may or may not be directly related to the changes they are going through at a specific time. It is particularly important for educators to be on the lookout for signs of depression, drug use, or other damaging activities, behaviors, or symptoms.

See also Skill 1.1

SKILL 1.5	**Applies knowledge of developmental characteristics of students to evaluate alternative instructional goals and plans**

See Skill 1.3

SKILL 1.6	**Selects appropriate instructional strategies, approaches, and delivery systems to promote students' development and learning**

To apply a one-dimensional instructional approach and a strict tunnel vision perspective of testing is to impose learning limits on students.

No two students are alike. It follows, then, that no students learn alike. All students have the right to an education, but there cannot be a singular path to that education. A teacher must acknowledge the variety of learning styles and abilities among students within a class (and, indeed, the varieties from class to class) by applying multiple instructional and assessment processes to ensure that every child has appropriate opportunities to master the subject matter, demonstrate such mastery, and improve and enhance learning skills with each lesson.

Direct Instruction and Lectures

It is traditionally assumed a teacher will use direct instruction in the classroom. The amount of time devoted to it will vary according by the age of the class and other factors. Lecturing can be very valuable because it is the quickest way for transferring knowledge to students, and as they also learn note taking, the students are able to organize the new information. However, there are many cautions against using too much lecture in a class of any age. In the first place, attention span even of senior high school students is short when they are using only one sense—the sense of hearing. Teachers should limit how much lecture they use and how long the lectures last.

Most teachers find students enjoy the learning process when lecturing is limited, and the students themselves become active in and responsible for their own learning. Students' attitudes and perceptions about learning are the most powerful factors influencing academic focus and success.

Learners must believe that the tasks that they are being asked to perform have some value and that they have both the ability and resources to perform them. If a student believes a task is unimportant, he or she will not put much effort into it. In addition, if a student thinks he lacks the ability or resources to successfully complete a task, even attempting the task becomes too great a risk. Not only must the teacher understand the students' abilities and interests, He or she must also help students develop positive attitudes and perceptions about learning tasks.

> *When instructional objectives center on students' interests and are relevant to their lives, effective learning occurs.*

Differentiated Instruction

The effective teacher will seek to connect all students to the subject matter using multiple techniques, with the goal being that each student, through his or her own abilities, will relate to one or more techniques and excel in the learning process.

See also Skill 8.3

Cooperative Learning

See Skill 11.3

Alternative Assessments

ALTERNATIVE ASSESSMENT is an assessment where students create an answer or a response to a question or task. This is as opposed to traditional, inflexible assessments where students choose a prepared response from among a selection of responses, such as matching, multiple-choice, or true or false.

> **ALTERNATIVE ASSESSMENT:** an assessment where students create an answer or a response to a question or task

Characteristics of alternative assessments

When implemented effectively, an alternative assessment approach will exhibit these characteristics, among others:

- Requires higher-order thinking and problem-solving

- Provides opportunities for student self-reflection and self-assessment

- Uses real world applications to connect students to the subject

- Provides opportunities for students to learn and examine subjects on their own, as well as to collaborate with their peers

- Encourages students to continuing learning beyond the requirements of the assignment

- Clearly defines objective and performance goals

Teachers realize the value of giving assignments that meet the individual abilities and needs of students. After instruction, discussion, questioning, and practice have been provided, rather than assigning one task to all students, teachers are asking students to generate tasks that will show their knowledge of the information presented. Students are given choices and thereby have the opportunity to demonstrate more effectively the skills, concepts, or topics that they, as individuals, have learned. It has been established that student choice increases student originality, intrinsic motivation, and higher mental processes.

COMPETENCY 2

UNDERSTAND LEARNING PROCESSES, AND USE THIS UNDERSTANDING TO PROMOTE STUDENT DEVELOPMENT AND LEARNING

SKILL 2.1 Analyzes ways in which development and learning processes interact

It is important for teachers to consider students' development and readiness when making instructional decisions. If an educational program is child-centered, it will surely address the developmental abilities and needs of the students because it will take its cues from students' interests, concerns, and questions.

Making an educational program child-centered involves building on the natural curiosity children bring to school and asking children what they want to learn.

Implementing Child-Centered Curriculum

Teachers help students to identify their own questions, puzzles, and goals, and they then structure for them widening circles of experiences and investigations of those topics. Teachers manage to infuse all of the skills, knowledge, and concepts that society mandates into a child-centered curriculum. This does not imply that teachers are passive and only respond to students' explicit cues; teachers also draw on their understanding of children's developmental characteristic needs and individual enthusiasms to design experiences that lead children into areas they might not otherwise choose, but that they do enjoy and find engaging. Teachers also bring their own interests and enthusiasms into the classroom to share and act as a motivational means of guiding children.

Planning

Implementing such a child-centered curriculum requires careful and deliberate planning. Planning serves as a means of organizing instruction and influences classroom teaching. Well thought-out planning includes:

- Specifying behavioral objectives

- Specifying students' entry behavior (knowledge and skills)

- Selecting and sequencing learning activities so as to move students from entry behavior to objective

- Evaluating the outcomes of instruction in order to improve planning

SKILL 2.2 Analyzes processes by which students construct meaning and develop skills, and applies strategies to facilitate learning in given situations *(e.g., by building connections between new information and prior knowledge; by relating learning to world issues and community concerns; by engaging students in purposeful practice and application of knowledge and skills; by using tools, materials and resources)*

Behavioral Learning

Historically, two main theories readily help describe how students construct knowledge, acquire skills, and develop habits of mind. The first theory is behavioral learning. BEHAVIORAL LEARNING theory suggests that people learn socially, by stimulation, or through repetition. For example, if you touch a hot stove, you learn not to repeat that action. Another example would be when a person makes a social error that leads to teasing or taunting; that person would likely learn acceptable social conventions. Learning by watching another complete an activity would be a third example of behavioral learning theory.

> **BEHAVIORAL LEARNING:** theory that suggests that people learn socially, by stimulation, or through repetition

Coginitive Learning

The second broad theory is cognitive learning. COGNITIVE LEARNING theories suggest that learning takes place within the mind. It goes further to explain that the mind processes ideas through brain mapping and connections with other material and experiences. In other words, with behaviorism, learning is somewhat external. For example, we see something, and then we copy it. With cognitive theories, learning is internal. We see something, analyze it in our minds, and make sense of it for ourselves. Then, if we choose to copy it, we do, but we do so having internalized (or thought about) the process.

> **COGNITIVE LEARNING:** theory that suggests that learning takes place within the mind

Behavioral and Cognitive Theories in Today's Classroom

Today, even though behavioral theories exist, most educators believe that children learn cognitively. Based on this information, teachers introduce new topics by relating those topics to information students may have already been exposed to or with which they are already familiar. In this way, the teacher is expecting that students will be able to better integrate this new information into their memories by attaching it to something that is already there. Or, when teachers apply new learning to real-world situations, they are expecting that the information will make more sense because it has been related to a real situation.

> *Today, even though behavioral theories exist, most educators believe that children learn cognitively.*

In all of the examples given in this standard, the importance is the application of new learning to something concrete. In essence, what is going on with these examples is that the teacher is slowing building on knowledge or adding knowledge to what students already know. Cognitively, this makes a great deal of sense. Think of a file cabinet. When we already have files for certain things, it's easy for us to find a file and put new information into it. When we're given something that doesn't fit into one of the preexisting files, we struggle to know what to do with it. The same is true with human minds.

SKILL 2.3 **Demonstrates knowledge of different types of learning strategies** *(e.g., rehearsal, elaboration, organization, metacognition)* **and how learners use each type of strategy**

Teachers should be familiar with several approaches to learning. The interdisciplinary curriculum planning approach creates a meaningful balance of both curriculum depth and breadth. Take for instance the following scenario:

Mrs. Jackson presents her Language Arts class with an assignment for collaborative group work. She provides them with the birth and death dates of the author Ernest Hemingway and asks them to determine how old he was when he died. She gives them five minutes as a group to work on the final answer. After five minutes, she asks each group for their answer and writes the answers on the board. Each group gives a different answer. When Mrs. Jackson comes to the last group, a female student asks, "Why do we have to do math in a Language Arts class?"

If the students had applied the knowledge learned from their basic math classes, they easily would have been able to solve the Language Arts question. The teacher was providing the students with a constructivist model by having them apply their knowledge of problem solving to pertinent information for a language arts' class. This type of learning should be an integral part of instructional practice in an interdisciplinary classroom.

Cognitive Learning and Interdisciplinary Curriculum

Centuries of educational research have shown a strong correlation between the need for interdisciplinary instruction and the application of cognitive learning skills. Understanding how students process information and create learning was the goal of early educators. Earlier researchers looked at how the brain connected information with meaning and found that learning occurs along intricate neural pathways. These paths formulate processing and meaning from data input into the brain. The implications of this information on teaching and student learning are vast. It can help teachers learn to work with students to break down subject content into bits of information that can be memorized, learned, and then applied to a former learning experience. Then the information is processed into integral resources of previously acquired information.

Brain learning theorists believe students formulate schematic structures of hundreds, often thousands, of interconnected and integrated bits of information that provide a framework for learning and meaning. The research of Ausubel (1968) explains the schematic structure of processing and "cognitive hooks" where students create links of connection in applying prior knowledge to new learning experiences.

Techniques for Interconnected Learning

Teachers who utilize a diversity of instructional strategies in the classroom provide students with multiple styles of learning modalities, which for students can translate into academic and life successes.

Providing students with learning toolkits, such as clustering/mind mapping techniques, that provide organizational tools for large quantities of information is vital to the visual or tactile-kinesthetic learner. The figure shows a cluster of how students might establish associations between major and minor contexts using an example of the current events in Iraq.

The Making of a Conflict—Iraq

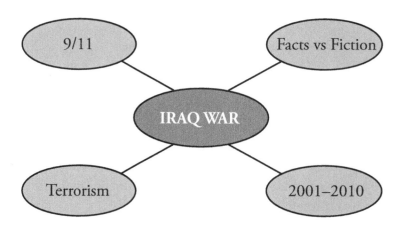

When students are provided opportunities in brainstorming sessions to construct meaning around specific content, they are able to create new meaning and expand upon prior knowledge of the event.

SKILL **Analyzes factors that affect student learning** *(e.g., learning styles,*
2.4 *contextually supported learning versus de-contextualized learning)*, **and**
adapting instructional practices to promote learning in given
situations

Many factors affect student learning including how students learn, how learning is presented, and how much background knowledge and experiences they have. Several educational learning theories can be applied to classroom practices. One classic learning theory is Piaget's stages of development, which comprise the following four learning stages:

1. Sensory motor stage (from birth to age 2)

2. Preoperation stage (ages 2 to 7 or early elementary)

3. Concrete operational stage (ages 7 to 11 or upper elementary)

4. Formal operational stage (ages 7 to 15 or late elementary/high school)

Piaget believed children passed through this series of stages as they developed from the most basic forms of concrete thinking to the most sophisticated levels of abstract thinking.

Brain-Based Learning Theory

Two of the most prominent learning theories in education today are Brain-based Learning and the Multiple Intelligence Theory. Recent brain research suggests that increased knowledge about the way the brain retains information will enable educators to design the most effective learning environments. As a result, researchers have developed twelve principles that relate knowledge about the brain to teaching practices.

Recent brain research suggests that increased knowledge about the way the brain retains information will enable educators to design the most effective learning environments.

The twelve principles of brain-based learning:
- *The brain is a complex adaptive system*
- *The brain is social*
- *The search for meaning is innate*
- *We use patterns to learn more effectively*
- *Emotions are crucial to developing patterns*
- *Each brain perceives and creates parts and whole simultaneously*
- *Learning involves focused and peripheral attention*
- *Learning involves conscious and unconscious processes*

Continued on next page

> • We have at least two ways of organizing memory
> • Learning is developmental
> • Complex learning is enhanced by challenge (and inhibited by threat)
> • Every brain is unique
>
> *Caine & Caine, 1994, Mind/Brain Learning Principles*

Educators can use these principles to help design methods and environments in their classrooms to maximize student learning.

Multiple Intelligence Theory

The Multiple Intelligence Theory, developed by Howard Gardner, suggests that students learn in (at least) seven different ways. These include:

- Visually/spatially
- Musically
- Verbally
- Logically/mathematically
- Interpersonally
- Intrapersonally
- Bodily/kinesthetically

Constructivism

Another learning theory is that of Constructivism. The theory of constructivist learning allows students to construct learning opportunities. For constructivist teachers, the belief is that students create their own reality of knowledge and how to process and observe the world around them. Students are constantly constructing new ideas, which serve as frameworks for learning and teaching.

Researchers have shown that the constructivist model is composed of four components:

CONSTRUCTIVIST LEARNING
Learner creates knowledge
Learner constructs and makes meaningful new knowledge to existing knowledge
Learner shapes and constructs knowledge by life experiences and social interactions
In constructivist learning communities, the student, teacher, and classmates establish knowledge cooperatively on a daily basis

Kelly (1969) states "human beings construct knowledge systems based on their observations parallels Piaget's theory that individuals construct knowledge systems as they work with others who share a common background of thought and processes." Constructivist learning is dynamic and ongoing. For constructivist teachers, the classroom becomes a place where students are encouraged to interact with the instructional process by asking questions and posing new ideas to old theories. The use of cooperative learning that encourages students to work in supportive learning environments using their own ideas to stimulate questions and propose outcomes is a major aspect of a constructivist classroom.

> *Constructivist learning for students is dynamic and ongoing. For constructivist teachers, the classroom becomes a place where students are encouraged to interact with the instructional process by asking questions and posing new ideas to old theories.*

Metcognition

Yet another learning theory is that of metacognition. The metacognition learning theory deals with "the study of how to help the learner gain understanding about how knowledge is constructed and about the conscious tools for constructing that knowledge." (Joyce and Weil 1996) The metacognitive approach to learning involves the teacher's understanding that teaching the student to process his or her own learning and mastery of skill provides the greatest learning and retention opportunities in the classroom. Students are taught to develop concepts and teach themselves skills in problem solving and critical thinking. The student becomes an active participant in the learning process and the teacher facilitates that conceptual and cognitive learning process.

Social and Behavioral Theories

Finally, social and behavioral theories look at the social interactions of students in the classroom that instruct or impact learning opportunities in the classroom. The psychological approaches behind both theories are subject to individual variables that are learned and applied, either proactively or negatively, in the classroom. The stimulus of the classroom can be conducive to learning or evoke behavior that is counterproductive for both students and teachers. Students are social beings who normally gravitate to action in the classroom, so teachers must be cognizant in planning classroom environments that provide both focus and engagement in maximizing learning opportunities.

See Skill 1.6, which discusses a variety of instructional strategies teachers can employ to meet the diverse needs of students who learn in different ways.

See Skill 2.2, which discusses how students benefit from learning that is linked to current issues, background knowledge, and relevant purposes (contextualized learning).

SKILL 2.5 **Recognizes how various teacher roles** *(e.g., direct instructor, facilitator)* **and student roles** *(e.g., self-directed learner, group participant, passive observer)* **may affect learning processes and outcomes**

The Teacher's Role

Teaching consists of a multitude of roles. Teachers must plan and deliver instruction in a creative and innovating way so that students find learning both fun and intriguing. The teacher must also research various learning strategies, decide which to implement in the classroom, and balance that information according to the various learning styles of the students. Teachers must facilitate all aspects of the lesson including preparation and organization of materials, delivery of instruction, and management of student behavior and attention.

Simultaneously, the teacher must observe student learning, interactions, and on-task behavior while making mental or written notes regarding what is working in the lesson and how the students are receiving and utilizing the information. This will provide the teacher with immediate feedback as to whether to continue with the lesson, or if it is necessary to slow the instruction or present the lesson in another way. Teachers must also work collaboratively with other adults in the room and utilize them to maximize student learning. The teacher's job requires the teacher to establish a delicate balance among all these factors.

How the teacher handles this balance depends on the teaching style of the teacher and lesson. Cooperative learning will require the teacher to have organized materials ready, perhaps even with instructions for the students, as well. The teacher should conduct a great deal of observations during this type of lesson. Direct instruction methods will require the teacher to take an enthusiastic, yet organized, approach to the lesson. When teaching directly to students, the teacher must take care to keep the lesson student-centered and intriguing while presenting accurate information.

The Student's Role

Like the teacher, the student has more than one role in a child-centered classroom. In collaborative settings, each student is expected to participate in class or group discussions. Through participation, students begin to realize their contributions have a place in a comprehensive discussion of a topic. Participation engages students in active learning, while increasing their self-confidence as they realize their ideas are necessary for group success.

Students also play the role of observer. As previously stated, behavioral theorists believe that through observation, a human's mind begins to make sense of the world around them as they decide to mimic or avoid certain behaviors. In a classroom, students observe many positive outcomes from behavior, as well as questioning, discussion, and hands-on activities.

An important goal for students should be to become self-directed in their learning. Teachers help students obtain this goal by providing them with ample opportunities to seek out their academic interests with various types of projects and assignments. Self-directed learners gain a lot from their inquiries since the topic usually interests them, and when students take over certain aspects of their own education, they gain a sense of empowerment and ownership over their learning. This is an important role in the classroom because the sense of ownership promotes a sense of lifelong learning in students.

> *Self-directed learners gain a lot from their inquiries since the topic usually interests them, and when students take over certain aspects of their own education, they gain a sense of empowerment and ownership over their learning.*

> **SKILL 2.6** **Recognizes effective strategies for promoting independent thinking and learning** *(e.g., by helping students develop critical-thinking, decision-making, and problem-solving skills; by enabling students to pursue topics of personal interest)* **and for promoting students' sense of ownership and responsibility in relation to their own learning**

Various materials and technologies should be utilized to encourage problem solving and critical thinking about subject content. Within each curriculum chosen by a district comes an expectation that students must master both benchmarks and standards of various learning skills. There is an established level of academic performance and proficiency in public schools that students are required to master in today's classrooms.

> *Teachers should have a toolkit of instructional strategies at their disposal.*

Research of national and state standards indicate that students are required to master additional benchmarks and learning objectives in the subject areas of science, foreign language, English language arts, history, art, health, civics, economics, geography, physical education, mathematics, and social studies in state assessments. (Marzano & Kendall, 1996)

Critical Thinking Skills

A CRITICAL THINKING SKILL is a skill target that teachers use to help students develop and sustain learning within specific subject areas and then can be applied to other subject areas. For example, when learning to understand algebraic concepts in solving a math word problem on how much fencing material is needed to build a fence around a backyard area that is 8' × 12', a math student must understand the order of numerical expression and how to simplify algebraic expressions.

> **CRITICAL THINKING SKILL:** a skill target that teachers use to help students develop and sustain learning within specific subject areas and then can be applied to other subject areas

Teachers can provide instructional strategies that show students how to group the fencing measurements into an algebraic word problem that, with minor addition, subtraction, and multiplication, can produce a simple number equal to the amount of fencing materials needed to build the fence.

Examples of critical thinking

Students use basic skills to understand things that are read, such as a reading passage, a math word problem, or directions for a project. However, students apply additional thinking skills to fully comprehend how what was read could be applied to their own life, how to make comparatives, or what choices could be made based on the factual information given. These are called critical thinking skills, because students think about the thinking process; teachers are instrumental in helping students use these skills in everyday activities. Examples of these types of skills may include:

- Analyzing bills for overcharges

- Comparing shopping ads or catalogue deals

- Finding the main idea from readings

- Applying what's been learned to new situations

- Gathering information or data from a diversity of sources to plan a project

- Following a sequence of directions

- Looking for cause and effect relationships

- Comparing and contrasting information in synthesizing information

Addressing Student Needs

Attention to learner needs during planning is foremost and includes:

- Identification of that which the students already know or need to know

- Matching learner needs with instructional elements such as content, materials, activities, and goals

- Determining whether students have performed at an acceptable level, following instruction

Because most teachers want their educational objectives to include higher level thinking skills, teachers need to direct students toward these higher levels on a taxonomy, such as Bloom's. Questioning is an effective tool to build up students to these higher levels.

Using questioning

Low-order questions are useful to begin the process. They ensure that the student is focused on the required information and understands what needs to be included in the thinking process. For example, if the objective is for students to be able to read and understand the story *Goldilocks and the Three Bears*, the teacher may begin with low-order questions (i.e., "What are some things Goldilocks did while in the bears' home?" [Knowledge] or "Why didn't Goldilocks like the Papa Bear's chair?" [Analysis]).

Through a series of questions, the teacher can move the students toward the top of the taxonomy. (For example, "If Goldilocks had come to your house, what are some things she may have used?" [Application], "How might the story have differed if Goldilocks had visited the three fishes?" [Synthesis], or "Do you think Goldilocks was good or bad? Why?" [Evaluation]). Through questioning, the teacher can control the thinking process of the class. As students become more involved in the discussion they are systematically being lead toward higher levels of thinking.

> *Low-order questions are useful to begin the process. They ensure the student is focused on the required information and understands what needs to be included in the thinking process.*

Tracking Growth

The ability to create a personal charting of students' academic and emotional growth using performance-based assessment and individualized portfolios becomes a toolkit for both students and teachers. Teachers can use semester portfolios to help gauge student academic progress and personal growth. When a student is studying to master a math concept and is able to create visuals of the learning that transcend the initial concept to create a bridge connecting a higher level of thinking and application of knowledge, then the teacher can share a moment of enjoyable math comprehension with the student.

> *The ability to create a personal charting of students' academic and emotional growth using performance-based assessment and individualized portfolios becomes a toolkit for both students and teachers.*

Using graphic organizers and web guides that center around a concept and the application of the concept is an instructional strategy teachers can use to guide students into further inquiry of the subject matter. Imagine the research of the German chemist Fredrich August Kekule when he looked into a fire one night and discovered the molecular structure of benzene. Imagine fostering that same creativity in students and helping students understand the art of visualization and building their creativity of discovery. One of your students may discover the cure for AIDS or cancer or create reading programs for the next generation of readers!

Helping students become effective note-takers and teaching different perspectives for spatial techniques is a proactive teacher strategy in which art and visualization become natural art forms for learning.

> *In today's computer environment, students must understand that computers cannot replace the creative thinking and skill application of the human mind.*

COMPETENCY 3

UNDERSTAND HOW FACTORS IN THE HOME, SCHOOL, AND COMMUNITY MAY AFFECT STUDENTS' DEVELOPMENT AND READINESS TO LEARN; AND USE THIS UNDERSTANDING TO CREATE A CLASSROOM ENVIRONMENT WITHIN WHICH ALL STUDENTS CAN DEVELOP AND LEARN

SKILL 3.1 **Recognizes the impact of socio-cultural factors** (*e.g., culture, heritage, language, socioeconomic profile*) **in the home, school, and community on students' development and learning**

Socio-cultural factors provide a definitive impact on a students' psychological, emotional, affective, and physiological development, along with a students' academic learning and future opportunities.

Often, students absorb the culture and social environment around them without deciphering contextual meaning of the experiences. When provided with a diversity of cultural contexts, students are able to adapt and incorporate multiple meanings from cultural cues that may differ vastly from their own socioeconomic backgrounds.

The Complex Dynamics of the Modern Classroom

The educational experience for most students is a complicated and complex experience with a diversity of interlocking meanings and inferences. If one aspect of the complexity is altered, it affects other aspects. These changes may affect how a student or teacher views an instructional or learning experience. With the current demographic profile of today's school communities, the complexity of understanding, interpreting, and synthesizing the nuances from the diversity of cultural lineages can provide difficulties in both communication and learning that could impede the acquisition of skills for students.

Importance of student inclusion

Teachers should create personalized learning communities where every student is a valued member and contributor of the classroom experiences.

In classrooms where socio-cultural attributes of the student population are incorporated into the fabric of the learning process, dynamic interrelationships are created that enhance the learning experience and the personalization of learning. When students are provided with academic and social opportunities to incorporate cultural attributes into the learning, everyone in the classroom benefits from the shared experiences and expanded viewpoint of a world experience and culture that vastly differs from their own.

Effects of personalized learning communities

Researchers continue to show that personalized learning communities increase the learning effect for students; decrease drop-out rates among marginalized students; and decrease unproductive student behavior, which can result from cultural misunderstandings or miscues between students. When students are able to step outside their comfort zones and share themselves, they grow exponentially in social understanding and cultural connectedness. Examining the world of a homeless student or empathizing with an English Language Learner (ELL) who has just immigrated to the United States can be important experiences for students.

Personalized learning communities provide supportive learning environments that address the academic and emotional needs of students. As socio-cultural knowledge is conveyed continuously in the interrelated experiences and shared cooperatively and collaboratively in student groupings or individualized learning, the current and future benefits will reinforce the importance of understanding the "whole" child, inclusive of the social and the cultural context.

> *Promoting diversity of learning and cultural competency in the classroom for students and teachers creates a world of multicultural opportunities and learning.*

> **SKILL 3.2** **Analyzes ways in which students' personal health, safety, nutrition, and past or present exposure to abusive or dangerous environments may affect their development and learning in various domains** *(e.g., physical, cognitive, linguistic, social, emotional, and moral)* **and their readiness to learn**

Helping students to develop healthy self-images and self-worth are integral to the learning and development experiences. Learning for students who are experiencing negative self-image and peer isolation is not necessarily the top priority, such as when students are feeling bullied or negated in the school community. When a student is attending school from a homeless shelter or is lost in the middle of a parent's divorce or feeling a need to conform to fit into a certain student group, the student is compromised and may be unable to effectively navigate the educational process or engage in the required academic expectations.

> *Helping students to develop healthy self-images and self-worth are integral to the learning and development experiences.*

Addressing Student Self-image Issues

Most schools will offer health classes that address issues such as:

- Sexuality
- Self-image
- Peer pressure
- Nutrition

- Wellness
- Gang activity
- Drug engagement
- Other relevant teen experiences

Students are required to take a health class as a core class and graduation requirement; the incentive from the district's and school's standpoint is that students will be exposed to issues that directly affect them. Unfortunately, one health class is not enough to effectively convey the multiplicity of issues that could create a psychological or physiological trauma for a teenager. School budgets and financial issues provide the minimum educational experience for students today. Students are lost in the process.

Resources outside the school system

Some schools have contracted with outside agencies to develop collaborative partnerships to bring in after-school tutorial classes. One example of this might be gender- and cultural-specific groupings where students can deal authentically with integration of cultural and ethnic experiences and lifestyles. Drug intervention programs and speakers on gang issues have created dynamic opportunities for school communities to bring the "undiscussable" issues to the forefront and help schools say "No to Drugs and Gangs." Both students and teachers must be taught about the world of teenagers and understand the social, psychological, and learning implications that underscore the process of academic acquisition for societies' most vulnerable citizens.

> *Both students and teachers must be taught about the world of teenagers and understand the social, psychological, and learning implications that underscore the process of academic acquisition for societies' most vulnerable citizens.*

Neglected and abused students

Unfortunately, many students are exposed to abuse and dangerous situations. Child abuse may manifest itself as a phenomenon known as chronic shock syndrome. The individual's nervous system becomes geared up to handle the extra flow of hormones and electrical impulses resulting in a fight or flight reaction. Each time the abuse happens, it creates a shift in the biology of the brain and allied systems. Essentially, the victim becomes allergic (hypersensitized) to stress of the kind that prevailed during the period of abuse. Recent research indicates such a shift is reflected in brain chemistry and structural changes and may last a lifetime.

Abused vs. neglected

The abused child differs from the neglected one. While the neglected child suffers from understimulation, the abused one suffers from overstimulation. The neglected child will be:

- Withdrawn
- Quiet
- Almost sedate

In contrast, the abused child may be:

- Angry
- Aggressive
- Energetic
- Hard to control
- Rebellious

In each case, the environment of abuse or neglect shapes the behavior of the child away from home. Often, out of reflex, the child will flinch when seeming to anticipate a blow, or may be unable to accept or understand healthy attention directed to him or her. To sense what the child's feelings and experiences may be, the teacher merely needs to watch the child's reaction to a loud noise, someone's aggression, or the response when offered some companionship by another child.

Signs of physical abuse

Obvious signs of physical abuse are marks from:

- Hand
- Kitchen utensil
- Fist
- Extension cord
- Belt
- Any other imaginable implement for striking and inflicting pain on a child
- Coat hanger

To effectively help the child, the suspicion has to be backed up with hard evidence. Unusual marks in geometric shapes may indicate the presence of an implement for spanking such as a spoon, homemade paddle, extension cord, or coat hanger. Marks on the arms and legs may indicate being whipped there. Teachers should always be suspicious about bruises.

Evaluating injuries

Bruises on the neck and face usually do not come from a child tripping and falling. Rather, they are usually the result of intentional hitting—and even choking. Noting the sizes and shapes of bruises and using simple imagination may reveal the source of the injury. The observer should notice whether the bruise has reddened areas, indicating ruptured capillaries, or is uniformly colored but shaded a darker color toward the perimeter. The rupture of capillaries indicates a strong hit, while the shaded bruise indicates a softer compression.

The educator who discovers any of these conditions should start with a reasonable suspicion that abuse is occuring. He or she would then gather specific indicators and firm evidence. Take note of the size of the injury and describe it in concrete terms. For instance, describe a bruise as being the size of a quarter or an orange.

Signs of neglect

When identifying the neglected child, teachers can look for signs of malnourishment. For instance, a child may gorge at lunch, yet still be thin and underweight. This student may be quiet and shy, shabbily groomed, and unconcerned about his or her appearance. Poor nutrition at home may result in an unusually high number of colds. It is of utmost importance to guarantee that immunizations are current, as they probably have been overlooked. Children who are neglected are usually not very social, may isolate themselves, and may not respond to invitations to join other children in play. These are not necessarily signs of neglect since any child can display these traits from time to time. However, if they are accompanied by a persistant social anxiety, this may indicate that something is happening at home.

Signs of sexual abuse

In cases of sexual abuse the most blatant warning sign is oversexualization by the child. They become interested in sexually related matters long before their developmental stage would predict. They may be seen to quietly masturbate at prepubescent ages and may even act out sexually with other children of their own age. If a child suddenly begins to engage in promiscuous sexual behavior, this is a sign that he or she is being molested. Sexual abuse of children is widespread and takes many forms. Kissing episodes by a parent or other adult, when out of normal context, are just as damaging as more overt forms of contact. The sexualized leer or stare by a perverted parent or adult can also be damaging. Deal with all situations of sexual abuse with extreme care. It is advisable to seek help from a trained professional who knows how to approach such matters. Incorrectly conducted information gathering can be detrimental to a prosecution.

See also Skill 1.1

See also Skill 1.1

SKILL 3.3	Recognizes the significance of family life and the home environment for student development and learning *(e.g., nature of the expectations of parents, guardians, and caregivers; degree of their involvement in the student's education)*

The student's capacity and potential for academic success within the overall educational experience are products of her or his total environment: classroom and school system; home and family; neighborhood and community in general. All of these segments are interrelated and can be supportive, one of the other, or divisive, one against the other. As a matter of course, the teacher will become familiar with all aspects of the system, the school, and the classroom pertinent to the students' educational experience. This would include not only process and protocols but also the availability of resources provided to meet the academic, health, and welfare needs of students. It is incumbent upon the teacher to look beyond the boundaries of the school system to identify additional resources, as well as issues and situations, that will affect (directly or indirectly) a student's ability to succeed in the classroom.

> *It is incumbent upon the teacher to look beyond the boundaries of the school system to identify additional resources, as well as issues and situations, that will affect (directly or indirectly) a student's ability to succeed in the classroom.*

Examples of Resources

Libraries, museums, zoos, planetariums, etc.

Clubs, societies and civic organizations, and community outreach programs of businesses, corporations, and government agencies are all programs that can provide excellent materials and resources to help address diversity issues.

Departments of social services operating within the local community

These agencies can provide background and program information relevant to social issues that may affect individual students. This information can be used as a resource for classroom instruction regarding life skills, at-risk behaviors, etc.

Initial contacts for resources outside of the school system will usually come from within the system itself, such as from administration, teacher organizations, department heads, and other colleagues.

Examples of Issues or Situations

Students from multicultural backgrounds

Curriculum objectives and instructional strategies may be inappropriate and unsuccessful when presented in a single format that relies on the student's understanding and acceptance of the values and common attributes of a specific culture that is not his or her own.

Parental and family influences

Attitude, resources, and encouragement available in the home environment may contribute to a student's success or failure at school.

Family income level

Families with higher incomes are able to provide increased opportunities for students. Students from lower-income families will need to depend on the resources available from the school system and the community. These resources should be orchestrated by the classroom teacher in cooperation with school administrators and educational advocates in the community.

Family educational level

Family members with higher levels of education often serve as models for students and have high expectations for academic success. And families with specific aspirations for children (often regardless of their own educational background) encourage students to achieve academic success and are most often active participants in the process.

Family stability level

A family in crisis (caused by economic difficulties, divorce, substance abuse, physical abuse, etc.) creates a negative environment that may have a profound impact on all aspects of a student's life and particularly his or her ability to function academically. The situation may require professional intervention. It is often the classroom teacher who will recognize a family in crisis and instigate an intervention by reporting this to school or civil authorities.

> *Regardless of the positive or negative impacts on the student's education from outside sources, it is the teacher's responsibility to ensure that all students in the classroom have an equal opportunity for academic success.*

Regardless of the positive or negative impacts on the student's education from outside sources, it is the teacher's responsibility to ensure that all students in the classroom have an equal opportunity for academic success. This begins with the teacher's statement of high expectations for every student and develops through planning, delivery, and evaluation of instruction that provides for inclusion and ensures that all students have equal access to the resources necessary for successful acquisition of the academic skills being taught and measured in the classroom.

SKILL 3.4 Analyzes how school-wide structures *(e.g., tracking)* and classroom factors *(e.g., homogeneous versus heterogeneous grouping, student-teacher interactions)* may affect students' self-concept and learning

Homogeneous Grouping

Classroom climate can have a significant influence on successful student learning. Interactions among and relationships between students are an important factor of a positive classroom climate. In past classroom practices, it was common for students to be grouped according to ability. This practice is sometimes referred to as tracking or HOMOGENOUS GROUPING. For example, students who found math challenging would be in the "low" math group, average math students would be in the "grade-level" math group, and excelling math learners would make up the "advanced" group.

> **HOMOGENOUS GROUPING:** a classroom organizational concept where students are grouped according to ability

Drawbacks

This type of grouping can lead to problems with students' self-concept and motivation in class. Students who found themselves in the low group would feel ashamed or stupid. At the same time, students in the advanced group may feel superior and boast of their successes in front of other students, and they may feel stressed over needing to perform. In summary, this type of grouping typically leads to a combination of feelings including resentment, stress, inferiority, and failure; feelings that do not enhance learning.

Homogenous grouping typically leads to a combination of feelings including resentment, stress, inferiority, and failure; feelings that do not enhance learning.

Heterogeneous Grouping

It's not that teachers can never group students by ability. Used once in a while, this method does allow students to work at a comfortable level. However, teachers often find that HETEROGENEOUS GROUPING (grouping by mixed abilities) allows all students to feel successful. In mixed groups, students can learn from more advanced students, while advanced students can still be provided with opportunities to excel in an activity.

Cooperative learning is an excellent setting for heterogeneous groups as students work together to solve problems or complete activities while benefitting from all learning abilities. In this setting, all students feel they are successful in their learning, and feelings of confidence, friendship, and achievement are experienced.

HETEROGENEOUS GROUPING: a classroom organizational concept where students are grouped according to mixed ability

Cooperative learning is an excellent setting for heterogeneous groups as students work together to solve problems or complete activities while benefitting from all learning abilities.

> SKILL 3.5 **Identifies effective strategies for creating classroom environment that promotes student development and learning by taking advantage of positive factors** (e.g., culture, heritage, language) **in the home, school, and community and minimizing the effect of negative factors** (e.g., minimal family support)

Academic Expectations

In a document prepared for the Southern Regional Education Board, titled *Strategies for Creating a Classroom Culture of High Expectations*, Myra Cloer Reynolds summarized the process necessary to meet stated educational objective when she wrote, "Motivation and classroom management skills are essential to creating and sustaining an environment of high expectations and improvement in today's schools."

In some school systems, very high expectations are placed on certain students and minimal expectations placed on others. Often, the result is predictable: students achieve as they are expected to achieve. A teacher is expected to provide the same standards of excellence in education for all students. This standard cannot be met or upheld unless the teacher has (and conveys) high expectations for all students.

Student expectations affecting performance

Considerable research has been done, over several decades, regarding student performance. Time and again, a direct correlation has been demonstrated between the teacher's expectations for a particular student and that student's academic performance. This may be unintended and subtle, but the effects are manifested and measurable.

> *A direct correlation has been demonstrated between the teacher's expectations for a particular student and that student's academic performance.*

For example, a teacher may not provide the fullest effort on behalf of the student when he or she has low expectations of success. And the student may "buy into" this evaluation of his or her potential, possibly becoming scholastically further burdened by low self-esteem. Other students, with more self-confidence in their own abilities, might still go along with this "free ride"—willing to do only what is expected of them and unwittingly allowing this disservice to hamper their academic progress.

Employing high expectations in the classroom

A teacher can convey high expectations to students in a variety of ways. Much has to do with the attitude of the teacher and positive interactions with the students—clearly stating expectations and reinforcing this at every opportunity.

METHODS FOR IMPLEMENTING HIGH EXPECTATIONS	
Notify the class of your high expectations for their academic success	Let students know that they can acquire all the skills in which you will be instructing them and that you take personal responsibility and pride in their success.
Speak to the class about the opportunity to support your goals for their success	Let students know that you appreciate when they approach you with questions, problems, or doubts about their performance, understanding of class work, or ability to succeed. That sort of request enables you to help them directly, and helps you succeed as a teacher.
Never lower standards or "dilute" instruction for certain students	It is the teacher's responsibility to ascertain the means to bring the student's academic performance up to standard.
Use all forms of teacher communication with students to reinforce your high expectations for them—as a class and especially as individuals	What we internalize as individuals, we utilize in group settings.

The teacher should provide positive reinforcement about the progress that the student is making regarding the high expectations for his or her academic achievement. If the work itself is below expectations—perhaps even substandard—provide positive, constructive feedback about what should be done to meet expectations.

Express your confidence in the student's ability. A negative comment, like a negative attitude, is unacceptable on the part of the teacher. The teacher may deem it necessary to speak one-on-one with the student regarding his or her performance. Remember, however, no student ever feels motivated when reading the words "*see me*" on an exam or assignment.

An example of an opportunity to communicate expectations might be when writing comments on exams and papers being returned to individual students.

Developmental Responsiveness

Members of the faculty and staff are assigned to provide mentoring, advice, and advocacy in response to the varying needs of students during their middle level educational experience. Along with in-house professionals who are prepared to meet the developmental requirements of a diverse middle level student population, many school systems provide programs and individuals who reach out to parents and families and the community on behalf of the students.

Curriculum is developed that is socially significant and relevant to the personal interests of middle level students. Classroom teachers plan, prepare, and deliver instructional modules that are directed toward specific issues of middle level childhood development (physical, intellectual, emotional, etc.

Wherever possible, interdisciplinary instructional modules (devised, developed, and presented by teachers from different disciplines—each providing his or her own skill sets to achieve comprehensive understanding of the subjects and issues) should be employed to provide the most efficient use of faculty resources and the most effective means of introducing the students to all aspects and skills related to a subject.

Within the school system, administrators, faculty, and the individual classroom teacher strives to develop an environment that provides for personalized support of each students' intellectual, physical, emotional, social, and ethical development.

Equity

Equity in the learning community addresses the following issues:

- Equal Access: Requires that no impediment (physical, cultural, intellectual, social, economic, etc.) or bias can restrict some students from access that is available to others.

- Equal Treatment: Ensures that no student is valued above or below the others. Physical, intellectual, cultural, economic, or other criteria may not be applied in determining how a student is treated. Equally high academic expectations are afforded to all students, with the assurance that this objective is achievable and will be supported by the teacher and the educational system.

- Equal Opportunity to Learn: Requires that every student have equal access to all resources, physical and intellectual, as well as equal instruction and support from the classroom teacher and staff.

- Equal Outcomes: Require that instruction and evaluation are structured to ensure all students acquire the skills being taught.

Policy and statutes regarding equity

While equal treatment and equal access for all individuals is mandated under various state and federal statutes, not every issue has been considered and addressed. These statutes can be difficult to interpret. Inconsistencies between the letter of the law and the intent of the law may exist.

Significant differences in the implementation and conduct of policy and procedure within institutions can also hamper the effectiveness of the laws and the intent with which these statutes were created. Equity may not be fully achieved if practices are instituted or changed superficially, only to comply with statutory regulations, rather than internalized and embraced by the entire learning community as an opportunity to improve the educational system.

Implementing equity in the classroom

In an educational environment, from the classroom throughout the entire school system, no impediments to achieving equity should exist. The primary responsibility of the educator is to ensure that all aspects of the educational process, and all information necessary to master specified skills, are readily accessible to all students. There should be no conflict between laws mandating equity and educational philosophy. Policies, practices, and procedures instituted to comply with (or surpass the requirements of) these laws support our educational objectives. By creating, internalizing, and practicing the values of an academic culture with high expectations for all students and inclusion of all students in every aspect of the educational process, we provide for equity in education and fulfill our primary responsibility as educators.

See also Skills 5.3 and 5.4

> *Significant differences in the implementation and conduct of policy and procedure within institutions can hamper the effectiveness of the laws and the intent with which these statutes were created.*

> SKILL 3.6 **Analyzes ways in which peer interactions** (e.g., acceptance versus isolation, bullying) **may promote or hinder a student's development and success in school, and determining effective strategies for dealing with peer-related issues in given classroom situations**

Middle-level students develop a deep social and emotional association with their peers. While young people are often self-conscious and perceive deficits in their intelligence, physical makeup, and personalities when compared to their peers, they also want to be accepted by their peers. Usually, they establish productive, positive, social and working relationships with one another. Often, they are inclined to consider the perceptions and reactions of peers and value their opinions above all else.

The Importance of Peer Relations

While many schools provide training in social skills for students who experience peer rejection, the success of these programs is often limited by the lack of social context in the exercises. Sometimes, participants become further stigmatized rather than helped. A recent study in the *Journal of Primary Prevention* evaluated and documented the effectiveness of classroom-level rather than individual-oriented approaches. Team-led groups consisting of "accepted" and "rejected" students in twenty-four middle-school classrooms met weekly to participate in nonacademic, cooperative activities and cooperative academic work. The study found that, after the experiment, there was a significant increase in the number of students who reported that "almost all" or "all" of their peers respected them and their opinions.

> *Some students not only perceive themselves as outsiders but are, in fact, treated as such by their peers.*

Acceptance by and interaction with one's peers is an overwhelming priority in the life of most middle-level students. And pursuit of this social necessity is not restricted to school-time; it permeates their entire lives.

Peer relations in the classroom

But it is within the classroom setting where the positive and negative aspects of peer relations can be monitored, evaluated, and focused through planning and instruction into constructive, enabling relationships.

This area of social growth will continue to increase in significance throughout the student's academic career. The foundation for the student's successful development in this area is established through the efforts of the classroom teacher to plan and develop positive peer group relationships and to provide opportunities and support for cooperative small group projects that not only develop cognitive ability

> *The ability to work and relate effectively with peers contributes greatly to the child's sense of competence.*

but promote peer interaction. The ability to work and relate effectively with peers contributes greatly to the child's sense of competence. In order to develop this sense of competence, students need to be successful in acquiring the information base and social skill sets which promote cooperative effort to achieve academic and social objectives.

Activities to enhance peer relations

All activities that the teacher plans for groups of students or the entire class should be informed by consideration of peer-related issues and provide for the introduction, utilization, and development of social as well as academic skills. Each such exercise must have stated, measurable objectives. There are a variety of resources available to the classroom teacher planning such activities. There is a tremendous variety of single medium and multimedia, modular planning, and instruction packages available through educational publishers. Not to be overlooked are the programs and activities developed by colleagues within the school system and beyond (via the Internet, for example).

> SKILL 3.7 **Demonstrates knowledge of health, sexuality, and peer-related issues for students** (e.g., self-image, physical appearance and fitness, peer-group conformity) **and the interrelated nature of these issues; and recognizes how specific behaviors related to health, sexuality, and peer issues** (e.g., eating disorders, drug and alcohol use, gang involvement) **can affect development and learning**

See Skill 3.2

COMPETENCY 4

UNDERSTAND LANGUAGE AND LITERACY DEVELOPMENT, AND USE THIS KNOWLEDGE IN ALL CONTENT AREAS TO DEVELOP THE LISTENING, SPEAKING, READING, AND WRITING SKILLS OF STUDENTS, INCLUDING STUDENTS FOR WHOM ENGLISH IS NOT THEIR PRIMARY LANGUAGE

SKILL 4.1 | **Identifies factors that influence language acquisition, and analyzes ways students' language skills affect their overall development and learning**

One of the most important things to know about the differences between first language (L1) and second language (L2) acquisition is that people usually will master L1, but they will almost never be fully proficient in L2. However, if children can be trained in L2 before the age of seven, their chances at full mastery will be much higher. Children learn languages with little effort, which is why they can be babbling during one year and speaking with complete, complex ideas just a few years later. It is important to know that language is innate, meaning that our brains are ready to learn a language from birth. Yet a lot of language learning is behavioral, meaning that children imitate adults' speech.

> One of the most important things to know about the differences between first language and second language acquisition is that people usually will master L1, but they will almost never be fully proficient in L2.

L2 Acquisition

L2 acquisition is much harder for adults. Multiple theories of L2 acquisition have been developed by researchers such as Jim Cummins. Cummins argues that there are two types of language that usually need to be acquired by students learning English as a second language: Basic Interpersonal Communication Skills (BICS) and Cognitive Academic Language Proficiency (CALP). BICS is general, everyday language used to communicate simple thoughts. In contrast, CALP is the more complex, academic language used in school. It is harder for students to acquire CALP, and many teachers mistakenly assume that students can learn complex academic concepts in English if they have already mastered BICS. The truth is that CALP takes much longer to master and, in some cases, particularly with little exposure in certain subjects, it may never be mastered.

Five principles of L2 aquisition

Another set of theories is based on Stephen Krashen's research in L2 acquisition. Most people understand his theories based on five principles:

1. The **ACQUISITION-LEARNING HYPOTHESIS:** This states that there is a difference between learning a language and acquiring it. Children "acquire" a first language easily—it's natural. But adults often have to "learn" a language through coursework, studying, and memorizing. One can acquire a second language, but often it requires more deliberate and natural interaction with that language.

2. The **MONITOR HYPOTHESIS:** This is when the learned language "monitors" the acquired language. In other words, this is when a person's "grammar check" kicks in and keeps awkward, incorrect language out of a person's L2 communication.

3. The **NATURAL ORDER HYPOTHESIS:** This suggests that the learning of grammatical structures is predictable and follows a "natural order."

4. The **INPUT HYPOTHESIS:** Some people call this "comprehensible input." This means that a language learner will learn best when the instruction or conversation is just above the learner's ability. That way, the learner has the foundation to understand most of the language, but will still have to figure out, often in context, what the more difficult elements mean.

5. The **AFFECTIVE FILTER HYPOTHESIS:** This suggests that people will learn a second language when they are relaxed, have high levels of motivation, and have a decent level of self-confidence.

ACQUISITION-LEARNING HYPOTHESIS: there is a difference between learning a language and acquiring it

MONITOR HYPOTHESIS: the learned language "monitors" the acquired language; a person's "grammar check" kicks in and keeps awkward, incorrect language out of a person's L2 communication

NATURAL ORDER HYPOTHESIS: the learning of grammatical structures is predictable and follows a "natural order"

INPUT HYPOTHESIS: a language learner will learn best when the instruction or conversation is just above the learner's ability

AFFECTIVE FILTER HYPOTHESIS: people will learn a second language when they are relaxed, have high levels of motivation, and have a decent level of self-confidence

English as a Second Language

Teaching students who are learning English as a Second Language (ESOL) poses some unique challenges, particularly in a standards-based environment. The key is realizing that no matter how little English a student knows, the teacher should teach with the student's developmental level in mind. This means that instruction should not be "dumbed-down" for ESOL students. Different approaches should be used, however, to ensure that these students get multiple opportunities to learn and practice English and still learn content.

Approaches to ESOL students

Many ESOL approaches are based on social learning methods. By being placed in mixed level groups or by being paired with a student of another ability level, students will get a chance to practice English in a natural, nonthreatening environment. Students should not be pushed into these groups to use complex language or to experiment with words that are too difficult. They should simply get a chance to practice with simple words and phrases.

Additional accommodations for ESOL students

ESOL students may need additional accommodations with assessments, assignments, and projects. For example, teachers may find that written tests provide little to no information about a student's understanding of the content. Therefore, an oral test may be better suited for ESOL students. When students are somewhat comfortable and capable with written tests, a shortened test may actually be preferable; take note that they will need extra time to translate.

Most lay people believe that in high school and college, learning a language strictly involves drills, memorization, and tests. While this is a common method (some people call it a structural, grammatical, or linguistic approach), it certainly does not work for all students.

> In teacher-directed instructional situations, visual aids, such as pictures, objects, and video, are particularly effective in helping students make connections between words and items with which they are already familiar.

SKILL 4.2 Identifies expected stages and patterns of second-language acquisition, including analyzing factors that affect second-language acquisition

The Five Stages of Second-Language Development

There is wide agreement that there are generally five stages of second-language development.

THE FIVE STAGES OF SECOND-LANGUAGE DEVELOPMENT	
Preproduction	While these students may actually understand what someone says to them (for the most part), they have a much harder time talking back in the target language. Teachers must realize that if a student cannot "produce" the target language, it does not mean that they aren't learning. Most likely, they are. They are taking it in, and their brains are trying to figure out what to do with all the new language.
Early Production	This is where the student can actually start to produce the target language. It is quite limited, and teachers most likely should not expect students to produce eloquent speeches during this time.
Speech Emergence	Longer, more complex sentences are used, particularly in speech—and in social situations. But remember that students aren't fully fluent in this stage, and they cannot handle complex academic language tasks.

Continued on next page

Intermediate Fluency	This is where more complex language is produced. Grammatical errors are common.
Advanced Fluency	While students may appear to be completely fluent, they will still need academic and language support from teachers.

Many people say that there are prescribed amounts of time by which students should reach each stage. However, keep in mind that it depends on the level at which students are exposed to the language. For example, students who get opportunities to practice with the target language outside of school may have greater ease in reaching the fifth stage more quickly. In general, though, it does take years to reach the fifth stage, and students should never be expected to have complete mastery within one school year.

Factors that Affect Second-Language Acquisition

Many factors affect someone's ability to pick up a second or third language. Age is one common factor. It is said that after a certain age (usually seven), learning a second language becomes much more difficult. But many social factors, such as anxiety, influence language learning. Often, informal social settings are more conducive to second-language learning. Motivation is another factor. A final important factor, particularly for teachers, is the strategies one uses to learn a language. For example, memorizing words out of context is not as effective as using words strategically for a real-life purpose.

For more information on second-language acquisition see:

www.everythingesl.net or http://www.nwrel. org/request/2003may/ overview.html.

> **SKILL 4.3** Identifies approaches that are effective in promoting English Language Learners' development of English language proficiency, including adapting teaching strategies and consulting and collaborating with teachers in the ESL program

From high school and college, most of us think that learning a language strictly involves drills, memorization, and tests. As mentioned earlier this works for some students, but certainly not for all.

Commonly Used Second Language Teaching Methods

Cognitive approach

Although dozens of methods have been developed to help people learn additional languages, these are some of the more common approaches used in today's K-12 classrooms. COGNITIVE APPROACHES to language learning focus on concepts. While words and grammar are important, when teachers use the cognitive approach, they focus on using language for conceptual purposes—rather than learning words and grammar for the sake of simply learning new words and grammatical structures. This approach focuses heavily on students' learning styles and it cannot necessarily be pinned down as having specific techniques. Rather, it is more of a philosophy of instruction.

Functional approach

Many approaches are noted for their motivational purposes. In a general sense, when teachers work to motivate students to learn a language, they do things to help reduce fear and to assist students in identifying with native speakers of the target language. A very common method is often called the FUNCTIONAL APPROACH. In this approach, the teacher focuses on communicative elements. For example, a first grade ESOL teacher might help students learn phrases that will assist them in finding a restroom, asking for help on the playground, etc. Many functionally based adult ESOL programs help learners with travel-related phrases and words.

Total physical response

Another very common motivational approach is TOTAL PHYSICAL RESPONSE. This is a kinesthetic approach that combines language learning and physical movement. In essence, students learn new vocabulary and grammar by responding with physical motion to verbal commands. Some people say it is particularly effective because the physical actions help to create good brain connections with the words.

In general, the best methods do not treat students as if they have a language deficit. Rather, the best methods build upon what students already know, and they help to instill the target language as a communicative process rather than a list of vocabulary words that have to be memorized.

The Importance of Consistency

In addition to these methods, it is important—particularly when second language learners have multiple teachers, such as in middle or high school—that teachers communicate and collaborate in order to provide a great level of consistency. It is particularly difficult for second language learners to go from one class to the next,

COGNITIVE APPROACH: an approach to teaching a second language that focuses on concepts and using language for conceptual purposes

FUNCTIONAL APPROACH: an approach to teaching a second language that focuses on communicative elements

In a general sense, when teachers work to motivate students to learn a language, they do things to help reduce fear and to assist students in identifying with native speakers of the target language.

TOTAL PHYSICAL RESPONSE: this approach to teaching a second language combines language learning and physical movement where there are different sets of expectations and varied methods of instruction and still focus on the more complex elements of learning language.

When students have higher levels of anxiety regarding the learning of a second language, they will be less likely to focus on the language; rather, they will be focusing on whatever it is that is creating their anxiety. This does not mean that standards and expectations should be different for these students in all classes; it simply means that teachers should have common expectations so that students know what to expect in each class and don't have to think about the differences between classes.

Another hugely important reason for teachers to collaborate, particularly with the ESOL specialists, is to ensure that students are showing consistent development across classes. Where there is inconsistency, teachers should work to uncover what it is that is keeping the student from excelling in a particular class.

Young Second Language Learners

> The most important concept to remember regarding the difference between learning a first and second language is that, if the learner is approximately age seven or older, learning a second language will occur very differently in the learner's brain than it would in a younger student.

A language-learning function exists in young children that appears to go away as they mature. Learning a language before age seven is almost guaranteed, with relatively little effort. The mind is like a sponge, and it soaks up language very readily. Some theorists, including the famous linguist Noam Chomsky, argue that the brain has a universal grammar and that only vocabulary and very particular grammatical structures, related to specific languages, need to be introduced in order for a child to learn a language. In essence, a child's mind has slots that language fills in, which is definitely not the case with learning a second language after about seven years old.

Older Second Language Learners

Learning a second language as a preadolescent, adolescent, or adult requires quite a bit of translation from the first language to the second. Vocabulary and grammar particulars are memorized, not necessarily internalized (at least, as readily as a first language). In fact, many (though not all) people who are immersed in a second language never fully function as fluent in the language. They may appear to be totally fluent, but often there will be small traits that are hard to pick up and internalize.

It is fairly clear that learning a second language successfully does require fluency in the first language. This is because, as stated above, the second language is translated from the first in the learner's mind. First language literacy is also a crucial factor in second language learning, particularly second language literacy.

When helping second language learners make the "crossover" in language fluency or literacy from first language to second language, it is important to help them identify strategies they use in the first language and apply those to the second language. It is also important to note similarities and differences in phonetic principals in the two languages. Sometimes it is helpful to encourage students to translate; other times, it is helpful for them to practice production in the target language. In either case, teachers must realize that learning a second language is a slow and complicated process.

> *Teachers must realize that learning a second language is a slow and complicated process.*

> SKILL 4.4 **Recognizes the role of oral language development, including vocabulary development, and the role of the alphabetic principle, including phonemic awareness and other phonological skills, in the development of English literacy; and identifies expected stages and patterns in English literacy development**

Five Areas of Reading Instruction

In 2000, the National Reading Panel released its now well-known report on teaching children to read. In a way, this report slightly put to rest the debate between phonics and whole-language. It argued, essentially, that word-letter recognition was as important as was understanding of what the text means. The report's "Big 5" critical areas of reading instruction are:

Phonemic awareness

The acknowledgement of sounds and words, for example, a child's realization that some words rhyme is one of the skills that fall under this category. Onset and rhyme are skills that might help students learn that the sound of the first letter "b" in the word "bad" can be changed with the sound "d" to make it "dad." The key in **PHONEMIC AWARENESS** is that when you teach it to children, it can be taught with the students' eyes closed. In other words, it's all about sounds, not about ascribing written letters to sounds.

> **PHONEMIC AWARENESS:** a student's acknowledgement of sounds and words

Phonics

As opposed to phonemic awareness, the study of **PHONICS** must be done with the eyes open. It's the connection between the sounds and letters on a page. In other words, students learning phonics might see the word "bad" and sound each letter out slowly until they recognize that they just said the word.

> **PHONICS:** a student's connection between the sounds and letters on a page

Fluency

When students practice **FLUENCY**, they practice reading connected pieces of text. In other words, instead of looking at a word as just a word, they might read a sentence straight through. The point of fluency is for the student to comprehend what she is reading. She would need to be able to "fluently" piece words in a sentence together quickly. If a student is NOT fluent in reading, he would sound each letter or word out slowly and pay more attention to the phonics of each word. A fluent reader, on the other hand, might read a sentence out loud using appropriate intonations.

> **FLUENCY:** a student's ability to read connected pieces of text and comprehend what is read

> *The best way to test for fluency is to have a student read something out loud, preferably a few sentences in a row—or more.*

The best way to test for fluency is to have a student read something out loud, preferably a few sentences in a row—or more. Sure, most students just learning to read will probably not be very fluent right away; but with practice, they will increase their fluency. Even though fluency is not the same as comprehension, it is said that fluency is a good predictor of comprehension. Think about it: If you're focusing too much on sounding out each word, you're not going to be paying attention to the meaning.

Comprehension

COMPREHENSION simply means that the reader can ascribe meaning to text. Even though students may be good with phonics, and even know what many words on a page mean, some of them are not able to demonstrate comprehension because they do not have the strategies that would help them to comprehend. For example, students should know that stories often have structures (beginning, middle, and end). They should also know that when they are reading something and it does not make sense, they will need to employ "fix-up" strategies where they go back into the text they just read and look for clues. Teachers can use many strategies to teach comprehension, including questioning, asking students to paraphrase or summarize, utilizing graphic organizers, and focusing on mental images.

> **COMPREHENSION:** a student's ability to ascribe meaning to text

Vocabulary

Students will be better at comprehension if they have a stronger working **VOCABULARY**. Research has shown that students learn more vocabulary when it is presented in context, rather than in vocabulary lists, for example. Furthermore, the more students get to use particular words in context, the more they will remember each word, and utilize it in the comprehension of sentences that contain the words.

> **VOCABULARY:** a student's knowledge of the definition of individual words and the ability to utilize them in context

Teaching Reading Instruction

Methods used to teach these skills are often featured in a BALANCED LITERACY CURRICULUM that focuses on the use of skills in various instructional contexts. For example, with independent reading, students independently choose books that are at their reading levels; with guided reading, teachers work with small groups of students to help them with their particular reading problems; with whole group reading, the entire class will read the same text and the teacher will incorporate activities to help students learn phonics, comprehension, fluency, and vocabulary. In addition to these components of balanced literacy, teachers incorporate writing so that students can learn the structures of communicating through text.

> **BALANCED LITERACY CURRICULUM:** an approach to teaching that focuses on the use of skills in various instructional contexts

Vocabulary Instruction

CONTENT AREA VOCABULARY is the specific vocabulary related to particular concepts of various academic disciplines (social science, science, math, art, etc).

While teachers tend to think of content area vocabulary as something that should just be focused on at the secondary level (middle and high school), even elementary school–aged students studying various subjects will understand concepts better when the vocabulary used to describe them is explicitly explained. But it is true that in the secondary level, where students go to teachers for the various subjects, content area vocabulary becomes more emphasized.

> **CONTENT AREA VOCABULARY:** the specific vocabulary related to particular concepts of various academic disciplines (social science, science, math, art, etc.)

Often, educators believe that vocabulary should just be taught in the Language Arts class, not realizing that:

1. There is not enough time for students to learn the enormous vocabulary in order to be successful with a standards-based education

2. The teaching of vocabulary, related to a particular subject, is a very good way to help students understand the subject better

Common questions about vocabulary instruction

How should content area teachers teach vocabulary?

First and foremost, teachers should teach students strategies to determine the meanings for difficulty vocabulary when they encounter it on their own. Teachers can do this by teaching students how to identify the meanings of words in context (usually through activities where the word is taken out and the students have to figure out a way to make sense of the sentence). In addition, dictionary skills must be taught in all subject areas. Teachers should also consider teaching vocabulary is not just the teaching of words: rather, it is the teaching of complex concepts, each with histories and connotations.

When teachers explicitly teach vocabulary, it is best if they can connect new words to words, ideas, and experiences with which students are already familiar.

When teachers explicitly teach vocabulary, it is best if they can connect new words to words, ideas, and experiences with which students are already familiar. This will help to reduce the strangeness of the new words. Furthermore, the more concrete the examples, the more likely students will be to use the word in context.

Finally, students need plenty of exposure to the new words. They need to be able to hear and use the new words in many naturally produced sentences. The more one hears and uses a sentence in context, the more the word is solidified in the person's long-term vocabulary.

What can teachers expect in their students' literacy development? Are there benchmarks that can be expected by age?

The answer to these questions is fuzzy. While teachers can anticipate that certain skills can be mastered by certain ages, all children are different. When development is too far off the general target, then intervention may be necessary.

For more detailed information on literacy development see:

http://www.learningpt.org/pdfs/literacy/readingbirth-tofive.pdf

By their first year, babies can identify words and notice the social and directive impacts of language. By their second year, children have decent vocabularies, make believe that they are reading books (especially if their role models read), and can follow simple oral stories. By their third year, children have more advanced skills in listening and speaking. Within the next few years, children are capable of using longer sentences, retelling parts of stories, counting, and "scribbling" messages. They are capable of learning the basics of phonemic awareness.

At about five years old, children are really ready to begin learning phonics. Many teachers mistake phonics as being just a step in the process toward comprehension, when in fact, children are fully capable of learning how to comprehend and make meaning at the same age. Phonics, though, ideally will be mastered by second to third grade.

> **SKILL 4.5 Identifies factors that influence students' literacy development, and demonstrating knowledge of research-validated instructional strategies for addressing the literacy needs of students at all stages of literacy development, including applying strategies for facilitating students' comprehension of texts before, during, and after reading, and using modeling and explicit instruction to teach students how to use comprehension strategies effectively**

The point of comprehension instruction is not necessarily to focus just on the text(s) students are using at the very moment of instruction, but rather to help them learn the strategies that they can use independently with any other text.

COMMON METHODS OF TEACHING INSTRUCTION	
Summarization	Students go over the main point of the text, along with strategically chosen details that highlight the main point. This is not the same as paraphrasing, which is saying the same thing in different words. Teaching students how to summarize is very important because it will help them look for the most critical areas in a text and in nonfiction. For example, it will help them distinguish between main arguments and examples. In fiction, it helps students to learn how to focus on the main characters and events and distinguish those from the lesser characters and events.
Question Answering	While this tends to be overused in many classrooms, it is still a valid method of teaching students to comprehend. Students answer questions regarding a text, either out loud, in small groups, or individually on paper. The best questions are those that cause students to think about the text (rather than just find an answer within the text).
Question Generating	This is the opposite of question answering, although students can then be asked to answer their own questions or the questions of peers. In general, we want students to constantly question texts as they read. This is important because it causes students to become more critical readers. To teach students to generate questions helps them to learn the types of questions they can ask, and it gets them thinking about how best to be critical of texts.
Graphic Organizers	Graphic organizers are graphical representations of content within a text. For example, Venn diagrams can be used to highlight the difference between two characters in a novel or two similar political concepts in a social studies textbook. Or, a teacher can use flow-charts with students to talk about the steps in a process, such as the steps of setting up a science experiment or the chronological events of a story. Semantic organizers are similar in that they graphically display information. The difference, usually, is that semantic organizers focus on words or concepts. For example, a word web can help students make sense of a word by mapping out from the central word all the similar and related concepts to that word.
Text Structure	Often in nonfiction—particularly in textbooks—and sometimes in fiction, text structures will give important clues to readers about what to look for. Students may not know how to make sense of all the types of headings in a textbook and do not realize that, for example, the side-bar story about a character in history is not the main text on a particular page in the history textbook. Teaching students how to interpret text structures gives them tools with which to tackle similar texts.
Monitoring Comprehension	Students need to be aware of their comprehension, or lack of it, in particular texts. So, it is important to teach students what to do when suddenly text stops making sense. For example, students can go back and reread the description of a character. Or, they can go back to the table of contents or the first paragraph of a chapter to see where they are headed.

Continued on next page

Textual Marking	This is where students interact with the text as they read. For example, armed with sticky notes, students can insert questions or comments regarding specific sentences or paragraphs within the text. This helps students focus on the importance of the small things, particularly when they are reading larger works (such as novels in high school). It also gives students a reference point on which to go back into the text when they need to review something.
Discussion	Small group or whole-class discussion stimulates thoughts about texts and gives students a larger picture of the impact of those texts. For example, teachers can strategically encourage students to discuss related concepts to the text. This helps students learn to consider texts within larger societal and social concepts. Or teachers can encourage students to provide personal opinions in discussion. By listening to various students' opinions, this will help all students in a class to see the wide range of possible interpretations and thoughts regarding one text.

Many people mistakenly believe that the terms "research-based," "research-validated," or "evidence-based" relate mainly to specific programs, such as early reading textbook programs. While research does validate that some of these programs are effective, much research has been conducted regarding the effectiveness of particular instructional strategies. In reading, many of these strategies have been documented in the report from the National Reading Panel (2000).

Just because a strategy has not been validated as effective by research, however, does not necessarily mean that it is not effective with certain students in certain situations. The number of strategies out there far outweighs researchers' ability to test their effectiveness. Some of the strategies listed above have been validated by rigorous research, while others have been shown consistently to help improve students' reading abilities in localized situations. There simply is not enough space to list all the strategies out there that have been proven effective; just know that the strategies described above are very commonly cited as working in a variety of situations.

> **SKILL 4.6** Recognizes similarities and differences between the English literacy development of native English speakers and English Language Learners, including how literacy development in the primary language influences literacy development in English, and applies strategies for helping English Language Learners transfer literacy skills in the primary language to English

See Skill 4.3

The educational community has not done the best job at transitioning students into reading tasks that require accessing information, making real-world judgments, or comprehending directions. Typically, children are taught to read with fiction and then suddenly are handed science and social science textbooks. Teachers believe the students will be able to handle the material successfully.

Judging Sources

While it is a bit of an exaggeration to say that teachers do not use nonfiction in younger grades, it is true that many students are completely unprepared to use textbooks with complete ease. Furthermore, when teachers start to assign research projects in upper elementary, middle school, and/or high school, they forget that students not only struggle with comprehending nonfiction sources, they also struggle with assessing the reliability of sources. This is why, in these days where students are often better at using the Internet than some of their teachers, the sources of students' research projects are not always reliable. While they can easily navigate around the Web, they do not always have the ability to decide whether a Web site is professional or not.

While they can easily navigate around the Web, students do not always have the ability to decide whether a Web site is professional or not.

The reason for this is simple: inexperience with having to judge sources, combined with the lack of instruction regarding the proper selection of sources. To go a bit deeper, another reason for this is that students do not always know strategies for reading content-area material.

Example of student challenges in judging sources

Let's take middle school subjects, for example. The English-Language Arts teacher, who instructs students in the elements of fiction, such as character, setting, and plot, is teaching her students strategies for understanding fiction. Likewise, that same teacher who conducts lessons on rhyme and imagery in poetry is teaching her students the strategies for reading poetry. When do students get the opportunity to study the ways in which we come to understand the material in the science textbook or the math textbook?

Too often, we assume that they will naturally be able to read those materials. And too often, teachers then find that our students are completely lost in a science textbook. With today's textbooks, the struggle to make sense of the material goes

With today's textbooks, the struggle to make sense of the material goes further: to supposedly keep students' attention, textbooks contain flashy graphics, side-bars with somewhat related information, discussion questions, vocabulary entries, etc. Some students simply do not know which parts of the text are required reading and which are peripheral.

further: to supposedly keep students' attention, textbooks contain flashy graphics, side-bars with somewhat related information, discussion questions, vocabulary entries, etc. Surprisingly, some students simply do not know which parts of the text are required reading and which are peripheral.

Strategies to help students

To improve this situation, it is strongly recommended that teachers explicitly teach the strategies needed to make sense of nonfiction sources. Some of the strategies are:

STRATEGIES TO TEACH NONFICTION SOURCES	
Text Structure	This refers to both the arrangement of a book (e.g., chapters, sub-headings, etc.) as well as the method of paragraphs (e.g., a paragraph that introduces a concept and explains it, versus one that compares and contrasts one concept with another).
Summarization	This is much harder for students than it may seem. Too often, students believe that summarization is simply the retelling of information that has been read. In actuality, summarization requires that the student identify the most important details, identify the main point, and highlight the pieces of a text that give light to that main point.
Source Identification	Although this isn't a term that gets used too much, the concept is very important. Teachers must instruct students explicitly in methods of determining whether a Web site, for example, is reliable or not. Methods for doing so include discussing author credentials, page layout, Web site links, etc.
Vocabulary	Teachers need to train students to look up words they are unfamiliar with or use textbook-provided glossaries. When students are unfamiliar with vocabulary used in textbooks, comprehension is much slower.
Text Annotation	Students will be more active readers if they interact with the text they are reading in some fashion. Marking texts can help students identify for themselves what concepts they are already familiar with, what concepts they are unclear about, or what concepts interest them.
Background Knowledge	Students who find a way to activate background knowledge will be far more successful with reading nonfiction than those who do not. This is because background knowledge serves as a place to organize and attach new knowledge more quickly.

While many more strategies can be used, remember that students need explicit instruction in understanding and accessing nonfiction material.

COMPETENCY 5

UNDERSTAND DIVERSE STUDENT POPULATIONS, AND USE KNOWLEDGE OF DIVERSITY WITHIN THE SCHOOL AND THE COMMUNITY TO ADDRESS THE NEEDS OF ALL LEARNERS, TO CREATE A SENSE OF COMMUNITY AMONG STUDENTS, AND TO PROMOTE STUDENTS' APPRECIATION OF AND RESPECT FOR INDIVIDUALS AND GROUPS

> **SKILL 5.1** **Recognizes appropriate strategies for teachers to use to enhance their own understanding of students** *(e.g., learning about students' family situations, cultural backgrounds, individual needs)* **and to promote a sense of community among diverse groups in the classroom**

Effective teaching and learning for students begins with teachers who can demonstrate sensitivity for diversity in teaching and relationships within school communities. Student portfolios should include work that includes a multicultural perspective. Teachers also need to be responsive to including cultural and diverse resources in their curriculum and instructional practices.

Cultural Sensitivity in the Classroom

Exposing students to culturally sensitive room decorations or posters that show positive and inclusive messages is one way to demonstrate inclusion of multiple cultures. Teachers should also continuously make cultural connections that are relevant and empowering for all students while communicating academic and behavioral expectations. Cultural sensitivity is communicated beyond the classroom with parents and community members to establish and maintain relationships.

Defining diversity

Diversity can be defined as the following:

- Differences among learners, classroom settings, and academic outcomes

- Biological, sociological, ethnicity, socioeconomic status, psychological needs, learning modalities, and styles among learners

- Differences in classroom settings that promote learning opportunities, such as collaborative, participatory, and individualized learning groupings

- Expected learning outcomes for students that are theoretical, affective, and cognitive

Expressing diversity

In a culturally sensitive classroom, teachers maintain equity and fairness in student interactions and curriculum implementation. Assessments include cultural responses and perspectives that become further learning opportunities for students. Other artifacts that could reflect teacher and student sensitivity to diversity might consist of:

> Teachers should establish a classroom climate that is culturally respectful and engaging for all students.

- Student portfolios reflecting multicultural/multiethnic perspectives

- Journals and reflections from field trips and guest speakers from diverse cultural backgrounds

- Printed materials and wall displays from multicultural perspectives

- Parent or guardian letters in a variety of languages reflecting cultural diversity

- Projects that include cultural history and diverse inclusions

- Disaggregated student data reflecting cultural groups

- Classroom climate of professionalism that fosters diversity and cultural inclusion

Benefits of diversity

The encouragement of diversity education allows teachers a variety of opportunities to expand their experiences with students, staff, community members, and parents from culturally diverse backgrounds. These experiences can be proactively applied to promote cultural diversity inclusion in the classroom. Teachers are able to engage and challenge students to develop and incorporate their own diversity skills in building character and relationships with cultures beyond their own. In changing the thinking patterns of students to become more culturally inclusive in the twenty-first century, teachers are addressing the globalization of our world.

> **SKILL 5.2** Applies strategies for working effectively with students from all cultures, students of both genders, students from various socioeconomic circumstances, students from homes where English is not the primary language, and students whose home situations involve various family arrangements and lifestyles

A positive environment, where open, discussion-oriented, nonthreatening communication among all students can occur, is a critical factor in creating an effective learning culture. The teacher must take the lead and model appropriate actions and speech, while intervening quickly when a student makes a misstep and offends (often inadvertently) another.

Common Communication Issues

Communication issues that the teacher in a diverse classroom should be aware of include:

- Being sensitive to terminology and language patterns that may exclude or demean students. Regularly switch between the use of "he" and "she" in speech and writing. Know and use the current terms that ethnic and cultural groups use to identify themselves (e.g., "Latinos" vs. "Hispanics").

- Being aware of body language that is intimidating or offensive to some cultures, such as direct eye contact, and adjusting accordingly.

- Monitoring your own reactions to students to ensure equal responses to males and females, as well as differently performing students.

- Not "protecting" students from criticism because of their ethnicity or gender. Likewise, acknowledge and praise all meritorious work without singling out any one student. Both actions can make all students hyper-aware of ethnic and gender differences and cause anxiety or resentment throughout the class.

- Emphasizing the importance of discussing and considering different viewpoints and opinions. Demonstrate and express value for all opinions and comments and lead students to do the same.

Gender differences

When teaching in diverse classrooms, teachers must also expect to be working and communicating with all kinds of students. The first obvious difference among students is gender. Interactions with male students are often different from those with female students. Depending on the lesson, female students are more likely to be interested in working with partners or perhaps even individually. On the other hand, male students may enjoy a more collaborative or hands-on activity. The gender of the teacher may also come into play when working with male and female students. Of course, every student is different and may not fit into a stereotypical role; getting to know their students' preferences for learning will help teachers to truly enhance learning in the classroom.

Cultural differences

Most class rosters will consist of students from a variety of cultures. Teachers should get to know their students (of all cultures) so that they may incorporate elements of their cultures into classroom activities and planning. Also, getting to know about a student's background or cultural traditions helps to build a rapport with each student, as well as further educate the teacher about the world in which he or she teaches.

Teachers should get to know their students (of all cultures) so that they may incorporate elements of their cultures into classroom activities and planning.

Language differences

For students still learning English, teachers must make every attempt to communicate with that student daily. Whether it's with another student who speaks the same language, word cards, computer programs, drawings, or other methods, teachers must find ways to encourage each student's participation. Of course, the teacher must be sure the appropriate language services begin for the student in a timely manner, as well.

Socioeconomic differences

Teachers must also consider students from various socioeconomic backgrounds. These students are just as likely as anyone else to work well in a classroom; unfortunately, sometimes difficulties occur with these children when it comes to completing homework consistently. These students may need help deriving a homework system or perhaps need more attention on study or test-taking skills. Teachers should encourage these students as much as possible and offer positive reinforcements when they meet or exceed classroom expectations. Teachers should also watch these students carefully for signs of malnutrition, fatigue, or possible learning disorders.

See Skill 14.1 for more information regarding how differences among students affect communication in the classroom.

SKILL 5.3 Applies strategies for promoting students' understanding and appreciation of diversity and for using diversity that exists within the classroom and the community to enhance all students' learning

In personalized learning communities, relationships and connections between students, staff, parents, and community members promote lifelong learning for all students. Setting school climates that are inclusive of the multicultural demographic student population create positive and proactive mission and vision themes that align student and staff expectations.

Emphasizing Diversity

The following factors enable students and staff to emphasize and integrate diversity in student learning:

- Inclusion of multicultural themes in curriculum and assessments

- Creation of a learning environment that promotes multicultural research, learning, collaboration, and social construction of knowledge and application

- Providing learning tasks that emphasize student cognitive, critical-thinking, and problem-solving skills

- Learning tasks that personalize the cultural aspects of diversity and celebrate diversity in the subject matter and student projects

- Promotion of intercultural positive social peer interrelationships and connections

Communicating Diversity

Teachers communicate diversity in instructional practices and experiential learning activities that create curiosity in students who want to understand the interrelationship of cultural experiences. Students become self-directed in discovering the global world in and outside the classroom.

Intercultural communication model

In the **INTERCULTURAL COMMUNICATION MODEL**, students learn how different cultures engage in both verbal and nonverbal modes of communicating meaning. Students who become multilingual in understanding the stereotypes that have defined other cultures are able to create new bonding experiences that will typify a more integrated global culture. Students who understand how to effectively

School communities that promote an inclusion of diversity in the classroom, community, curriculum, and connections enable students to maximize their academic capabilities and educational opportunities.

Teachers understand that when diversity becomes an integral part of the classroom environment, students become global thinkers and doers.

INTERCULTURAL COMMUNICATION MODEL: a learning model in which students learn how different cultures engage in both verbal and nonverbal modes of communicating meaning

Teaching students how to incorporate learning techniques from a cultural aspect enriches the cognitive expansion experience since students are able to expand their cultural knowledge bases.

communicate with diverse cultural groups are able to maximize their own learning experiences by being able to transmit, both verbally and nonverbally, cues and expectations in project collaborations or in performance-based activities.

The learning curve for teachers in intercultural understanding is exponential in that they are able to engage all learners in the academic process and learning engagement. Teaching students how to incorporate learning techniques from a cultural aspect enriches the cognitive expansion experience since students are able to expand their cultural knowledge bases.

SKILL 5.4 Analyzes how classroom environments that respect diversity promote positive student experiences

Benefits of Promoting Diversity

When diversity is promoted in learning environments and curriculum, both students and teachers are the beneficiaries of increased academic success. Teachers who are able to create global thinkers are helping students identify cultural assumptions and biases that may direct the type of social and academic groupings. These groupings are occurring in the classroom and influence the type of thinking and ability of students to construct appropriate learning experiences. For example, if a student is struggling in math, a teacher can examine the cultural aspect of learning math. For some students, math is insignificant when socioeconomic issues of poverty and survival are the daily reality of their existence. When students see parents juggling finances, the only math that becomes important for them is that less is never enough to keep the lights on and mortgage paid.

Using classrooms as vital resources for cultural and ethnic inclusion can assist students in contributing cultural norms and artifacts to the acquisition of learning.

Incorporating diversity in the classroom

When there is equity in pedagogy, teachers are able to use a variety of instructional styles to facilitate diversity in both cooperative learning and individualized instruction that will provide more opportunities for positive student experiences and lead to future academic success. Empowering the school culture and climate by establishing an antibias learning environment as well as promoting multicultural learning activities will discourage disproportional and unfair labeling of certain students.

Toolkits

Teachers can use various toolkits to evaluate the ethnic and cultural inclusion in classroom. Effective promotion of diversity should translate into increased academic success and opportunities for all students. Looking at diverse or homogenous groupings in the classroom can provide teachers with opportunities to restructure cooperative learning groupings and increase diverse student interactions, which can provide increased improvements for school communities.

Culture grams and technology

Using culture grams to help students understand different cultures and research cultural diversity is a useful tool for helping teachers profile students' learning styles and engagement in the classroom. Students can also use technology to network and learn how students in other cultures or other states learn.

An interesting aspect of using culture grams is the manner in which it helps students connect to other cultures and their perceptions of students who identify with different cultures.

> The ability to communicate with other learners provides another way of compiling and categorizing cultural profiles that may assist teachers in identifying learning styles and how students acquire learning.

COMPETENCY 6

UNDERSTAND THE CHARACTERISTICS AND NEEDS OF STUDENTS WITH DISABILITIES, DEVELOPMENTAL DELAYS, AND EXCEPTIONAL ABILITIES (INCLUDING GIFTED AND TALENTED STUDENTS); AND USE THIS KNOWLEDGE TO HELP STUDENTS REACH THEIR HIGHEST LEVELS OF ACHIEVEMENT AND INDEPENDENCE

SKILL 6.1 **Demonstrates awareness of types of disabilities, developmental delays, and exceptional abilities and of the implications for learning associated with these differences**

Many types of disabilities are found in children and adults. Some disabilities are entirely physical, while others are entirely related to learning and the mind. Some involve a combination of both. When teachers notice abnormalities in the classroom, such as a student's incredible ability to solve a math problem without working it out (a potential attribute of giftedness) or another student's extreme trouble with spelling (a potential attribute of dyslexia), a teacher may suspect a disability is present.

Common Classroom Disabilities

Common learning disabilities include:

- Attention deficit hyperactivity disorder (where concentration can be very difficult)

- Auditory processing disorders (where listening comprehension is very difficult)

- Visual processing disorders (where reading and visual memory may be impaired)

- Dyslexia (where reading may be difficult)

Some physical disabilities include:

- Down's Syndrome

- Cerebral Palsy

Developmental disabilities might include the lack of ability to use fine motor skills.

Dealing with Giftedness and Disabilities

When giftedness is observed, teachers should also concern themselves with ensuring that such children receive the attention they need and deserve so they can continue to learn and grow.

The list of possible disabilities is almost endless. When noticed, teachers might seek the help of specialists within their school to determine if further testing or intervention is needed.

> **SKILL 6.2** Applies criteria and procedures for evaluating, selecting, creating, and modifying materials and equipment to address individual special needs, and recognizing the importance of consulting with specialists to identify appropriate materials and equipment, including assistive technology, when working with students with disabilities, developmental delays, or exceptional abilities

A teacher's responsibility to students extends beyond the four walls of the school building. In addition to offering well-planned and articulately delivered lessons, the teacher must consider the effects of both body language and spoken language on students' learning. Furthermore, today's educator must address the needs of diverse learners within a single classroom. The teacher is able to attain materials that may be necessary for the majority of the regular education students and some of the special needs children and, more and more frequently, one individual student. The effective teacher knows that there are currently hundreds of adaptive materials that could be used to help these students increase achievement and develop skills.

A teacher's responsibility to students extends beyond the four walls of the school building.

Materials to Address Student Learning Needs

Student-centered classrooms contain not only textbooks, workbooks, and literature materials, they also rely heavily on a variety of audio-visual equipment and computers. Tape recorders, language masters, and DVD players can help meet the learning styles of some of the students.

Student-centered classrooms contain not only textbooks, workbooks, and literature materials but also rely heavily on a variety of audio-visual equipment and computers.

Although most school centers cannot supply all of the possible materials all special needs students within their school may require, each district, more than likely, has a resource center where teachers can borrow special equipment. Most community-support agencies offer assistance in providing necessary equipment or materials to serve students and adults with special needs. Teachers must be familiar with procedures to obtain a wide range of materials including:

- School supplies
- Medical care
- Clothing
- Food
- Adaptive computers
- Books (such as Braille)

- Eye glasses
- Hearing aids
- Wheelchairs
- Counseling
- Transportation

Dealing with Individual Student Needs

A teacher's job would be relatively easy if simply instructing students in current curriculum objectives was his or her only responsibility. Today's educator must first ensure that the students are able to come to school, are able to attend to the curriculum, have their individual learning styles met, and are motivated to work to their fullest capacity.

Individualized Education Plans

Many special needs students have an Individualized Educational Plan (IEP) or a 504 Plan. These documents clearly state the students' educational objectives and learning needs, as well as the individuals responsible for meeting these objectives.

A well-written IEP will contain evidence that the student is receiving resources from the school and the community that will assist in helping to meet the physical, social, and academic needs of the student.

The challenges of meeting the needs of all students in the classroom require that the teacher himself be a lifelong learner. Ongoing participation in professional staff development, attendance at local, state, and national conferences, and continuing education classes help teachers grow in many ways including an awareness of resources available for students.

> *The challenges of meeting the needs of all students in the classroom require that the teacher himself be a lifelong learner.*

SKILL 6.3 Identifies teacher responsibilities and requirements associated with referring students who may have special needs and with developing and implementing Individualized Education Plans (IEPs), and recognizes appropriate ways to integrate goals from IEPs into instructional activities and daily routines

---

Individuals with Disabilities Act and Child Study Teams

Collaborative teams play a crucial role in meeting the needs of all students, and they are an important step in helping to identify students with special needs. Under the **INDIVIDUALS WITH DISABILITIES ACT (IDEA)**, which federally mandates special education services in every state, it is the responsibility of public schools to ensure consultative, evaluative, and, if necessary, prescriptive services to children with special needs.

In most school districts, this responsibility is handled by a collaborative group of professionals called the **CHILD STUDY TEAM (CST)**. If a teacher or parent suspects a child is experiencing academic, social, or emotional problems a referral can be made to the CST. The CST will determine what evaluations or tests are necessary, if any, and will also discuss the results. Based on these results, the CST will suggest a plan of action if one is necessary.

> **INDIVIDUALS WITH DISABILITIES ACT (IDEA):** a federal act that mandates special education services in every state, it states that it is the responsibility of public schools to ensure consultative, evaluative, and, if necessary, prescriptive services to children with special needs

> **CHILD STUDY TEAM (CST):** a collaborative group of professionals who determine a plan of action for special needs children

Inclusion, Mainstreaming, and Least Restrictive Environment

Inclusion, mainstreaming, and least restrictive environment are interrelated policies under the IDEA, with varying degrees of statutory imperatives.

- Inclusion: the right of students with disabilities to be placed in the regular classroom

- **Least restrictive environment:** the mandate that children be educated to the maximum extent appropriate with their nondisabled peers

- **Mainstreaming:** a policy whereby disabled students can be placed in the regular classroom, as long as such placement does not interfere with the student's educational plan

Dealing with Special Student Needs

Academic Intervention Plan

One plan of action is an **ACADEMIC INTERVENTION PLAN (AIP)**. An AIP consists of additional instructional services that are provided to the student in order to help her better achieve academically. Often these plans are developed if the student has met certain criteria (such as scoring below the state reference point on standardized tests or performing more than two levels below grade-level).

> **ACADEMIC INTERVENTION PLAN (AIP):** consists of additional instructional services that are provided to the student in order to help her better achieve academically

504 Plan

Another plan of action is a 504 plan. A 504 plan is a legal document based on the provisions of the Rehabilitation Act of 1973 (which preceded IDEA). A **504 PLAN** is a plan of instructional services to assist students with special needs in a regular education classroom setting. When a student's physical, emotional, or other impairments (such as Attention Deficit Disorder) impact his ability to learn in a regular education classroom setting, that student can be referred for a 504 meeting. Typically, the CST and perhaps even the student's physician or therapist, will participate in the 504 meeting and review the student's specific needs to determine if a 504 plan will be written.

> **504 PLAN:** a plan of instructional services to assist students with special needs in a regular education classroom setting

Individualized Education Plan

Finally, a child referred to CST may qualify for an **INDIVIDUALIZED EDUCATION PLAN (IEP)**. An IEP is a legal document that delineates the specific, adapted services a student with disabilities will receive. An IEP differs from a 504 plan in that the child must be identified for special education services to qualify for an IEP, and all students who receive special education services must have an IEP. Each IEP must contain statements pertaining to the student's present performance level, annual goals, related services and supplementary aids, testing modifications, a projected date of services, and assessment methods for monitoring progress. At least once each year, the CST and guardians must meet to review and update a student's IEP.

> **INDIVIDUALIZED EDUCATION PLAN (IEP):** a legal document that delineates the specific, adapted services a student with disabilities will receive

> **SKILL 6.4** Demonstrates knowledge of basic service delivery models *(e.g., inclusion models)* for students with special needs, and identifies strategies and resources *(e.g., special education staff)* that help support instruction in inclusive settings

Special education teachers, resource specialists, school psychologists, and other special education staff are present on school campuses to be resources for students who have special educational needs. Occasionally, new teachers fear that when a resource specialist seeks to work with them, it means that the resource specialist does not think they are doing an adequate job in dealing with students with **Individualized Education Plans (IEPs)**. Quite the contrary is true. Many IEPs require that resource specialists work in students' general education classrooms. Considering that school is more than just about the learning of content standards—that it is often about socialization and the development of citizens for a democratic society—it is both counterproductive and unfair to exclude students from regular classrooms, even if they need some individualized assistance from a special education resource teacher.

Dealing with IEPS

First and foremost, teachers must be familiar with what is stated in their students' IEPs.

First and foremost, teachers must be familiar with what is stated in their students' IEPs. For example, some IEPs have explicit strategies that teachers should use to help the students learn effectively. Additionally, teachers may want to provide additional attention to these students to ensure that they are progressing effectively. Sometimes, it may be necessary to reduce or modify assignments for students with disabilities. For example, if a teacher were to assign fifteen math problems for homework, the assignment might be more effective if it is five problems for the students with disabilities. Teachers can use multiple strategies, group students in flexible situations, and pair them with others who can be of greater assistance.

Most resource specialists are trained particularly to work with general education teachers and most want to be able to do that in the most effective, nonthreatening way.

Finally, welcome and include the suggestions and assistance of the special education staff. Most resource specialists are trained particularly to work with general education teachers and most want to be able to do that in the most effective, nonthreatening way.

Other Special Education Services

Special education services are offered in many ways, and a student's IEP will determine their least restrictive environment. **Inclusion** refers to the situation where a student with special needs remains in the regular education classroom with the support of special education support staff (sometimes in the form of a personal or class aid). Sometimes, a student requires some resource room, or pull out, services. In these cases, students are taken into smaller class settings where personalized services are delivered in their greatest area(s) of difficulty. Students who have difficulty functioning in a regular education classroom are placed in smaller classrooms for the full school day. These are sometimes referred to as LD classrooms or **LEARNING DISABLED CLASSROOMS**.

> **SKILL 6.5** Demonstrates knowledge of strategies to ensure that students with special needs and exceptional abilities are an integral part of the class and participate to the greatest extent possible in all classroom activities

Per federal law, students with disabilities should be included as much as possible in the general education curriculum of their schools. While this may be difficult for new teachers (likewise, it may be difficult for new teachers to include gifted students in the general education curriculum), it is extremely important to do so.

Per federal law, students with disabilities should be included as much as possible in the general education curriculum of their schools.

Including Special Needs Students in the Classroom

Flexible grouping

FLEXIBLE GROUPING is a unique strategy to ensure that students with special needs are fully accommodated. While flexible grouping can indeed involve groups for various learning activities that will change (depending on the activity, or just depending on the need to rotate groups), when teachers consistently build in various group structures in order to accommodate various learning needs, their students will get varied and multiple opportunities to talk about, reflect upon, and question new learning. In some cases, teachers may wish to pair students with special needs with other students who are proficient in particular subjects; at other times, they may desire to pair students with others who have similar levels of proficiency.

FLEXIBLE GROUPING: a strategy whereby the teacher consistently builds in various group structures in order to accommodate various learning needs

Behavior issues

Behavior issues often cause students with special needs to be excluded from full class participation. It is important for teachers to note that, often, students with special needs do not want to be excluded and, often, they do not want to be "bad." Rather, they are seeking attention or they are bored. In either case, classroom activities must be developed with these concerns in mind. All students, in fact, will be more engaged with hands-on, real-world learning activities. Often,

It is important for teachers to note that, often, students with special needs do not want to be excluded and, often, they do not want to be "bad."

when teachers give students even small amounts of choice, such as letting them choose one of three topics to write about, students feel empowered. Students with special needs are no different.

Being "caught up"

Finally, many students with special needs want to stay "caught up" with the rest of the class, but occasionally they cannot. In such cases, it is imperative that teachers find ways that will allow these students to know that they are on the same page as the rest of the class. Reducing the amount of work for students with special needs is often productive; pairing such students with more proficient students can also be assistive.

Students with exceptional abilities

Students with exceptional abilities can be a great challenge for teachers. These students need to continue to learn, even if it is above and beyond the rest of the class.

Students with exceptional abilities can be a great challenge for teachers. It is very unfair to assume that since these students already "get it" that they can be ignored. These students need to continue to learn, even if it is above and beyond the rest of the class. Furthermore, they will often resent being so much smarter than the rest of the class because they are "called on" more or they are treated as if they do not need any attention. First, while these students are a fantastic resource for the rest of the class, being a resource is not their role in the classroom. They are there to learn, just like the rest of the class. They occasionally need different work to engage them and stimulate their minds. They do not simply need more work; this is unfair to them and it is insulting.

See also Skill 6.4

DOMAIN II
INSTRUCTION AND ASSESSMENT

PERSONALIZED STUDY PLAN

KNOWN MATERIAL/ SKIP IT

PAGE	COMPETENCY AND SKILL	
71	**7: Understand how to structure and manage a classroom to create a safe, healthy, and secure learning environment**	☐
	7.1: Analyzes relationships between classroom management strategies	☐
	7.2: Recognizes issues related to the creation of a classroom climate	☐
	7.3: Demonstrates knowledge of basic socialization strategies	☐
	7.4: Organizes a daily schedule that considers the developmental characteristics of learners	☐
	7.5: Evaluates methods for managing transitions, and handling routine classroom tasks and unanticipated situations	☐
	7.6: Analyzes the effects of the physical environment	☐
81	**8: Understand curriculum development, and apply knowledge of factors and processes in curricular decision making**	☐
	8.1: Applies procedures used in classroom curricular decision making	☐
	8.2: Evaluates curriculum materials and resources for their effectiveness in addressing the developmental and learning needs	☐
	8.3: Applies strategies for modifying curriculum based on learner characteristics	☐
	8.4: Applies strategies for integrating curricula	☐
87	**9: Understand the interrelationship between assessment and instruction and how to use formal and informal assessment to learn about students, plan instruction, monitor student understanding in the context of instruction, and make effective instructional modifications**	☐
	9.1: Demonstrates understanding that assessment and instruction must be closely integrated	☐
	9.2: Demonstrates familiarity with basic assessment approaches	☐
	9.3: Uses knowledge of the different purposes of various assessments	☐
	9.4: Uses rubrics	☐
	9.5: Recognizes strategies for planning lessons and activities based on assessment results	☐

PERSONALIZED STUDY PLAN

KNOWN MATERIAL/ SKIP IT

PAGE	COMPETENCY AND SKILL	
100	**10: Understand instructional planning and apply knowledge of planning processes to design effective instruction that promotes the learning of all students**	☐
	10.1: Recognizes key factors to consider in planning instruction	☐
	10.2: Analyzes and applies given information about specific planning factors to select appropriate instructional approach(es) and develop specific lesson and unit plans	☐
	10.3: Identifies the background knowledge and prerequisite skills required by a given lesson	☐
	10.4: Uses assessment information before, during, and after instruction	☐
	10.5: Analyzes a given lesson or unit plan	☐
	10.6: Applies strategies for collaborating with others to plan and implement instruction	☐
110	**11: Understand various instructional approaches, and use this knowledge to facilitate student learning**	☐
	11.1: Analyzes the uses, benefits, or limitations of a specific instructional approach	☐
	11.2: Recognizes appropriate strategies for varying the role of the teacher	☐
	11.3: Applies procedures for promoting positive and productive small-group interactions	☐
	11.4: Compares instructional approaches	☐
117	**12: Understand principles and procedures for organizing and implementing lessons, and use this knowledge to promote student learning and achievement**	☐
	12.1: Evaluates strengths and weaknesses of various strategies	☐
	12.2: Recognizes the importance of organizing instruction	☐
	12.3: Evaluates various instructional resources	☐
	12.4: Demonstrates understanding of the developmental characteristics of students	☐
	12.5: Applies strategies for adjusting lessons	☐

PERSONALIZED STUDY PLAN

KNOWN MATERIAL/ SKIP IT

PAGE	COMPETENCY AND SKILL	
127	**13: Understand the relationship between student motivation and achievement and how motivational principles and practices can be used to promote and sustain student cooperation in learning**	☐
	13.1: Distinguishes between motivational strategies that use intrinsic and extrinsic rewards	☐
	13.2: Analyzes the effects of using various intrinsic and extrinsic motivational strategies	☐
	13.3: Recognizes factors that promote or diminish student motivation	☐
	13.4: Recognizes the relationship between direct engagement in learning and students' interest	☐
	13.5: Applies procedures for enhancing student interest	☐
	13.6: Recognizes the importance of encouragement in sustaining students' interest	☐
	13.7: Recognizes the important of utilizing peers to benefit students' learning	☐
136	**14: Understand communication practices that are effective in promoting student learning and creating a climate of trust and support in the classroom, and how to use a variety of communication modes to support instruction**	☐
	14.1: Analyzes how cultural, gender, and age differences affect communication	☐
	14.2: Applies strategies to promote effective classroom interactions	☐
	14.3: Analyzes teacher-student interactions with regard to communication issues	☐
	14.4: Recognizes purposes for questioning and selecting appropriate questioning techniques	☐
	14.5: Applies strategies for adjusting communication to enhance student understanding	☐
	14.6: Demonstrates knowledge of the limits of verbal understanding of students at various ages and with different linguistic backgrounds	☐

PERSONALIZED STUDY PLAN

✗ **KNOWN MATERIAL/ SKIP IT**

PAGE	COMPETENCY AND SKILL	
143	**15: Understand uses of technology, including instructional and assistive technology, in teaching and learning; and apply this knowledge to use technology effectively and to teach students how to use technology to enhance their learning**	☐
	15.1: Demonstrates knowledge of educational uses of various technology tools	☐
	15.2: Recognizes purposes and uses of common types of assistive technology	☐
	15.3: Recognizes issues related to the appropriate use of and the legal and ethical use of technology resources	☐
	15.4: Identifies and addresses equity issues related to the use of technology	☐
	15.5: Identifies effective instructional uses of current technology	☐
	15.6: Applies strategies for helping students acquire, analyze, and evaluate electronic information	☐
	15.7: Evaluates students' technologically produced products	☐

COMPETENCY 7
UNDERSTAND HOW TO STRUCTURE AND MANAGE A CLASSROOM TO CREATE A SAFE, HEALTHY, AND SECURE LEARNING ENVIRONMENT

SKILL 7.1 **Analyzes relationships between classroom management strategies** *(e.g., in relation to discipline, student decision making, establishing and maintaining standards of behavior) and student learning, attitudes, and behaviors*

Classroom Management

Classroom management plans should be in place when the school year begins. Developing a management plan requires a proactive approach. A proactive approach involves:

- Deciding what behaviors will be expected of the class as a whole

- Anticipating possible problems

- Teaching the expected behaviors early in the school year

- Implementing behavior management techniques that focus on positive procedures that can be used at home as well at school

Establishing rules

It is important to involve the students in the development of the classroom rules. The benefits include:

- Helping students understand the rationale for the rules

- Allowing students to assume responsibility for the rules because they had a part in developing them; when students are involved in establishing rules, they will be more likely to follow them

Once the rules are established, enforcement and reinforcement for following them should begin right away.

Establishing consequences and rewards

Consequences should be introduced when the rules are introduced; they should be clearly stated and understood by all of the students. The severity of the

> *The severity of the consequence should match the severity of the offense and must be enforceable.*

consequence should match the severity of the offense and must be enforceable. The teacher must apply the consequence consistently and fairly, so the students will know what to expect when they choose to break a rule.

Like consequences, students should understand what rewards to expect for following the rules. The teacher should never promise a reward that cannot be delivered and should follow through with the reward as soon as possible. Consistency and fairness are also necessary for rewards to be effective. Students will become frustrated and give up if they see that rewards and consequences are not delivered fairly and quickly.

Displaying the classroom management plan

About four to six classroom rules should be posted where students can easily see and read them. These rules should be stated positively and describe specific behaviors so they are easy to understand. Certain rules may also be tailored to meet target goals and IEP requirements of individual students. (For example, a new student who has had problems with leaving the classroom may need an individual behavior contract to assist him with adjusting to the class rule about remaining in the assigned area.) As the students demonstrate the behaviors, the teacher should provide reinforcement and corrective feedback.

Classroom rules should be stated positively and describe specific behaviors so they are easy to understand.

Reviewing the classroom management plan

Periodic "refresher" practice can be done as needed, for example, after a long holiday or if students begin to "slack off." A copy of the classroom plan should be readily available for substitute use, and the classroom aide should also be familiar with the plan and procedures.

The teacher should clarify and model the expected behavior for the students. In addition to the classroom management plan, a management plan should be developed for special situations, (i.e., fire drills) and transitions (i.e., going to and from the cafeteria). Periodic review of the rules, as well as modeling and practice, may be conducted as needed, such as after an extended school holiday.

Things not to do

Procedures that use social humiliation, withholding of basic needs, pain, or extreme discomfort should never be used in a behavior management plan. Emergency intervention procedures used when the student is a danger to himself or others are not considered behavior management procedures. Throughout the year, the teacher should periodically review the types of interventions being used assess their effectiveness and make revisions as needed.

Procedures that use social humiliation, withholding of basic needs, pain, or extreme discomfort should never be used in a behavior management plan.

SKILL 7.2 **Recognizes issues related to the creation of a classroom climate** *(e.g., with regard to shared values and goals, shared experiences, patterns of communication)*

Develop Success-Oriented Activities

SUCCESS-ORIENTED ACTIVITIES are tasks that are selected to meet the individual needs of the student. During the time a student is learning a new skill, tasks should be selected so that the student will be able to earn a high percentage of correct answers during the teacher questioning and seatwork portions of the lesson. Later, the teacher should also include work that challenges students to apply what they have learned and stimulate their thinking.

Factors that influence individual student success include:

- Skill knowledge

- Strategy use

- Motivation

- Personal interests

The student who can't be bothered with reading the classroom textbook may be highly motivated to read the driver's handbook for his or her license or the rulebook for the latest video game. Students who did not master their multiplication tables will likely have problems working with fractions.

In the success-oriented classroom, mistakes are viewed as a natural part of the learning process. The teacher can also show that adults make mistakes by correcting errors without getting unduly upset. The students feel safe to try new things because they know that they have a supportive environment and can correct their mistakes.

Success-oriented activities

Activities that promote student success:

- Are based on useful, relevant content that is clearly specified and organized for easy learning

- Allow sufficient time to learn the selected skill for the highest rate of success

- Allow students the opportunity to work independently, self-monitor, and set goals

- Provide for frequent monitoring and corrective feedback

- Include collaboration in group activities or peer teaching

SUCCESS-ORIENTED ACTIVITIES: tasks that are selected to meet the individual needs of the student

A classroom is a learning community where each member contributes to the goals, experiences, and learning of the other members; teachers should design learning activities that promote these common aspects among its members.

In the success-oriented classroom, mistakes are viewed as a natural part of the learning process.

When the teacher communicates the expectation that the students can be successful learners and chooses activities that will help them be successful, achievement is increased.

Students with learning problems often attribute their successes to luck or ease of the task. Their failures are often blamed on their supposed lack of ability, difficulty of the task, or the fault of someone else. Successful activities, attribution retraining, and learning strategies can help these students to discover that they can become independent learners.

> **SKILL 7.3** **Demonstrates knowledge of basic socialization strategies, including how to support school interaction and facilitate conflict resolution among learners, and applies strategies for instructing students on the principles of honesty, personal responsibility, respect for others, observance of laws and rules, courtesy, dignity, and other traits that will enhance the quality of their experiences in, and contributions to, the class and the greater community**

Assessing Social Skills

A class of students with emotional disabilities may present several deficits in a few areas or a few deficits in many areas.

Teaching social skills can be rather difficult because social competence requires a repertoire of skills in a number of areas. The socially competent person must be able to get along with family and friends, function in a work environment, take care of personal needs, solve problems in daily living, and identify sources of help. A class of students with emotional disabilities may present several deficits in a few areas or a few deficits in many areas. Therefore, the teacher must begin with an assessment of the skill deficits and prioritize the ones to teach first.

TYPE OF ASSESSMENT	DESCRIPTION
Direct Observation	Observe student in various settings with a checklist.
Role Play	Teacher observes students in structured scenarios.
Teacher Ratings	Teacher rates student with a checklist or formal assessment instrument.
Sociometric Measures	*Peer Nomination:* Student names specific classmates who meet a stated criterion (i.e., playmate). Score is the number of times a child is nominated. *Peer Rating:* Students rank all their classmates on a Likert-type scale (e.g., 1-3 or 1-5 scale) on stated criterion. Individual score is the average of the total ratings of their classmates. *Paired-Comparison:* Student is presented with paired classmate combinations and asked to choose who is most or least liked in the pair.

Table continued on next page

Context Observation	Student is observed to determine if the skill deficit is present in one setting but not others.
Comparison with Other student	Student's social skill behavior is compared to two other students in the same situation to determine if there is a deficit or if the behavior is not really a problem.

Teaching Social Skills

Social skills instruction can include teaching:

- Conversation skills

- Assertiveness

- Play and peer interaction

- Problem-solving and coping skills

- Self-help

- Task-related behaviors

- Self-concept related skills (i.e., expressing feelings, accepting consequences)

- Job-related skills

One advantage of schooling organizations for students is to facilitate social skills and social development. While teachers cannot take the largest role for developing such traits as honesty, fairness, and concern for others, they are extremely important in the process.

Recommendations for teaching social skills

The first recommendation is to be a very good role model. As we all know, actions do indeed speak louder than words.

Second, teachers need to communicate expectations and be firm about them. When teachers ignore certain "infractions" and make a big deal about others, they demonstrate to students that it isn't about manners and social skills but rather discipline and favoritism. All students need to feel safe, cared about, and secure with their classmates. Teachers are the best people to ensure that students understand how to be generous, caring, considerate, and sociable individuals.

> *Teachers are the best people to ensure that students understand how to be generous, caring, considerate, and sociable individuals.*

Importance of Classroom Organization

Instructional momentum requires an organized system for material placement and distribution. Inability to find an overhead transparency, a necessary chart page, or the handout worksheet for the day not only stops the momentum but is very irritating to students. Disorganization of materials frustrates both teacher and students. Effective teachers deal with daily classroom procedures efficiently and quickly because then students will spend the majority of class time engaged in academic tasks, which will likely result in higher achievement.

Strategies for organization

In the lower grades, an organized system uses a classroom helper for effective distribution and collection of books, equipment, supplies, etc. At higher grade levels, the teacher is concerned with materials such as textbooks, written instructional aids, worksheets, computer programs, etc., which must be produced, maintained, distributed, and collected for future use.

One important consideration is the production of sufficient copies of duplicated materials to satisfy classroom needs. Another is the efficient distribution of worksheets and other materials. The teacher may decide to hand out materials as students are in their learning sites (desks, etc.) or have distribution materials at a clearly specified place (or small number of places) in the classroom. In any case, there should be firmly established procedures, completely understood by students, for receiving classroom materials.

Establishing a classroom routine

An effective teacher will also consider the needs and abilities of her students when developing routines or a daily schedule. For routines, a teacher might motivate a low-achieving student with a coveted task (such as taking down the attendance sheet or a recommendation for Safety Patrol) in order to increase confidence in that child. This increased confidence could lead to an increased interest in school and improved learning. Likewise, a teacher should also consider the needs of his or her students when developing the aspects of the daily schedule. For instance, if faced with a "hard to calm down" group, a teacher might schedule quiet reading time after recess. Being aware of their students' trends and characteristics in developing a classroom routine can significantly affect student learning.

Effective teachers deal with daily classroom procedures efficiently and quickly because then students will spend the majority of class time engaged in academic tasks, which will likely result in higher achievement.

An effective teacher will also consider the needs and abilities of her students when developing routines or a daily schedule.

SKILL 7.5 **Evaluates, selects, and uses various methods for managing transitions** *(e.g., between lessons, when students enter and leave the classroom)*, **and handling routine classroom tasks and unanticipated situations**

Effectives Use of Classroom Time

Effective teachers use class time efficiently. This results in higher student subject engagement and will likely result in more subject matter retention. One way that teachers use class time efficiently is through a smooth transition from one activity to another; this is also known as management transition.

Management transition

MANAGEMENT TRANSITION is defined as the teacher shifting from one activity to another in a systemic, academically oriented way. One factor that contributes to efficient management transition is the teacher's management of instructional material. Effective teachers gather their materials during the planning stage of instruction. Doing this, a teacher avoids flipping through things and looking for the items necessary for the current lesson. Momentum is lost and student concentration is broken when this occurs.

> **MANAGEMENT TRANSITION:** shifting from one activity to another in a systemic, academically-oriented way

Additionally, teachers who keep students informed of the sequencing of instructional activities maintain systematic transitions because the students are prepared to move on to the next activity. For example, the teacher says, "When we finish with this guided practice together, we will turn to page twenty-three and each student will do the exercises. I will then circulate throughout the classroom helping on an individual basis. Okay, let's begin." Following an example such as this will lead to systematic smooth transitions between activities because the students will be turning to page twenty-three when the class finishes the practice without a break in concentration.

Group fragmentation

Another method that leads to smooth transitions is to move students in groups and clusters rather than one by one. This is called GROUP FRAGMENTATION. For example, if some students do seat work while other students gather for a reading group, the teacher moves the students in predetermined groups. Instead of calling the individual names of the reading group, which would be time consuming and laborious, the teacher simply says, "Will the blue reading group please assemble at the reading station. The red and yellow groups will quietly do the vocabulary assignment I am now passing out." As a result of this activity, the classroom is ready to move on in a matter of seconds rather than minutes.

> **GROUP FRAGMENTATION:** a method for ensuring smooth transitions, whereby a teacher moves students in groups and clusters rather than one by one

TRANSITION SIGNALS: a teacher utterance or gesture that indicates movement of the lesson from one topic or activity to another by indicating where the lesson is and where it is going

Additionally, the teacher may employ academic **TRANSITION SIGNALS**, defined as teacher utterances that indicate movement of the lesson from one topic or activity to another by indicating where the lesson is and where it is going. For example, the teacher may say, "That completes our description of clouds, now we will examine weather fronts." Like the sequencing of instructional materials, this keeps the student informed on what is coming next so the students will move to the next activity with little or no break in concentration.

Therefore, effective teachers manage transitions from one activity to another in a systematically oriented way through efficient management of instructional matter, sequencing of instructional activities, moving students in groups, and by employing academic transition signals.

Through an efficient use of class time, achievement is increased because students spend more class time engaged in on-task behavior.

Examples of transitions

TRANSITIONS refer to changes in class activities that involve movement. Some examples are:

TRANSITIONS: changes in class activities that involve movement

- Breaking up from large group instruction into small groups for learning centers and small-group instructions

- Classroom to lunch, to the playground, or to elective classes

- Finishing reading at the end of one period and getting ready for math the next period

- Emergency situations such as fire drills

Successful transitions are achieved by using proactive strategies. Early in the year, the teacher pinpoints the transition periods in the day and anticipates possible behavior problems, such as students habitually returning late from lunch. After identifying possible problems with the environment or the schedule, the teacher plans proactive strategies to minimize or eliminate those problems.

After identifying possible problems with the environment or the schedule, the teacher plans proactive strategies to minimize or eliminate those problems.

Proactive planning also gives the teacher the advantage of being prepared, addressing behaviors before they become problems, and incorporating strategies into the classroom management plan right away. Transition plans can be developed for each type of transition and the expected behaviors for each situation taught directly to the students.

Analyzes the effects of the physical environment, including different spatial arrangements, on student learning and behavior

Physical Attributes of the Classroom

The physical setting of the classroom contributes a great deal toward the propensity for students to learn. An adequate, well-built, and well-equipped classroom will invite students to learn. This has been called **INVITATIONAL LEARNING**.

Important classroom factors

Among the important factors to consider in the physical setting of the classroom are:

- Adequate physical space

- Repair status

- Lighting adequacy

- Adequate entry and exit access (including handicap accessibility)

- Ventilation/climate control

- Coloration

Adequate physical space

A classroom must have adequate physical space so students can conduct themselves comfortably. Some students are distracted by windows, pencil sharpeners, doors, etc. Some students prefer the front, middle, or back rows.

Repair status

The teacher has the responsibility to report any items of classroom disrepair to maintenance staff. Broken windows, falling plaster, exposed sharp surfaces, leaks in ceiling or walls, and other items of disrepair present hazards to students.

Lighting adequacy

Another factor that must be considered is adequate lighting. Report any inadequacies in classroom illumination. Florescent lights placed at acute angles often burn out faster. A healthy supply of spare tubes is a sound investment.

Adequate entry and exit access

Local fire and safety codes dictate entry and exit standards. In addition, all corridors and classrooms should be wheelchair accessible for students and others who use them. Older schools may not have this accessibility.

> **INVITATIONAL LEARNING:** a theory of learning that centers on adequate, well-built, and well-equipped classrooms that invite students to learn

> *A classroom must have adequate physical space so students can conduct themselves comfortably.*

Ventilation/climate control

Another consideration is adequate ventilation and climate control. Some classrooms in some states use air conditioning extensively. Sometimes it is so cold as to be considered a distraction. Specialty classes such as science require specialized hoods for ventilation. Physical education classes have the added responsibility for shower areas and specialized environments that must be heated, such as pool or athletic training rooms.

Coloration

Classrooms with warmer subdued colors contribute to students' concentration on task items. Neutral hues for coloration of walls, ceiling, and carpet or tile are generally used in classrooms to minimize distractions.

Furniture

> *In the modern classroom, a great deal of furniture, equipment, supplies, appliances, and learning aids help the teachers teach and students learn.*

In the modern classroom, a great deal of furniture, equipment, supplies, appliances, and learning aids help the teachers teach and students learn. The classroom should be provided with furnishings that fit the purpose of the classroom. For example, the kindergarten classroom may have a reading center, a playhouse, a puzzle table, student work desks and tables, a sandbox, and any other relevant learning and interest areas.

Whatever the arrangement of furniture and equipment, the teacher must provide for adequate traffic flow. Rows of desks must have adequate space between them to enable students to move and the teacher to circulate. All areas must be open to line-of-sight supervision by the teacher.

In all cases, proper care must be taken to ensure student safety. Furniture and equipment should be situated safely at all times. No equipment, materials, boxes, etc., should be placed where there is danger of them falling. Doors must have entry and exit accessibility at all times.

Emergency responses

The major emergency responses include two categories for student movement: tornado warning response, and building evacuation, which includes most other emergencies (fire, bomb threat, etc.).

Tornado warning response

For tornadoes, the prescribed response is to evacuate all students and personnel to the first floor of multistory buildings, and to place students along walls away from windows. All people, including the teacher, should then crouch on the floor and cover their heads with their hands. These are standard procedures for severe weather, particularly tornadoes.

Building evacuation

Most other emergency situations require evacuation of the school building. Teachers should be thoroughly familiar with evacuation routes established for each classroom in which they teach. Teachers should accompany and supervise students throughout the evacuation procedure and check to see that all students under their supervision are accounted for. Teachers should then continue to supervise students until the building may be reoccupied (upon proper school or community authority) or until other procedures are followed for students to officially leave the school area and cease to be the supervisory responsibility of the school. Elementary students evacuated to another school can wear nametags and parents or guardians should sign them out at a central location.

> *Teachers should be thoroughly familiar with evacuation routes established for each classroom in which they teach.*

COMPETENCY 8
UNDERSTAND CURRICULUM DEVELOPMENT, AND APPLY KNOWLEDGE OF FACTORS AND PROCESSES IN CURRICULAR DECISION MAKING

> **SKILL 8.1** **Applies procedures used in classroom curricular decision making** *(e.g., evaluating the current curriculum, defining scope and sequence)*

Curriculum Development

Curriculum development today must consider many factors including:

- Alignment
- Scope
- Sequence
- Design

Alignment

First, curriculum must be aligned to state standards, state and local assessments, and district and school goals. **CURRICULUM ALIGNMENT** simply means that there is reflection in the curriculum of these elements. In other words, what students learn should reflect state requirements. Usually, this also means that what students learn

> **CURRICULUM ALIGNMENT:** the alignment of curriculum to state and local standards and district and school goals

is tested on state assessments. If the district wanted all students to learn how to live in a multicultural society, curriculum would address that theme in a variety of ways; this would be an example of alignment to district and school goals.

Scope and Sequence

SCOPE: the "horizontal" aspect of curriculum

SEQUENCE: the outline of what should be taught before and after a particular subject

Second, SCOPE is the "horizontal" aspect of curriculum. For example, if a topic of study in a biology class is invertebrate animals, the scope would define everything that must be taught for students to adequately understand this concept. On the other hand, SEQUENCE is the outline of what should be taught before and after a particular subject. So, for example, a sequence in math might suggest that students should learn addition and subtraction before multiplication and division. Likewise, basic math topics, like those just described, should be taught before decimals and fractions. A sequence would put all of these elements into an appropriate order.

Design

DESIGN: considers the progression from the beginning of a unit of study to the end of the same unit of study

DESIGN considers the progression from the beginning of a unit of study to the end of the same unit of study. First, curriculum should be designed with the end in mind. What do you want students to know and be able to do when finished? How would they prove that they know the material or have the skill? If that information has been defined, it is much easier to design a curriculum. Too often, curricula is designed only considering forward steps in a process without concern for what students should be getting out of the curriculum.

Curriculum Implementation

As a teacher implements a curriculum, the teacher should be familiar with these three main components:

MAIN COMPONENTS OF CURRICULUM IMPLEMENTATION	
The Philosophy or Principal Aims of the Curriculum	What the students should get out of the curriculum
The Knowledge Base of the Curriculum	Teachers must be deeply familiar with what they are teaching to students, in order to be effective in getting students to learn it
The Plan, Scope, and Sequence of the Curriculum	What would students have learned prior? Where will they go next?

SKILL 8.2 Evaluates curriculum materials and resources for their effectiveness in addressing the developmental and learning needs of given students

Addressing State Requirements

In considering suitable learning materials for the classroom, the teacher must have a thorough understanding of the state-mandated competency-based curriculum. According to state requirements, certain objectives must be met in each subject taught at every designated level of instruction. It is necessary that the teacher become well acquainted with the curriculum that is assigned. The teacher must also be aware that it is unlawful to require students to study from textbooks or materials other than those approved by the State Department of Education.

In considering suitable learning materials for the classroom, the teacher must have a thorough understanding of the state-mandated competency-based curriculum.

Assessing Students

Keeping in mind the state requirements concerning the objectives and materials, the teacher must determine the abilities of the incoming students assigned to his class or supervision. It is essential to be aware of each student's entry behavior—that is, their current level of achievement in the relevant areas. The next step is to take a broad overview of students who are expected to learn before they are passed on to the next grade or level of instruction. Finally, the teacher must design a course of study that will enable students to reach the necessary level of achievement, as displayed in their final assessments or exit behaviors. Textbooks and learning materials must be chosen to fit into this context.

The teacher must determine the abilities of the incoming students assigned to his or her class or supervision.

Selecting Learning Materials

Once students' abilities are determined, the teacher will select the learning materials for the class. In choosing materials, teachers should also keep in mind that not only do students learn at different rates, but also they bring a variety of cognitive styles to the learning process. Prior experiences influence the individual's cognitive style, or method of accepting, processing, and retaining information.

In choosing materials, teachers should also keep in mind that not only do students learn at different rates, but also they bring a variety of cognitive styles to the learning process.

Textbooks

Most teachers chose to use textbooks that are suitable to the age and developmental level of specific student populations. Textbooks reflect the values and assumptions of the society that produces them, while they also represent the knowledge and skills considered to be essential in becoming an educated adult. Finally, textbooks are useful to the school bureaucracy and the community, for they make public and accessible the private world of the classroom.

Multimedia materials

Aside from textbooks, a wide variety of materials are available to today's teachers. Computers are now commonplace, and some schools can now afford DVDs to bring alive the content of a reference book in text, motion, and sound. Hand-held calculators eliminate the need for drill and practice in number facts, while they also support a problem solving and process to mathematics. Videocassettes and VCRs are common and permit the use of home-produced or commercially produced tapes. Textbook publishers often provide films, recordings, and software to accompany the text, as well as maps, graphics, and colorful posters to help students visualize what is being taught. Teachers can usually scan the educational publishers' brochures that arrive at their principal's or department head's office on a frequent basis. Another way to stay current in the field is by attending workshops or conferences. Teachers will be enthusiastically welcomed on those occasions when educational publishers are asked to display their latest productions and revised editions of materials.

Display Materials

Yesterday's libraries are today's media centers.

In addition, yesterday's libraries are today's media centers. Teachers can usually have opaque projectors delivered to the classroom to project print or pictorial images (including student work) onto a screen for classroom viewing. Some teachers have chosen to replace chalkboards with projectors that reproduce the print or images present on the plastic sheets known as transparencies, which the teacher can write on during a presentation or have machine-printed in advance. In either case, the transparency can easily be stored for later use. In an art or photography class (or any class in which it is helpful to display visual materials), slides can easily be projected onto a wall or a screen. Cameras are inexpensive enough to enable students to photograph and display their own work, as well as keep a record of their achievements in teacher files or student portfolios.

SKILL 8.3 Applies strategies for modifying curriculum based on learner characteristics

Differentiation

DIFFERENTIATION: describes the variations of curriculum and instruction that can be provided to an entire class of students

The effective teacher will seek to connect all students to the subject matter by using multiple techniques, with the goal being that each student, through their own abilities, will relate to one or more techniques and excel in the learning process. While all students need to have exposure to the same curriculum, not all students need to have the curriculum taught in the same way. **DIFFERENTIATION** is the term used to describe the variations of curriculum and instruction that can be provided to an entire class of students.

Ways to differentiate

The following are three primary ways to differentiate:

THREE PRIMARY WAYS TO DIFFERENTIATE	
Content	The specifics of what is learned. Whole units or concepts should not be modified; however, within certain topics, specifics can be modified.
Process	The route to learning the content. This means that not everyone has to learn the content in exactly the same method.
Product	The result of the learning. Usually, a product is the result or assessment of learning. For example, not all students are going to demonstrate complete learning on a quiz; likewise, not all students will demonstrate complete learning on a written paper.

Keys to differentiation

There are two keys to successful differentiation:

TWO KEYS TO SUCCESSFUL DIFFERENTIATION	
Knowing what is essential in the curriculum	Although certain things can be modified, other things must remain in-tact in a specific order. Disrupting central components of a curriculum can actually damage a student's ability to learn something successfully.
Knowing the needs of the students	While this can take quite some time to figure out, it is very important that teachers pay attention to the interests, tendencies, and abilities of their students so that they understand how each of their students will best learn.

Keeping the Class as a Community

Many students will need certain concepts explained in greater depth; others may pick up on concepts rather quickly. For this reason, teachers will want to adapt the curriculum in a way that allows students with the opportunity to learn at their own pace, while also keeping the class together as a community. This can be difficult, but the more creative a teacher is with the ways in which students can demonstrate mastery, the more fun the experience will be for students and teachers. Furthermore, teachers who tailor lesson plans, activities, groupings, and other elements of curriculum to each student's need will reach students more successfully.

Applies strategies for integrating curricula *(e.g., incorporating interdisciplinary themes)*

Implementing Curricula

Keeping in mind what is understood about the students' abilities and interests, the teacher needs to design a course of study that presents units of instruction in an orderly sequence. The instruction should be planned to advance all students toward the next level of instruction, although exit behaviors need not be identical because of the inevitability of individual student differences.

The instruction should be planned to advance all students toward the next level of instruction, although exit behaviors need not be identical because of the inevitability of individual student differences.

Beyond textbooks and lectures

Studies have shown that students learn best when what is taught in lecture and textbook reading is presented more than once in a variety of formats. In some instances, students themselves may be asked to reinforce what they have learned by completing some original production—for example, by drawing pictures to explain some scientific process, by writing a monologue or dialogue to express what some historical figure might have said on some occasion, by devising a board game to challenge the players' mathematical skills, or by acting out (and perhaps filming) episodes from a classroom reading selection. Students usually enjoy having their work displayed or presented to an audience of peers; thus, their productions may supplement and personalize the learning experiences that the teacher has planned for them.

Studies have shown that students learn best when what is taught in lecture and textbook reading is presented more than once in a variety of formats.

Selection of learning activities

The effective teacher takes care to select appropriate activities and classroom situations in which learning is optimized. The classroom teacher should manipulate instructional activities and classroom conditions in a manner that enhances group and individual learning opportunities. For example, the classroom teacher can organize group learning activities in which students are placed in a situation in which cooperation, sharing ideas, and discussion occurs. Cooperative learning activities can assist students in learning to share personal and cultural ideas and values in a classroom learning environment.

Teachers should combine instructional activities to reinforce information by providing students with relevant learning experiences throughout instructional activities.

The effective teacher plans his or her learning activities to introduce them in a meaningful instructional sequence.

COMPETENCY 9
UNDERSTAND THE INTERRELATIONSHIP BETWEEN ASSESSMENT AND INSTRUCTION AND HOW TO USE FORMAL AND INFORMAL ASSESSMENT TO LEARN ABOUT STUDENTS, PLAN INSTRUCTION, MONITOR STUDENT UNDERSTANDING IN THE CONTEXT OF INSTRUCTION, AND MAKE EFFECTIVE INSTRUCTIONAL MODIFICATIONS

> **SKILL 9.1** Demonstrates understanding that assessment and instruction must be closely integrated

Assessments

Assessment is key to providing differentiated and appropriate instruction to all students. Teachers should use a variety of assessment techniques to determine a student's existing knowledge and skills, as well as needs. Depending on the age of the student and the subject matter under consideration, diagnosis of readiness may be accomplished through pre-test, checklists, teacher observation, or student self-report. Diagnosis serves two related purposes—to identify those students who are not ready for the new instruction and to identify, for each student, what prerequisite knowledge is lacking.

Teachers should use a variety of assessment techniques to determine a student's existing knowledge and skills, as well as the needs.

Student assessment is an integral part of the teaching and learning process. Identifying student, teacher, or program weaknesses is only significant if the information so obtained is used to remedy the concerns. Lesson materials and lesson delivery must be evaluated to determine relevant prerequisite skills and abilities. The teacher must be capable of determining whether a student's difficulties lie with the new information or with a lack of significant prior knowledge. The ultimate goal of any diagnostic or assessment endeavor is improved learning. Thus, instruction is adapted to the needs of the learner based on assessment information.

The ultimate goal of any diagnostic or assessment endeavor is improved learning.

Principles of assessment

As is the case with purposes of assessment, a number of lists identify principles of assessment. Linn and Gronlund (1995) identify the following five principles of assessment.

1. Clearly specifying what is to be assessed has priority in the assessment process

2. An assessment procedure should be selected because of its relevance to the characteristics or performance to be measured

3. Comprehensive assessment requires a variety of procedures

4. Proper use of assessment procedures requires an awareness of their limitations

5. Assessment is a means to an end, not an end in itself

Stiggins (1997) introduces seven guiding principles for classroom assessment.

1. Assessments require clear thinking and effective communication

2. Classroom assessment is key

3. Students are assessment users

4. Clear and appropriate targets are essential

5. High-quality assessment is a must

6. Understand personal implication

7. Assessment as teaching and learning

> **SKILL 9.2 Demonstrates familiarity with basic assessment approaches, including the instructional advantages and limitations of various assessment instruments and techniques** *(e.g., portfolio, teacher-designed classroom tests, performance assessment, peer assessment, student self-assessment, teacher observation, criterion-referenced test, norm-referenced test)*

Types of Assessments

It is useful to consider the types of assessment procedures that are available to the classroom teacher. The types of assessment discussed below represent many of the more common types, but the list is not exhaustive.

FORMAL TESTS: tests that have been standardized using a large sample population

Tests

FORMAL TESTS are those tests that have been standardized using a large sample population. The process of standardization provides various comparative norms and scales for the assessment instrument.

The term informal test includes all other tests. Most publisher-provided tests and teacher-made tests are informal tests using this definition. Note clearly that an informal test is not necessarily unimportant. A teacher-made final exam, for example, is informal by definition simply because it has not been standardized.

Anecdotal records

ANECDOTAL RECORDS are notes recorded by the teacher concerning an area of interest or concern with a particular student. These records should focus on observable behaviors and should be descriptive in nature. They should not include assumptions or speculations regarding effective areas such as motivation or interest. These records are usually compiled over a period of several days to several weeks.

> **ANECDOTAL RECORDS:** notes recorded by the teacher concerning an area of interest or concern with a particular student

Rating scales and checklists

These assessments are generally self-appraisal instruments completed by the students or observations-based instruments completed by the teacher. The focus of these is frequently on behavior or effective areas such as interest and motivation.

Portfolio assessment

The use of student portfolios for some aspect of assessment has become quite common. The purpose, nature, and policies of portfolio assessment vary greatly from one setting to another. In general, though, a student's portfolio contains samples of work collected over an extended period of time. The nature of the subject, age of the student, and scope of the portfolio, all contribute to the specific mechanics of analyzing, synthesizing, and otherwise evaluating the portfolio contents.

In most cases, the student and teacher make joint decisions as to which work samples will go into the student's portfolios. A collection of work compiled over an extended time period allows teacher, student, and parents to view the student's progress from a unique perspective. Qualitative changes over time can be readily apparent from work samples. Such changes are sometimes difficult to establish with strictly quantitative records, such as those typical of the scores recorded in the teacher's grade book.

> *A collection of work compiled over an extended time period allows teacher, student, and parents to view the student's progress from a unique perspective.*

Questioning

One of the most frequently occurring forms of assessment in the classroom is oral questioning by the teacher. As the teacher questions the students, she collects a great deal of information about the degree of student learning and potential sources of confusion for the students. While questioning is often viewed as a component of instructional methodology, it is also a powerful assessment tool.

Direct Assessment Methods and Types

Tests and similar direct assessment methods represent the most easily identified types of assessment. Thorndike (1997) identifies three types of assessment instruments:

1. Standardized achievement tests

2. Assessment material packaged with curricular materials

3. Teacher-made assessment instruments

    – Pencil and paper test

    – Oral tests

    – Product evaluations

    – Performance tests

    – Effective measures

Kellough and Roberts (1991) take a slightly different perspective. They describe three avenues for assessing student achievement:

1. What the learner says

2. What the learner does

3. What the learner writes

Performance-based assessments

PERFORMANCE-BASED ASSESSMENTS: assessments that measure the learning outcomes of individual students in subject content areas

PERFORMANCE-BASED ASSESSMENTS are currently being used in a number of state testing programs to measure the learning outcomes of individual students in subject content areas. Washington State uses performance-based assessments for the WASL (Washington Assessment of Student Learning) in reading, writing, math, and science to measure student-learning performance. Attaching a graduation requirement to passing the required state assessment beginning with the class of 2008 has created high-stakes testing and educational accountability for both students and teachers in meeting the expected skill based requirements for 10th grade students taking the test.

In today's classrooms, performance-based assessments in core subject areas must have established and specific performance criteria that start with pre-testing in the subject area and maintaining of daily or weekly testing to gauge student progress toward learning goals and objectives. To understand a student's learning is to understand how a student processes information. Effective performance assessments will show the gaps or holes in student learning that allows for an intense concentration on providing fillers to bridge nonsequential learning gaps. Typical performance assessments include oral and written student work in the form of:

- Research papers
- Oral presentations
- Class projects
- Journals
- Student portfolio collections of work
- Community service projects

Criterion-referenced assessments

CRITERION-REFERENCED ASSESSMENTS examine specific student learning goals and performance compared to a norm group of student learners. According to Bond (1996), "Educators or policy makers may choose to use a Criterion-referenced test (CRT) when they wish to see how well students have learned the knowledge and skills that they are expected to have mastered." Many school districts and state legislation use CRTs to ascertain whether schools are meeting national and state learning standards. The latest national educational mandate of No Child Left Behind (NCLB) and Adequate Yearly Progress (AYP) use CRTs to measure student learning, school performance, and school improvement goals as structured accountability expectations in school communities. CRTs are generally used in learning environments to reflect the effectiveness of curriculum implementation and learning outcomes.

> **CRITERION-REFERENCED ASSESSMENTS:** tools that examine specific student learning goals and performance compared to a norm group of student learners

Norm-referenced assessments

NORM-REFERENCED TESTS (NRT) are used to classify student learners for homogenous groupings based on ability levels or basic skills into a ranking category. In many school communities, NRTs are used to classify students into AP (Advanced Placement), honors, regular, or remedial classes that can significantly impact future student educational opportunities or success. NRTs are also used by national testing companies such as Iowa Test of Basic Skills (Riverside), Florida Achievement Test (McGraw-Hill), and other major test publishers to test a national sample of students that are used to develop norms against standard test-takers. Stiggins (1994) states "Norm-referenced tests (NRT) are designed to highlight achievement differences between and among students to produce a dependable rank order of students across a continuum of achievement from high achievers to low achievers."

> **NORM-REFERENCED TESTS (NRT):** tools used to classify student learners for homogenous groupings based on ability levels or basic skills into a ranking category

Educators may use the information from NRTs to provide students with academic learning that accelerates student skills from the basic level to higher skill applications and thereby enables them to meet the requirements of state assessments and core subject expectations. NRT ranking ranges from 1–99 with 25 percent of students scoring in the lower ranking of 1–25 and 25 percent of students scoring in the higher ranking of 76–99.

> **SKILL 9.3** **Uses knowledge of the different purposes** *(e.g., screening, diagnosing, comparing, monitoring)* **of various assessments and knowledge of assessment concepts** *(e.g., validity, reliability, bias) to select the most appropriate assessment instrument or technique for a given situation*

Purposes for Assessment

A number of different classification systems identify the various purposes for assessment. A compilation of several lists identifies some common purposes, such as:

1. Diagnostic assessments: Determine individual weakness and strengths in specific areas

2. Readiness assessments: Measure prerequisite knowledge and skills

3. Interest and attitude assessments: Identify topics of high interest or areas in which students may need extra motivational activities

4. Evaluation assessments: Program- or teacher-focused, and help to determine progress made

5. Placement assessments: Used for grouping students or determining appropriate beginning levels in leveled materials

6. Formative assessment: Provide ongoing feedback on student progress and the success of instructional methods and materials

7. Summative assessment: Defines student accomplishment with the intent to determine the degree of student mastery or learning that has taken place

For most teachers, assessment purposes vary according to the situation. It may be helpful to consult several sources to help formulate an overall assessment plan. Kellough and Roberts (1991) identify the following six purposes for assessment:

1. To evaluate and improve student learning

2. To identify student strengths and weaknesses

3. To assess the effectiveness of a particular instructional strategy

4. To evaluate and improve program effectiveness

5. To evaluate and improve teacher effectiveness

6. To communicate to parents their children's progress

Validity and Reliability

A desirable assessment is both reliable and valid. Without adequate reliability and validity, an assessment provides unusable results. A **RELIABLE ASSESSMENT** provides accurate and consistent results; there is little error from one time it is given to the next. A **VALID ASSESSMENT** is one which tests what it intends to test.

> **RELIABLE ASSESS-MENT:** a test that provides accurate and consistent results

Reliability

Reliability can sometimes be described by a correlation. A perfect positive correlation equals + 1.00 and a perfect negative correlation equals -1.00. The reliability of an assessment tool is generally expressed as a decimal to two places (e.g., 0.85). This decimal number describes the correlation that would be expected between two scores if the same student took the test two times.

> **VALID ASSESSMENT:** tests what it intends to test

Test-retest method

Actually, we have several ways to estimate the reliability of an instrument. The method that is conceptually the most clear is the **TEST-RETEST METHOD**. When the same test is administered again to the same students, if the test is perfectly reliable, each student will receive the same score each time. Even as the scores of individual students vary some from one time to the next, it is desirable for the rank order of the students to remain unchanged. Other methods of estimating reliability operate off of the same conceptual framework.

> **TEST-RETEST METHOD:** a method of testing reliability whereby the same test is administered again to the same students

Split-half method

SPLIT-HALF METHODS divide a single test into two parts and compare them. Equivalent form methods use two versions of the same test and compare results. With some types of assessment, such as essays and observation reports, reliability concerns also deal with the procedures and criteria used for scoring. The interrater reliability asks the question: How much will the results vary depending on who is scoring or rating the assessment data?

> **SPLIT-HALF METHODS:** a method of testing reliability that divides a single test into two parts and compares them

Validity

Three commonly described types of validity are:

1. Content validity

2. Criterion validity

3. Construct validity

Content validity

CONTENT VALIDITY: the degree to which an assessment actually measures the skills it was designed to measure

CONTENT VALIDITY describes the degree to which the assessment actually measures the skills it was designed to measure, say, arithmetic. Story problems on an arithmetic test will lower its validity as a measure of arithmetic since reading ability will also be reflected in the results. However, note that it remains a valid test of the ability to solve story problems.

Criterion validity

CRITERION VALIDITY: the degree to which an assessment can predict performance on another measure or test

CRITERION VALIDITY is so named because of the concern with the test's ability to predict performance on another measure or test. For example, a college admissions test is highly valid if it predicts very accurately those students who will attain high GPAs at that college. The criterion in this case is college GPA.

Construct validity

CONSTRUCT VALIDITY: describes the usefulness or reality of what is being tested

CONSTRUCT VALIDITY is concerned with describing the usefulness or reality of what is being tested. The recent interest in multiple intelligences, instead of a single IQ score, is an example of the older construct of intelligence being reexamined as potentially several distinct constructs.

Readiness and Screening

A student's readiness for a specific subject is not an absolute concept but is determined by the relationship between the subject matter/topic and the student's prior knowledge, interest, motivation, attitude, experience, and other similar factors.

A student's readiness for a specific subject is not an absolute concept but is determined by the relationship between the subject matter/topic and the student's prior knowledge, interest, motivation, attitude, experience, and other similar factors.

Thus, the student's readiness to learn about the water cycle depends on whether the student already knows related concepts such as evaporation, condensation, and filtration. Readiness, then, implies that no gap exists between what the student knows and the prerequisite knowledge base for learning.

Pretesting

A pretest designed to assess significant and related prerequisite skills and abilities is the most common method of identifying the students' readiness. This assessment should focus not on the content to be introduced but on prior knowledge judged to be necessary for understanding the new content. A pretest that focuses on the new content may identify students who do not need the new instruction (who have already mastered the material), but it will not identify students with readiness gaps.

Basic skill readiness

The most common areas of readiness concerns are in the basic academic skill areas. Mastery of the basic skill areas is a prerequisite for almost all subject area learning. Arithmetic skills and some higher-level mathematic skills are generally necessary for science learning or for understanding history and related time concepts.

Reading skills are necessary throughout the school years and beyond. A student with poor reading skills is at a disadvantage when asked to read a textbook chapter independently. Writing skills, especially handwriting, spelling, punctuation, and mechanics, are directly related to success in any writing-based activity. A weakness in any of these basic skill areas may at first glance appear to be a difficulty in understanding the subject area.

A teacher who attempts to help the student master the subject matter through additional emphasis on the content will be misusing instructional time and frustrating the student. An awareness of readiness issues helps the teacher to focus on treating the underlying deficiency instead of focusing on the overt symptoms.

Addressing readiness gaps

Once a readiness gap has been identified, the teacher can provide activities designed to close the gap. Specific activities may be of almost any form. Since most learning builds upon previous learning, a few activities or segments of learning can be viewed solely as readiness or nonreadiness activities. Very few types of learning can be identified as solely readiness activities without legitimacy in their own right.

While growth and maturation rates vary greatly from individual to individual, some generalizations can be made concerning development characteristics of children. Most children appear to go through identifiable, sequential stages of growth and maturation, although not at the same rate.

Curriculum and readiness

For the curriculum developers, it is often necessary to make some generalizations about the development level of the students of a particular age group or grade level. These generalizations, then, provide a framework for establishing the expectations of the children's performance. Textbooks, scope and sequence charts,

> *The most common areas of readiness concerns are in the basic academic skill areas.*

> *For the curriculum developers, it is often necessary to make some generalizations about the development level of the students of a particular age group or grade level.*

school curriculum planners, and more, translate these generalizations into plans and expectations for the students. The curriculum plan that emerges identifies general goals and expectations for the average student.

One of the teacher's responsibilities in this situation is to determine an initial rough estimate of what is appropriate for a given group of students. The teacher should expect to modify and adjust the instructional program based on the needs and abilities of the students. A teacher may do this by:

- Grouping students for alternative instruction

- Adjusting or varying the materials (textbooks)

- Varying the teaching methods

- Varying the learning tasks

SKILL 9.4 **Uses rubrics, and interprets and uses information derived from a given assessment**

Subjective Tests and Rubrics

Subjective tests put the student in the driver's seat.

RUBRICS: a document that provides assessment criteria for high-scoring answers and projects

Subjective tests put the student in the driver's seat. These types of assessments usually consist of short answer questions, longer essays, or problem-solving items that require more critical thinking skills. Sometimes teachers provide **RUBRICS** that include assessment criteria for high-scoring answers and projects. Sometimes, the rubric is as simple as a checklist and, other times, a maximum point value is awarded for each item on the rubric. Either way, rubrics provide a guideline of the teacher's expectations for the specifics of the assignment. The teacher usually discusses and models what is expected to fulfill each guideline, as well as provides a detailed outline of these expectations for reference.

For example, students being asked to write a research paper might be provided with a rubric. An elementary teacher may assign a total of 50 points for the entire paper. The rubric may award 10 points for note taking quality, 10 points for research skills, 20 points for content covered, 5 points for creative elements, and 5 points for organization and presentation. Then a certain number of points will be awarded in accordance with the students' performance. Rubrics allow students to be scored in multiple areas, rather than simply on a final product.

Importance of Preparation

The bottom line is that studying and preparing for any type of test will equate to better student performance and achievement on tests. In addition, as teachers evaluate the students' work, they are able to see each student's strengths and weaknesses. This information allows teachers to differentiate instruction for each student in order to maximize their learning.

The bottom line is that studying and preparing for any type of test will equate to better student performance and achievement on tests.

> **SKILL 9.5** **Recognizes strategies for planning, adjusting, or modifying lessons and activities based on assessment results**

Curriculum Control

The degree to which the classroom teacher has control over the curriculum varies from setting to setting. Some schools have precisely defined curriculum plans and teachers are required to implement the instruction accordingly. A more common occurrence is that the textbooks become the default curriculum. A fourth-grade arithmetic book, for example, defines what must be taught in the fourth grade so that the fifth-grade teacher can continue the established sequence.

The teacher is responsible for implementing the formal curricula and for providing necessary scaffolding to enhance student learning. Since the basic element of educational structure is time, the teacher must distribute the necessary learning activities over the available amount of time. The teacher can do this by creating an overview of:

Whatever the source of limitations and requirements, the classroom teacher always has some control over the method of instructional delivery and the use of supplemental materials and procedures.

- What material is to be presented
- The total amount of time available (whether for the school year, grading period, unit, etc.)
- The relative importance of the components of the material
- The students' prior knowledge of portions of the material

Lesson planning and delivery

Planning an individual lesson is a continuation of the principles for curriculum design. The same considerations exist but on a smaller scale. Numerous lesson planning forms and guidelines are available and some may be mandated by schools or districts. Some procedures are restricted to lessons of a particular nature, such as teaching a skill. Others are more generally applicable and provide a framework appropriate for most instruction.

A typical lesson plan will include:

- Identification of objectives

- The content

- Materials and supplies

- Instructional delivery methods

- In-class reinforcement activities

- Homework assignments

- Evaluation of student learning

- Evaluation of the lesson and teacher effectiveness

Grouping for instruction

There are three common methods by which a teacher may address grouping for instruction:

THE COMMON METHODS FOR GROUPING	
Individualized Instruction	Individualization requires extensive assessment both for placement and, in an on-going capacity, to monitor student progress and to plan subsequent instructional activities. Few teachers have the resources and time necessary to fully individualize their instructional program.
Small Group Instruction	A compromise approach is to assign students to small groups and then modify the lesson plans to reflect the need of the group. This procedure offers some of the advantages of individualization without the extensive administrative demands. It is quite common, especially in content area instruction, for teachers to work with the whole class. This further reduces planning and management consideration and can ensure that all students are presented with the same information.
Whole Group Instruction	In whole group instruction, the teacher delivers the same content to the entire classroom. It requires the least amount of planning but meets the needs of the fewest students.

Addressing the varying needs of students

Teachers can use a number of procedures to address the varying needs of the students. Some of the more common procedures follow:

Vary assignments

A variety of assignments on the same content allows students to match learning styles and preferences with the assignment. If all assignments are writing assignments, for example, students who are hands-on or visual learners are at a disadvantage unrelated to the content base itself.

Cooperative learning

Cooperative learning activities allow students to share ideas, expertise, and insight within a nonthreatening setting. The focus tends to remain on positive learning rather than on competition.

Structured environment

Some students need and benefit from clear structure that defines the teacher's expectations and goals. The student who clearly understands expectations can work and plan accordingly.

Clearly stated assignments

Assignments should be clearly stated along with the expectation and criteria for completion. Reinforcement and practice activities should not be a guessing game for the students. The exception to this is, of course, those situations in which a discovery method is used.

Independent practice

Independent practice involving application and repetition is necessary for thorough learning. Students learn to be independent learners through practicing independent learning. These activities should always be within the student's abilities to perform successfully without assistance.

Repetition

Very little learning is successful with a single exposure. Learners generally require multiple exposures to the same information for learning to take place. However, this repetition does not have to be dull and monotonous. Varied assignments can provide repetition of content or skill practiced without repetition of specific activities. This helps keep learning fresh and exciting for the student.

Overlearning

As a principle of effective learning, overlearning recommends that students continue to study and review after they have achieved initial mastery. The use of repetition in the context of varied assignments offers the means to help students pursue and achieve overlearning.

See also Skills 10.4 and 10.5

COMPETENCY 10

UNDERSTAND INSTRUCTIONAL PLANNING AND APPLY KNOWLEDGE OF PLANNING PROCESSES TO DESIGN EFFECTIVE INSTRUCTION THAT PROMOTES THE LEARNING OF ALL STUDENTS

> **SKILL 10.1** **Recognizes key factors to consider in planning instruction** *(e.g., New York State Learning Standards for students, instructional goals and strategies, the nature of the content and skills to be taught, students' characteristics and prior experiences, students' current knowledge and skills as determined by assessment results, available time and other resources)*

Understanding Standards and Planning Accordingly

The first step in planning successful instruction is having a firm grasp on the ending objectives for which the students will be held accountable. While teachers may have the best of intentions in teaching numerous, exciting topics, there are only so many days in a school year. Furthermore, the more content the teacher covers (skimmed over, so that students can be exposed to everything), the weaker the deep and lasting understandings of content by the students.

Aligning with standards

Teachers may benefit from laying out all crucial standards throughout the year and aligning them in a fashion that allows for conceptual growth.

So, with that in mind, teachers may benefit from laying out all crucial standards throughout the year and aligning them in a fashion that allows for conceptual growth. Conceptual growth refers to concepts building upon one another. Certain topics simply should be taught before other topics.

Demonstrating proficiency

Next, teachers should consider how students will be required to demonstrate proficiency of the various concepts presented. This is important, as all instruction needs to focus on making sure that students can indeed demonstrate proficiency.

Assessing understanding

Finally, as lessons and units are planned, to be most efficient with time, teachers should determine how much students already understand about the topics being taught. This will help the teacher to determine how long the concept will take to fully teach. This will allow the teacher to develop lessons that build on students' background knowledge without requiring them to repeat it. It will also help teachers manage their ability to teach all of the required standards in a one-year time period.

See Skills 2.1 and 9.2 for information on readiness

> SKILL **Analyzes and applies given information about specific planning**
> 10.2 **factors (see above statement) to define lesson and unit objectives, select appropriate instructional approach(es) to use in a given lesson** (e.g., discovery learning, explicit instruction)**, determine the appropriate sequence of instruction and learning for given content or learners within a lesson and unit, and develop specific lesson and unit plans**

Lesson Plans

Teaching was once seen as simply developing lesson plans, teaching, going home early, and taking the summer off. However, the demands of a classroom involve much more than grading papers. To begin with, writing lesson plans is very complicated. Lesson plans are crucial in guiding instruction within the classroom. The **LESSON PLAN** outlines the steps a teacher will implement and what forms of assessment will be used in an instructional learning capacity. Teachers are able to both objectify and quantify learning goals and targets through the incorporating of effective performance-based assessments as well as the projected criteria for identifying when a student has learned the material presented.

LESSON PLAN: an outline of the steps a teacher will implement and what forms of assessment will be used in an instructional learning capacity

Components

Components of a lesson plan include:

- The unit description
- Learning targets
- Learning experiences
- Explanation of learning rationale
- Assessments

These all must be present to provide both quantifiable and qualitative data. These two data sources help the teacher to ascertain whether student learning has taken place and whether effective teaching has occurred for the students. National and state learning standards must be considered, because not only will the teacher and the students be measured by the students' scores at the end of the year, the school will also. So, not only must the teacher be knowledgeable about state and local standards, she must structure her own classes in ways that will satisfy those frameworks.

Long-Term Considerations

On the large scale, the teacher must think about the scope of his ambitious plans for the day, the week, the unit, the semester, the year. The teacher must also decide on the subject matter for the unit, semester, and year, making certain that it is appropriate to the age of the students, relevant to their real lives, and in their realm of anticipated interest. Should he introduce politically controversial issues or avoid them? He must make these decisions deliberatively on the basis of feedback from his students, while at the same time keeping sight of his objectives.

Behavioral objectives

The teacher must be very knowledgeable about the writing of behavioral objectives that fall within the guidelines of both the state and local expectations; additionally, the objectives must be measurable so he can know for sure whether he has accomplished what he set out to do.

The teacher must be very knowledgeable about the writing of behavioral objectives that fall within the guidelines of both the state and local expectations.

Aligning goals with student needs

Once long-range goals have been identified and established, it is important to ensure that all goals and objectives are also in conjunction with student ability and needs. Some objectives may be too basic for a higher-level student, while others cannot be met by students with a lower level of knowledge. There are many forms of evaluating student needs to ensure that all goals set are challenging yet achievable.

Teachers should check a student's cumulative file for reading level and prior subject area achievement. This provides a basis for goal setting but shouldn't be the only method used. Depending on the subject area, basic skills test, reading level evaluations, writing samples, and interest surveys can all be useful in determining if all goals are appropriate. Informal observation should always be used as well. Finally, it is important to take into consideration the student's level of motivation when addressing student needs.

Teachers should check a student's cumulative file for reading level and prior subject area achievement.

Adjusting objectives to specific needs

When given objectives by the school or county, teachers may wish to adapt them so that they can better meet the needs of their individual student population. For example, if a higher-level advanced class is given the objective, "State five causes of World War II," a teacher may wish to adapt the objective to a higher level. "State five causes of World War II and explain how they contributed to the start of the war." Subsequently, objectives can be modified for a lower level as well: "From a list of causes, pick three that specifically caused World War II."

Constructing and Organizing Objectives

When organizing and sequencing objectives the teacher needs to remember that skills are building blocks. Taxonomy of educational objectives can be helpful to construct and organize objectives. Knowledge of material, for example, memorizing definitions or famous quotes, is low on the taxonomy of learning and should be worked with early in the sequence of teaching. Eventually, objectives should be developed to include higher-level thinking such as:

- Comprehension (being able to use a definition)

- Application (being able to apply the definition to other situations)

- Synthesis (being able to add other information)

- Evaluation (being able to judge the value of something)

Strategies

EMERGENT CURRICULUM describes the projects and themes that classrooms may embark upon that have been inspired by the children's interests. The teacher uses all the tools of assessment available to her to learn as much as she can about her students and then continually assesses them over the period of the unit or semester. As she gets to know them, she listens to what their interests are and creates a curriculum in response to what she learns from her observations of her own students.

WEBBING is a recent concept related to the idea of emergent curriculum. The two main uses of webbing are planning and recording curriculum. Planning webs are used to generate ideas for activities and projects for the children from an observed interest such as rocks.

Teachers work together to come up with ideas and activities for the children and to record them in on a web format. Activities can be grouped by different areas of the room or by developmental domains. For example, clusters either fall under areas such as dramatic play or science areas or around domains such as language, cognitive, and physical development. Either configuration works; being consistent in each web is important.

This format will work as a unit, weekly, or monthly program plan. Any new activities that emerge throughout the unit can also be added to the web. The record will serve in the future to plan using activities that emerge from the children's play and ideas.

EMERGENT CURRICULUM: projects and themes that classrooms may embark upon that have been inspired by the children's interests

WEBBING: a curriculum-planning strategy whereby activities are grouped by different areas of the room or by developmental domains and recorded in a web format

> **SKILL 10.3** **Identifies the background knowledge and prerequisite skills required by a given lesson, and applying strategies for determining students' readiness for learning** *(e.g., through teacher observation, student self-assessment, pre-testing)* **and for ensuring students' success in learning** *(e.g., by planning sufficient time to pre-teach key concepts or vocabulary, by planning differentiated instruction)*

To determine the abilities of incoming students, it may be helpful to consult their prior academic records. Letter grades assigned at previous levels of instruction as well as scores on standardized tests may be taken into account. In addition, the teacher may choose to administer pretests at the beginning of the school year and, perhaps, also at the initial stage of each new unit of instruction. The textbooks available for classroom use may provide suitable pretests, tests of student progress, and post-tests.

Selecting Assessments

In selecting tests and other assessment tools, the teacher should keep in mind that different kinds of tests measure different aspects of student development.

In selecting tests and other assessment tools, the teacher should keep in mind that different kinds of tests measure different aspects of student development. The tests included in most textbooks chosen for the classroom are usually achievement tests. Few of these are the type of tests intended to measure the students' inherent ability or aptitude. Teachers will find it difficult to raise students' scores based on ability tests, but students' scores on achievement tests may be expected to improve with proper instruction and application in the area being studied.

Using a variety of tasks

In addition to administering tests, the teacher may assess the readiness of students for a particular level of instruction by having them demonstrate their ability to perform some relevant task.

In addition to administering tests, the teacher may assess the readiness of students for a particular level of instruction by having them demonstrate their ability to perform some relevant task. In a class that emphasizes written composition, for example, students may be asked to submit writing samples. These may be used not only to ensure the placement of the students into the proper level but as a diagnostic tool to help them understand what aspects of their composition skills may need improvement. Similarly, students in a speech class may be asked to make an impromptu oral presentation before beginning a new level or specific level of instruction. Others may be asked to demonstrate their psychomotor skills in a physical education class, display their computational skills in a mathematics class, and so on. Whatever the chosen task, the teacher will need to select or devise an appropriate assessment scale and interpret the results with care.

SKILL 10.4 Uses assessment information before, during, and after instruction to modify plans and to adapt instruction for individual learners

Assessment Language

Assessment language has been deeply rooted in key terms.

KEY ASSESSMENT TERMS	
Formative	Sets targets for student learning and creates an avenue to provide data on whether students are meeting the targets
Diagnostic testing	Determines students' skill levels and current knowledge
Normative	Establishes rankings and comparatives of student performances against an established norm of achievement
Alternative	Nontraditional method of helping students construct responses to problem-solving
Authentic	Real-life assessments that are relevant and meaningful in a student's life (for a student learning math percentages, calculating a 20% discount on a calculator creates a more personalized approach to learning)
Performance based	Judges according to preestablished standards
Traditional	Diversity of teacher assessments that either come with the textbooks or are directly created from the textbooks

Using Assessment to Adjust Instruction

Teachers need to be able to:

Assessment skills should be an integral part of teacher training.

- Monitor student learning using pre- and post-assessments of content areas

- Analyze assessment data in terms of individualized support for students and instructional practice for teachers

- Design lesson plans that have measurable outcomes and definitive learning standards

Assessment information should be used to provide performance-based criteria and academic expectations for all students in evaluating whether students have learned the expected skills and content of the subject area.

For example, in an Algebra I class, teachers can use assessment to see whether students have acquired enough prior knowledge to engage in the subject area. If the teacher provides students with a preassessment on algebraic expression and can then ascertain whether the lesson plan should be modified to include a pre-algebraic expression lesson unit to refresh student understanding of the content area, then the teacher can create, if needed, quantifiable data to support the need of additional resources to support student learning. Once the teacher has taught the unit on algebraic expression, a post-assessment test can be used to test student learning and a mastery exam can be used to test how well students understand and can apply the knowledge to the next unit of math content learning.

Varying and analyzing assessments

Teachers can use assessment data to inform and impact instructional practices by making inferences on teaching methods and gathering clues for student performance. By analyzing the various types of assessments, teachers can gather more definitive information on projected student academic performance. Instructional strategies for teachers would provide learning targets for student behavior, cognitive thinking skills, and processing skills that can be employed to diversify student-learning opportunities.

By analyzing the various types of assessments, teachers can gather more definitive information on projected student academic performance.

SKILL 10.5 **Analyzes a given lesson or unit plan in terms of organization, completeness, feasibility, etc.**

Lesson plans are important in guiding instruction in the classroom. Incorporating the nuts and bolts of a teaching unit, the lesson plans outline the steps of teacher implementation, assessment of teacher instructional capacity, and student learning capacity. Teachers are able to objectify and quantify learning goals and targets in terms of incorporating effective performance-based assessments and projected criteria for identifying when a student has learned the material presented.

Lesson plans are important in guiding instruction in the classroom.

Components of a Successful Lesson Plan

All components of a lesson plan—including the unit description, learning targets, learning experiences, explanation of learning rationale and assessments—must be designed to provide both quantifiable and qualitative data. These two data sources help the teacher ascertain whether student learning has taken place and whether effective teaching has occurred.

A typical format would include:

1. **Written instructional lesson plan:** Guidelines for what is being taught and how the students will be able to access the information.

Subsequent evaluations and assessments will determine whether students have learned or correctly processed the subject content being taught.

2. **Unit Description:** Desribes the learning and classroom environment.

   – **Classroom Characteristics:** The physical arrangements of the classroom, along with the student grouping patterns for the lesson being taught. Classroom rules and consequences should be clearly posted and visible.

   – **Student Characteristics:** Demographics of the classroom, which include student number, gender, cultural and ethnic backgrounds, along with independent education students with IEPs (Individualized Education Plans).

3. **Learning Goals/Targets/Objectives:** What are the expectations of the lessons? Are the learning goals appropriate to the state learning standards and district academic goals? Are the targets appropriate for the grade level and, subject content area and do they include a multicultural perspective and global viewpoint?

4. **Learning Experiences:** How will student learning be supported using the learning goals?

   – What prior knowledge or experiences will the students bring to the lesson? How will you check and verify that student knowledge?

   – How will you engage all students in the classroom? How will students who have been identified as marginalized in the classroom be engaged in the lesson unit?

   – How will the lesson plan be modified for students with IEPs and how will independent education students be evaluated for learning and processing of the modified lesson targets?

   – How will the multicultural aspect be incorporated into the lesson plan?

   – What interdisciplinary linkages and connections will be used to incorporate across other subject areas.

   – What types of assessments and evaluations will be used to test student understanding and processing of the lesson plan?

   – How will students be cooperatively grouped to engage in the lesson?

   – What Internet links are provided in the lesson plan?

5. **Rationales for Learning Experiences:** Provide data on how the lesson plan addresses student learning goals and objectives. Address whether the lesson provides accommodations for students with IEPs and provides support for marginalized students in the classroom.

6. Assessments: Constructing pre- and post-assessments that evaluate student learning as it correlates to the learning goals and objectives. Do the assessments include a cultural integration that addresses the cultural needs and inclusion of students?

SKILL Applies strategies for collaborating with others to plan and
10.6 implement instruction

Collaborative Learning

According to Walther-Thomas et al. (2000) *Collaboration for Inclusive Education,* ongoing professional development that provides teachers with opportunities to create effective instructional practice is vital and necessary, "A comprehensive approach to professional development is perhaps the most critical dimension of sustained support for successful program implementation." The inclusive approach incorporates learning programs that include all stakeholders in defining and developing high-quality programs for students. The figure below shows how an integrated approach of stakeholders can provide the optimal learning opportunity for all students.

Integrated Approach to Learning

Teachers

All Students

Parents

Community

The integrated approach

INTEGRATED AP-
PROACH: an approach to
learning whereby teacher,
parent, and community
support become the
integral apexes to student
learning

In the **INTEGRATED APPROACH** to learning, teachers, parents, and community support become the integral apexes to student learning. The focus and central core of the school community is triangular as a representation of how effective collaboration can work in creating success for student learners. The goal of student learning and achievement now become the heart of the school community. The direction of teacher professional development in constructing effective instruction is clearly articulated in a greater understanding of facilitating learning strategies that develop skills and education equity for students.

Classroom application of collaborative learning

Teachers need diversity in their instructional toolkits, which can provide students with clear instruction, mentoring, inquiry, challenge, performance-based assessment, and journal reflections on their learning processes. For teachers, having a collaborative approach to instruction fosters for students a deeper appreciation of learning, subject matter, and knowledge acquisition. Implementing a consistent approach to learning from all stakeholders will create equitable educational opportunities for all learners.

The ability to gain additional insight into how students learn and modalities of differing learning styles can increase a teacher's capacity to develop proactive instruction methods. Teachers who team-teach or have daily networking opportunities can create a portfolio of curriculum articulation and inclusion for students.

Research has shown that educators who collaborate become more diversified and effective in implementation of curriculum and assessment of effective instructional practices.

Networking

People in business are always encouraged to network in order to further their careers. The same can be said for teaching. If English teachers get together and discuss what is going on in their classrooms, those discussions make the whole much stronger than the parts. Even if there are no formal opportunities for such networking, it is wise for schools or even individual teachers to develop them and seek them out.

COMPETENCY 11

UNDERSTAND VARIOUS INSTRUCTIONAL APPROACHES, AND USE THIS KNOWLEDGE TO FACILITATE STUDENT LEARNING

SKILL 11.1 **Analyzes the uses, benefits, or limitations of a specific instructional approach** (e.g., direct instruction, cooperative learning, interdisciplinary instruction, exploration, discovery learning, independent study, lectures, hands-on activities, peer tutoring, technology-based approach, various discussion methods such as guided discussion, various questioning methods) **in relation to given purposes and learners**

Direct Instruction

Siegfried Engelmann and Dr. Wesley Becker are among the researchers who proposed **DIRECT INSTRUCTION**, a teaching method that emphasizes well-developed and carefully planned lessons with small learning increments. It assumes that learning outcomes are improved through clear instruction that eliminates misinterpretations. Their approach is currently used by thousands of schools. It recommends that teacher creativity and autonomy be replaced by a willingness to follow certain carefully prescribed instructional practices. At the same time, it encourages hard work, dedication, and commitment to students. It demands that teachers adopt and internalize the belief that all students, if properly taught, can learn.

> **DIRECT INSTRUCTION:** teaching method that emphasizes well-developed and carefully planned lessons with small learning increments

Discovery Learning

Beginning at birth, **DISCOVERY LEARNING** is a normal part of growing-up, and this naturally occurring phenomenon can be used to improve classroom outcomes. Discovery learning is based upon inquiry and has been a factor in most human advances. For example, Rousseau constantly questioned his world, particularly the philosophies and theories that were commonly accepted. Dewey, himself a great discoverer, wrote, "There is an intimate and necessary relation between the processes of actual experience and education." Piaget, Bruner, and Papert have all recommended this teaching method.

> **DISCOVERY LEARNING:** learning technique that involves students solving problems by using their own experience and prior knowledge to determine what truths can be learned

In discovery learning, students solve problems by using their own experience and prior knowledge to determine what truths can be learned. Bruner wrote "Emphasis on discovery in learning has precisely the effect on the learner of leading him to a constructionist, to organize what he is encountering in a manner not only designed to discover regularity and relatedness, but also to avoid the kind of information drift that fails to keep account of the uses to which information might have to be put."

Whole Group Discussion

Whole group discussion can be used in a variety of settings, but the most common is in the discussion of an assignment. With this strategy, learning is peer-based; thus, students gain a different perspective on the topic while also learning to respect the ideas of others. One obstacle to this teaching method is that the same students tend to participate or not participate each time. However, with proper teacher guidance during this activity, whole group discussions are highly valuable.

Case Method Learning

Disseminating and integrating knowledge can be achieved effectively by providing opportunities for students to apply what they learn in the classroom to real-life experiences. The **CASE METHOD** is an instructional strategy that engages students in active discussion about issues and problems of practical application. It can highlight fundamental dilemmas or critical issues and provide a format for role-playing of ambiguous or controversial scenarios. A successful class discussion involves planning on the part of the instructor and preparation on the part of the students. Instructors should communicate this commitment to the students on the first day of class by clearly articulating course expectations. Just as the instructor carefully plans the learning experience, the students must comprehend the assigned reading and show up for class on time, ready to learn.

> **CASE METHOD:** an instructional strategy that engages students in active discussion about issues and problems of practical application

Concept Mapping

Concept mapping is a common tool used by teachers in various disciplines, and many kinds of maps have been developed for this purpose. They are useful devices, but each teacher must determine which is appropriate for use in his/her own classroom. Following is a concept map that is often used in writing courses.

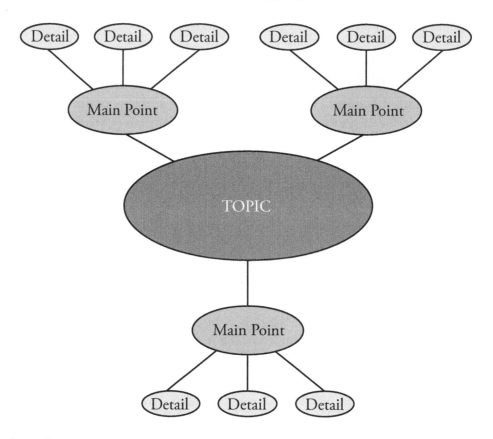

Concept Mapping

Inquiry

All learning begins with the student. What children know and what they want to learn are not constraints on what can be taught; they are the very foundation for learning.

DEWEY'S PRIMARY INTERESTS OF THE CHILD
The child's instinctive desire to find things out
In conversation, the propensity children have to communicate
In construction, their delight in making things
Their gifts of artistic expression

Questioning

Questioning is a teaching strategy as old as Socrates. In fact, the Socratic method is a well-known form of questioning. It is important for the teacher to deliberately and carefully plan in order to lead students in critical thinking.

Play

There are so many educational games available that the most difficult task is choosing which will fit into a classroom. Some are electronic, some are board games, and some are designed to be played by a child individually. Even in those cases, a review of the results by the entire classroom can be a useful learning experience.

Learning Centers

LEARNING CENTERS are extremely important in flexible classrooms. In this set-up, students have some time during which they can choose their own activity. Under a teacher's guidance, learners can even take out-of-class time for creating the centers, collecting the necessary items, and then setting up the area.

> **LEARNING CENTERS:** an instructional method whereby students have time during which they can choose their own activity

Small Group Work

Today's classrooms are usually diverse and small group work is vital. Children can be grouped according to their developmental level. If the small groups themselves are diverse, this gives students who are struggling an opportunity to learn from students who are already proficient. The better-prepared student will learn from becoming a resource for the weaker student. In turn, the weaker student may sometimes be more likely to accept help from another student. This frees the teacher to perform other tasks.

Revisiting

Revisiting should occur during and at the end of a unit and at the end of a semester. This gives students more than one opportunity to grasp principles and skills and to integrate them.

Reflection

Teaching can move along so rapidly that students may fail to incorporate what they've learned. They may also lack the time to think about what they can bring to the topic. Providing time for reflection and guiding students in developing these tools is a wise teaching method.

Projects

Seeing a unit as a project is also very useful. It opens the door to approaching learning as multitasking. For example, in a unit on birds, not only will students learn about birds, they will have an opportunity to observe them, they can try their hands at drawing them, and they can learn to differentiate one from the other. It's easy to see how a lifetime interest in birdwatching can take root from such a project. This is more effective than simply reading and talking about the topic.

> **SKILL 11.2** **Recognizes appropriate strategies for varying the role of the teacher** *(e.g., working with students as instructor, facilitator, observer; working with other adults in the classroom)* **in relation to the situations and the instructional approach used**

The Various Roles of Teachers

Teaching consists of a multitude of roles. Teachers must plan and deliver instruction in a creative and innovative way so that students find learning both fun and intriguing. The teacher must also research various learning strategies, decide which to implement in the classroom, and balance that information according to the various learning styles of the students. Teachers must facilitate all aspects of the lesson including preparation and organization of materials, delivery of instruction, and management of student behavior and attention.

Simultaneously, the teacher must also observe for student learning, interactions, and on-task behavior, while making mental or written notes regarding what is working in the lesson and how the students are receiving and utilizing the information. This will provide the teacher with immediate feedback as to whether to continue with the lesson, or if it is necessary to slow the instruction or present the lesson in another way. Teachers must also work collaboratively with other adults in the room and utilize them to maximize student learning. The teacher's job requires the teacher to establish a delicate balance among all these factors.

Effects of teaching style

How the teacher handles this balance depends on the teacher's style and the lesson. Cooperative learning will require the teacher to have organized materials ready, perhaps even with instructions for the students, as well. The teacher should conduct a great deal of observation during this type of lesson. Direct instruction methods will require the teacher to have an enthusiastic, yet organized, approach to the lesson. When teaching directly to students, the teacher must take care to keep the lesson student-centered and intriguing while presenting accurate information.

Applies procedures for promoting positive and productive small-group interactions *(e.g., establishing rules for working with other students in cooperative learning situations)*

Cooperative Learning

Cooperative learning situations, as practiced in today's classrooms, grew out of searches conducted by several groups in the early 1970s. Cooperative learning situations can range from very formal applications such as STAD (Student Teams-Achievement Divisions) and CIRC (Cooperative Integrated Reading and Composition) to less formal groupings known variously as "group investigation," "learning together," "discovery groups."

Classroom application of cooperative learning

Because cooperative learning techniques are so widely diffused in the schools, it is necessary to orient students in the skills cooperative learning groups use to operate smoothly and, thereby, enhance learning. Students who cannot interact constructively with other students will not be able to take advantage of the learning opportunities provided by the cooperative learning situations and will furthermore deprive their fellow students of the opportunity for cooperative learning.

These skills form the hierarchy of cooperation in which students first learn to work together as a group, so they may then proceed to levels at which they may engage in simulated conflict situations. This cooperative setting allows different points of view to be constructively entertained.

> *Cooperative learning as a general term is now firmly recognized and established as a teaching and learning technique in American schools.*

Teaching cooperative learning

To teach cooperative skills, the teacher should:

- Ensure that students see the need for the skill

- Ensure that students understand what the skill is and when it should be used

- Set up practice situations and encourage mastery of the skill

- Ensure that students have the time and the needed procedures for discussing (and receiving feedback on) how well they are using the skill

- Ensure that students persevere in practicing the skill until the skill becomes a natural action

Cooperative learning can promote positive social goals when used effectively as a teaching and learning tool. When the teacher promotes interaction of students among ethnic and social groups, students tend to respond positively by forming friendships and having enhanced respect for other sociological groups. Thus, the

> *A further goal of cooperative learning techniques is to establish and enhance mutual respect for other students.*

teacher who effectively manages cooperative learning groups has not only promoted cognitive learning, but has also promoted desirable behaviors in terms of mutual respect for all students.

SKILL 11.4 Compares instructional approaches in terms of teacher and student responsibilities, expected student outcomes, usefulness for achieving instructional purposes, etc.

In order for students to learn, teachers must facilitate learning in the classroom and provide continued motivation to learn and synthesize knowledge as national citizens and world learners.

Albert Einstein, the highly noted German physicist on the theory of relativity, once wrote, "The general level of world information is high but usually biased, influenced by national prejudices serving to make us citizens of our nation but not of our world." In order for students to learn, teachers must facilitate learning in the classroom and provide continued motivation to learn and synthesize knowledge as national citizens and world learners.

Establishing a Conducive Learning Environment

COLLABORATIVE LEARNING: defines student roles and academic outcomes by creating multiple learning perspectives and integration of cultural and ethnic inclusion in the learning process

Teacher responsibility in today's classroom includes establishing a learning conducive environment that is both positive and proactive where class values and rules are determined by the student community and visibly posted in the classroom. COLLABORATIVE LEARNING defines student roles and academic outcomes by creating multiple learning perspectives and integration of cultural and ethnic inclusion in the learning process. Helping students to develop cognitive learning skills that include both local and global problem solving of academic and interpersonal skills will provide students with safe interactive learning environments to process and acquire skills that will create worldwide learners.

Developing an Action Plan

The focus on student performance begins with a vision and mission that supports the direction of NCLB (No Child Left Behind) where all educational directives are focused on improving academic achievement and success for all students. The next goal for teachers and school communities is to develop an action plan that incorporates the following:

- Clearly defined goals and objects for student learning and school improvement

- Clear alignment of goals and objectives

- Developing clear timelines and accountability for goal implementation steps

- Constructing an effective evaluation plan for assessing data around student performance and established objectives for student learning outcomes

- Defining a plan B in case plan A falls short of meeting the goals and objectives for student achievement and school improvement

The priorities for school communities should continue to be consistent with the desired results of their action plans. Analyzing teacher instructional practices and curriculum adoptions will provide data for evaluating the effectiveness of student learning and access to academic goals and objectives.

COMPETENCY 12
UNDERSTAND PRINCIPLES AND PROCEDURES FOR ORGANIZING AND IMPLEMENTING LESSONS, AND USE THIS KNOWLEDGE TO PROMOTE STUDENT LEARNING AND ACHIEVEMENT

SKILL 12.1 **Evaluates strengths and weaknesses of various strategies for organizing and implements a given lesson** *(e.g., in relation to introducing and closing a lesson, using inductive and deductive instruction, building on students' prior knowledge and experiences)*

Things to Consider when Planning a Lesson

There are many things to consider when planning a lesson. First, lessons must have objectives. Those objectives state what students should be able to know and do by the time the lesson is finished. It is not good enough to simply know particular objectives for the sake of planning a lesson. If those objectives are not placed appropriately in the context of a coherent learning plan (i.e., a course of study, a unit, or an aligned curriculum), the lesson will mean very little in the overall depth of knowledge or skill of a student.

Second, when lessons have objectives, those objectives must be observable. To observe that an objective is accomplished, a teacher will need an assessment. Let's take an example of a seventh grade Language Arts teacher.

AN EXAMPLE OF LESSON PLANNING

This teacher has been working on a unit of argumentative writing. He wants his students at the end of the unit to be able to write a coherent, effective five-paragraph essay that argues an opinion about a current topic in the news. The lesson for the day is the thesis sentence. His objective is that students will be able to write a coherent thesis sentence that argues an opinion about a current issue. The assessment might be multi-faceted.

First, students are given four different sentences, three of which are potential thesis sentences, and one of which is an example sentence. If students can identify the sentence that is not a thesis sentence, they have been able to slightly show mastery of the objective. To continue ensuring that students have mastery of the objective, the assessment might also include a sample topic with some examples. Students would have to write a thesis sentence that could be supported by the given example sentences. Additionally, the students might be given another topic, and then they would have to consider their opinion on the topic and write a thesis sentence regarding that opinion. Having the assessment in mind before designing the lesson will ensure that the teacher is focusing exclusively on teaching material that is extremely pertinent to the objective(s).

Introducing a lesson

The introduction to a lesson is very important for three primary reasons. First, students need to be engaged. They need to know that the material they will be learning in the lesson is interesting and important. They need to be given a reason to motivate themselves to learn it.

Second, students need to know what they are going to study—they need to know what they are expected to learn. This is an area that teachers often forget. In their rush to get to the "meat" of the lesson, they forget that students may not really know what it is that they are going to be assessed on. Knowing this helps them focus.

Third, students need to have their background knowledge activated. If they have ways in which to attach new knowledge to existing knowledge throughout the lesson, they will be more successful in retaining and utilizing the new knowledge.

Concluding a lesson

Ending a lesson can be equally complex. This is where assessment comes into play. And even though teachers should constantly assess their students, even on a lesson-by-lesson basis, not all assessments need to be long, graded, something that students should prepare for, or something students should be worried about.

Some assessments simply should quickly tell the teacher what students know and do not know about the lesson that has just been taught. Also, the end of lessons should help students know where the instruction will go next (i.e., the content of

Some assessments should simply quickly tell the teacher what students know and do not know about the lesson that has just been taught.

the next lesson, so they can see where their new knowledge is headed), and they should know how the new knowledge is valued and useful.

Inductive and deductive lessons

The difference between inductive and deductive lessons lies in the way in which the new learning is attained. DEDUCTIVE LESSONS move from the general to the specific, while INDUCTIVE LESSONS move in the opposite direction.

What does this mean for instruction? Sometimes, it is important for students to learn the small pieces first and then to understand that bigger picture. Other times, it is important for students to understand the bigger picture first and then learn the smaller pieces.

When the students learn the smaller pieces first and then are exposed to the bigger picture this is inductive instruction. When the bigger picture is introduced first, and then the particulars are explained, that is deductive instruction.

Choosing inductive or deductive

How would the teacher decide what method to use? Let's take an example of the Civil War in a social studies class. The teacher wouldn't want to teach all the battles first and then inform students that these are part of a larger war. For this subject, he would probably use deductive instruction. However, when teaching students a second language, it might be more important to teach smaller pieces first and then, once those small pieces are mastered, ask the students to try to use those in a sentence for a real communicative purpose.

> **DEDUCTIVE LESSONS:** lessons that move from the general to the specific

> **INDUCTIVE LESSONS:** lessons that move from the specific to the general

> SKILL **Recognizes the importance of organizing instruction to include**
> 12.2 **multiple strategies for teaching the same context so as to provide the kind and amount of instruction and practice needed by each student in the same class**

Student learning is an intricate, multifaceted process. Teachers instruct based upon their students' background knowledge. The first step teachers may take in approaching a new topic or skill is to simply ask the students what they already know and list their responses. This will provide the teacher with a beginning point from which they can build instruction. The next step will include the teacher's delivery of the topic, subject matter, or skill information. Following these steps, the teacher will always provide the necessary time and resources for student practice. Student practice is perhaps the most crucial means by which information is internalized.

The Importance of Student Practice

There are unlimited forms of **PRACTICE**. Just as the teacher intricately planned her instructional delivery based upon student needs, the teacher will also carefully plan the practice activities necessary to enhance the learning experience. These practice activities will depend largely on the students' developmental stage and on the skill or knowledge being practiced. Although practice activities are intended to reinforce what the teacher has taught, for many students the practice—the interactive process of doing something—is the point at which learning occurs. Therefore, the importance of practice activities cannot be underestimated. Teachers must monitor students as they practice in order to observe both the difficulties that might arise as well as student proficiency. Based on the observations that teachers make during practice activities, it will be evident when additional instruction needs to occur and when the students are ready to go on to another concept or skill.

> **PRACTICE:** the interactive process of doing something and, the point at which learning occurs

> Teachers must monitor students as they practice in order to observe difficulties that might arise as well as student proficiency.

Repetition

Repetitive practice can occur in many forms. Sometimes the teacher will lead the students in choral chants whereby they repeat basic skills including addition, subtraction, and multiplication facts. This activity can also be effective in memorizing spelling words and academic laws. In addition to orally repeating information, these same kinds of skills can be acquired by students repeatedly writing multiplication tables, addition or subtraction facts, or spelling words. Older students may use these types of practice in memorizing algebraic formulas, geometric theorems, and scientific laws.

Repetitive practice may also occur over time. Teachers and students may revisit skills, concepts, or knowledge throughout a school year or even over several school years as a means of internalizing important information. Repetition may come in the form of discussing, rereading, or taking information to a higher level.

> Repetition may come in the form of discussing, rereading, or taking information to a higher level.

Short-term versus long-term retention

Most teachers are aware that short-term retention is the first phase of long-term retention. During the time period that short-term retention is being actualized, instruction and practice are ongoing. Once it appears that a skill or concept has become internalized, the teacher plans for future follow-up activities that will foster long-term retention. Long-term retention is not the result of haphazard instruction, but rather is the result of deliberate and planned instruction. Just as assessment is ongoing, so is instruction and learning.

Practice time

One of the best uses of practice time is to assign homework activities that will permit students to both reinforce learning and revisit skills and concepts. This allows the teacher to use classroom time for instruction of new ideas, while giving the students opportunities and motivation to practice important skills or concepts. Sometimes, while working on homework assignments with the assistance of a parent, students will develop a broader comprehension of a concept. Also during this valuable time, students may realize valid questions that can then be addressed during class time.

Teacher observations

The value of teacher observations cannot be underestimated. It is through the use of observations that the teacher is able to informally assess the needs of the students during instruction. These observations will drive the lesson and determine the direction that future lessons will take. Teacher observations also set the pace of instruction and ascertain the flow of both student and teacher discourse. After a lesson is carefully planned, teacher observation is the single most important component of an instructional presentation.

It is through the use of observations that the teacher is able to informally assess the needs of the students during instruction.

Looking for on-task behavior

One of the primary behaviors that teachers look for in an observation is on-task behavior. There is no doubt that student time on-task directly influences student involvement in instruction and enhances student learning. If the teacher observes that a particular student is not on-task, he will change the method of instruction accordingly. He may change from a teacher-directed approach to a more interactive approach. Questioning will increase in order to cull the participation of the students. If appropriate, the teacher will introduce manipulative materials to the lesson. In addition, teachers may switch to a cooperative group activity thereby removing the responsibility of instruction from the teacher and putting it on the students.

Changing Approaches

Teachers will also change instructional strategies based on the questions and verbal comments of the students. If the students express confusion or doubt or are unclear in any way about the content of the lesson, the teacher will immediately take another approach in presenting the lesson. Sometimes this can be accomplished by simply rephrasing an explanation. At other times, it will be necessary for the teacher to use visual organizers or models for understanding to be clear. Effective teachers are sensitive to the reactions and responses of their students and will almost intuitively know when instruction is valid and when it is not. Teachers will constantly check for student comprehension, attention, and focus throughout the presentation of a lesson.

Effective teachers are sensitive to the reactions and responses of their students and will almost intuitively know when instruction is valid and when it is not.

After the teacher has presented a skill or concept lesson, she will allow time for the students to practice the skill or concept. At this point, it is essential for the teacher to circulate among the students to check for understanding. If the teacher observes that any of the students did not clearly understand the skill or concept, then she must immediately readdress the issue using another technique or approach.

SKILL 12.3 **Evaluates various instructional resources** *(e.g., textbooks and other print resources, primary documents and artifacts, guest speakers, films and other audiovisual materials, computers and other technological resources)* **in relation to given content, learners** *(including those with special needs)*, **and goals**

Incorporating Media

The use of media in lesson presentation has become an instructional staple. In order to address the many learning styles that are present within a classroom, the teacher must incorporate the use of media. In today's society, where children have been stimulated and entertained by television, teachers must rely on this and other media to secure the interest of students.

> In order to address the many learning styles that are present within a classroom, the teacher must incorporate the use of media.

Low technology media

A wide variety of media is available in most schools, including overhead projectors, tape recorders, and videos. Other low technology media are important motivators in helping students maintain academic focus, such as posters, graphs, matrices, and charts. Not only are these visuals valuable as motivators, they are also organizers that can assist the students in understanding and retaining information.

High technology media

Many sophisticated high technology media are now available and are being actuated on lesson presentations throughout our schools. Computers connected to televisions or LCD panels allow teachers to present information in all content areas, including technology. DVD players connected to either computer monitors or televisions allow students to view a voluminous amount of visual material. Media is an integral tool in delivering instruction and is applied by both teachers and students.

> Media can never replace teachers but it can offer teachers alternative teaching strategies that students will respond to in a positive and enlightened manner.

The implementation of media into instruction offers both the students and the teacher variety. There is "something for everybody." Teachers can be on the cutting edge and address all learning styles and all learners will be stimulated by something within the structure and presentation of the lesson.

The Importance of Student Involvement

As previously stated, student learning increases when their interests and ideas are included as part of the focus of instruction. Undoubtedly, students learn more when they decide what they will learn because the desire to learn is already present. Not only should students be encouraged to decide what they will learn, they should also be given the opportunity to decide what methods they will use to learn. Frequently, students have ideas on how to acquire information and knowledge and how to demonstrate their understanding of newly acquired knowledge.

Students learning from students

More and more, students are generating the tasks that will aid them in learning and in assessing what they have learned. Teachers are also capitalizing upon the talents of students to enhance instruction. Research indicates that many times, students learn best from other students. It is natural for teachers to tap this valuable resource and to encourage students to share their expertise. Teachers are no longer the only or even the most effective deliverers of information. Students can help one another by working together in cooperative groups, by engaging in peer tutoring activities, or by giving presentations to the entire group. Students can help one another by working together in cooperative groups or by engaging in peer tutoring activities as well as by giving presentations to the entire group.

Student product as motivation

Some of the most influential motivating resources that can stimulate learning are student products. The process of creating a product can be exhilarating to the student engaged in the learning activity. The actual creation of the finished product can be a strong motivator to other students because of the excitement of the student who created the product. Enthusiasm and excitement are contagious. Nothing is more rewarding to a teacher than to observe students who are excited about learning and who become absorbed in the process.

Some of the most influential motivating resources that can stimulate learning are student products.

SKILL 12.4 **Demonstrates understanding of the developmental characteristics of students** *(e.g., with regard to attention and focus, writing or reading for extended periods of time)* **when organizing and implementing lessons**

Folk wisdom says that the number of minutes a person is able to sit still and do one thing is typically equal to that person's age. While this might not have any scientific validity, most kindergarten teachers would probably agree that, yes, six minutes is about all their students can handle!

Mentally Taxing Activities

The truth of the matter is that most people, young or old, have a hard time concentrating on difficult mental tasks for too long. For children, such things as learning to read or do math are mentally taxing, and too much of one activity at one time can be detrimental. Students will not focus and the teacher will end up having to reteach the lesson.

> *For children, such things as learning to read or do math are mentally taxing, and too much of one activity at one time can be detrimental.*

Varying activities

Generally, in younger grades, activities should change every 15–30 minutes. In older grades, activities should change every 20–40 minutes. The reason for this is not to encourage short attention spans but rather to encourage higher levels of intellectual focus for shorter periods of time, which can increase both retention and engagement.

It is important, however, for teachers in the younger grades to gradually increase the amount of time spent on reading or writing. In the younger grades, students will struggle to stay focused on a text, for example, simply because they have never been required to do such an activity. Their eyes in particular may get very tired. In writing, as well, hands and eyes will tire quickly, so gradual increases of time spent on these activities is a good idea. Over time, students will be able to handle more and more.

Example of varied activities

When designing and implementing lessons, it is crucial for teachers to develop multiple activities on the same content. For example, in a one-hour period to cover a reading lesson, a teacher can:

- Have a whole class discussion
- Have students write independently
- Spend time reading aloud
- Have students read quietly
- Have students do an activity with the text

Not only will this change of activity keep students' attention, it will provide them with unique ways to think about, integrate, and learn the material.

SKILL 12.5 **Applies strategies for adjusting lessons in response to student performance and student feedback** *(e.g., responding to student comments regarding relevant personal experiences, changing the pace of a lesson as appropriate)*

The Importance of Feedback

In the old days, students expected teachers to put a letter grade at the top of their papers and perhaps make grammatical corrections to written work. Those days are over. Teachers are now expected to provide feedback to help students learn more.

The amount of time teachers spent grading work yielded little new learning for students. The fear of a low grade alone is not viewed as sufficient to provide students with information as to what was done well and what may need additional work. Students need deeper interaction, particularly as areas of knowledge and skills taught are becoming more complex.

> Teachers are now expected to provide feedback to help students learn more.

Constructive feedback

How can a teacher provide appropriate feedback so that students will be able to learn from their assessments? First, language should be helpful and constructive. Critical language does not necessarily help students learn. They may become defensive or hurt and, therefore, they may be more focused on the perceptions than the content. Language that is constructive and helpful will guide students to specific actions and recommendations that would help them improve in the future.

> Language that is constructive and helpful will guide students to specific actions and recommendations that would help them improve in the future.

Timely feedback

When teachers provide timely feedback, they increase the chance that students will reflect on their thought processes as they originally produced the work. When feedback comes weeks after the production of an assignment, the student may not remember what it is that caused him to respond in a particular way.

Specific feedback

Specific feedback is particularly important. Comments like "This should be clearer" and "Your grammar needs to be worked on" provide information that students may already know. They may already know they have a problem with clarity. Commentary that provides very specific actions students could take to make something more clearly or to improve his or her grammar is more beneficial to the student.

Using feedback to promote learning

While written feedback will enhance student learning, having students do something with the feedback encourages an even deeper learning and reflection.

When teachers provide feedback on a set of assignments, for example, they enhance their students' learning by teaching students how to use the feedback. For example, returning a set of papers can actually do more than provide feedback to students on their initial performance. Teachers can ask students to do additional things to work with their original products, or they can even ask students to take small sections and rewrite based on the feedback. While written feedback will enhance student learning, having students do something with the feedback encourages an even deeper learning and reflection.

Managing feedback

Experienced teachers may be reading this and thinking, "When will I ever get the time to provide so much feedback?" Although detailed and timely feedback is important—and necessary—teachers do not have to provide it all the time to increase student learning. They can also teach students how to use scoring guides and rubrics to evaluate their own work, particularly before they hand it in to be graded.

Examples of proficient work

One particularly effective way of doing this is by having students examine models and samples of proficient work. Through the years, teachers should collect samples, remove names and other identifying factors, and show these examples to students so that they understand what is expected of them. Often, when teachers do this, they will be surprised to see how much students gain in terms of their ability to assess their own performance.

Revising and improving based on feedback

Finally, teachers can help students develop plans for revising and improving upon their work, even if it is not evaluated by the teacher in the preliminary stages. For example, teachers can have students keep track of words they commonly misspell or they can have students make personal lists of areas on which they feel they need to focus.

COMPETENCY 13

UNDERSTAND THE RELATIONSHIP BETWEEN STUDENT MOTIVATION AND ACHIEVEMENT AND HOW MOTIVATIONAL PRINCIPLES AND PRACTICES CAN BE USED TO PROMOTE AND SUSTAIN STUDENT COOPERATION IN LEARNING

SKILL 13.1 Distinguishes between motivational strategies that use intrinsic and extrinsic rewards, and identifying the likely benefits and limitations of each approach

---

Types of Motivation

EXTRINSIC MOTIVATION is motivation that comes from the expectation of rewards or punishments. The rewards and punishments can be varied. For example, in social situations, most human beings are extrinsically motivated to behave in common, socially accepted ways. The punishment for *not* doing so might be embarrassment or ridicule. The reward for doing so might be the acceptance of peers. In the classroom, rewards might be grades, candy, or special privileges. Punishments might be phone calls to parents, detention, suspension, or poor grades.

> **EXTRINSIC MOTIVATION:** motivation that comes from the expectation of rewards or punishments

INTRINSIC MOTIVATION is motivation that comes from within. For example, while some children only read if given extrinsic rewards (e.g., winning an award for the most pages read), other children read because they enjoy it.

> **INTRINSIC MOTIVATION:** motivation that comes from within

There are benefits and drawbacks of both methods of motivation. In reality, it should be noted that in an ideal world, all motivation would be intrinsic. But this is not the case. Consider having to clean your apartment, dorm room, or house. We might appreciate the "reward" of a clean living space at the end of the activity, but most of us do not particularly enjoy the process of cleaning and we only put up with it so that we get the end result.

In learning, of course we want all students to be intrinsically motivated. We would want students to not care about grades or prizes as much as we might want them to do their work, listen attentively, and read just because they want to learn. And while all teachers should work tirelessly to ensure that they develop intrinsic motivation as much as possible within their students, everyone knows that for certain students and subjects, extrinsic motivators must be used.

Using extrinsic motivators

What extrinsic motivators are useful in the classroom? If things like candy and prizes are *always* used to get students to pay attention in class, soon they will expect these things and possibly not pay attention in their absence. Likewise, if punishment is always used as a motivator, students may be consumed with fear rather than have the frame of mind that is most conducive to learning.

Benchmarks and standards are indeed useful for many teachers. Punishments, if they are reasonable, applied consistently, and students know what to expect, can be useful in making sure students behave appropriately. The best punishments, though, are ones in which a whole school has decided will be consistently used from classroom to classroom and grade level to grade level.

> *In general, teachers must walk a careful line with motivation. They must utilize extrinsic motivators when all possible intrinsic motivators have failed to work.*

SKILL 13.2 **Analyzes the effects of using various intrinsic and extrinsic motivational strategies in given situations**

Encouraging Intrinsic Motivation

As a rule, teachers should strive to encourage intrinsic motivation for students' learning. To do so lessens the need to use extrinsic motivators, such as frivolous rewards and harsh punishments.

Student engagement with the material

The best way to encourage intrinsic motivation is to engage students in the learning. Engagement happens most when students work with material that is of greatest interest to them and if they feel there is a useful application for such material. For example, teachers will notice intrinsic motivation in reading when students have found books that they relate to.

When teachers believe that certain students just will not read, often (though not always), those students have not found books that they like. Considering that hundreds of thousands of books are out there, most likely, each student can find at least one interesting book.

Extrinsic Motivators

Grades

The extrinsic motivator of grades can be a particularly large challenge for well-meaning high school teachers who have college-bound students. Such students may not care much about the learning as much as they do about the grades so that their college applications look more competitive. Unfortunately, across the country, this has resulted in very troubling behavior. Plagiarism and cheating have been noticed in high schools everywhere.

While teachers may want to encourage students to learn for the sake of the learning itself, they must contend with students who have been trained to "win at all costs." Teachers can therefore use many strategies—*not* to eradicate the very act of cheating, for example—but to encourage students to explore topics that are of interest to them or to create more meaningful, authentic assessments. Authentic assessments are those in which students have to use new learning in a real-world, deeply meaningful way.

Punishment

Finally, it must be noted that punishment as an extrinsic motivator, while necessary at some times, often creates greater problems in the future. Students who feel like they are constantly punished into better behavior or to do better academically lose interest in pleasing teachers, acting appropriately, or learning. It is always better, whenever possible, for teachers to work at engaging students first and then punishing if all options have been exhausted.

> Students who feel like they are constantly punished into better behavior or to do better academically lose interest in pleasing teachers, acting appropriately, or learning.

SKILL 13.3 **Recognizes factors** (e.g., expectations, methods of providing specific feedback) **and situations that tend to promote or diminish student motivation**

Teachers as Motivators

Teachers need to be aware that much of what they say and do can be motivating and may have a positive effect on students' achievement. Studies have been conducted to determine the impact of teacher behavior on student performance. Surprisingly, a teacher's voice can really make an impression on students. Teachers' voices have several dimensions—volume, pitch, rate, etc. A recent study on the effects of speech rate indicates that, although both boys and girls prefer to listen at the rate of about 200 words per minute, boys tend to prefer slower rates overall than girls. This same study indicates that a slower rate of speech directly affects processing ability and comprehension.

> Teachers need to be aware that much of what they say and do can be motivating and may have a positive effect on students' achievement.

Speech and body language

Other speech factors, such as communication of ideas, communication of emotion, distinctness and pronunciation, quality variation and phrasing, correlate with teaching criterion scores. These scores show that good teachers (good meaning teachers who positively impact and motivate students) use more variety in speech than do less effective teachers. A teacher's speech skills can be strong motivating elements. A teacher's body language has an even greater effect on student achievement and ability to set and focus on goals.

Teacher smiles provide support and give feedback about the teacher's affective state. A deadpan expression can actually be a detriment to the student's progress. Teacher frowns are perceived by students to mean displeasure, disapproval, and even anger. Studies also show that teacher posture and movement are indicators of the teacher's enthusiasm and energy, which emphatically influence:

- Student learning

- Attitudes

- Motivation

- Focus on goals

Teachers have a greater efficacy on student motivation than any person other than parents.

SKILL 13.4 Recognizes the relationship between direct engagement in learning and students' interest in lessons and activities

Motivating Students

Interactive Learning

Teachers can enhance student motivation by planning and directing interactive, "hands-on" learning experiences. Research substantiates that cooperative group projects decrease student behavior problems and increase student on-task behavior. Students who are directly involved with learning activities are more motivated to complete a task to the best of their ability.

Research substantiates that cooperative group projects decrease student behavior problems and increase student on-task behavior.

Supportive feedback

Students generally do not realize their own abilities and frequently lack self-confidence. Teachers can instill positive self-concepts in children and thereby enhance their innate abilities by providing certain types of feedback. Such feedback includes attributing students' successes to their effort and specifying what the student did that produced the success. Qualitative comments influence attitudes more than quantitative feedback such as grades.

Teacher enthusiasm

Despite a teacher's best efforts to provide important and appropriate instruction, there may be times when a teacher is required to teach a concept, skill, or topic that students perceive as trivial and irrelevant. These tasks can be effectively presented if the teacher exhibits a sense of enthusiasm and excitement about the content. Teachers can help spark the students' interest by providing anecdotes and interesting digressions.

> *Research indicates that as teachers become significantly more enthusiastic, students exhibit increased on-task behavior.*

Addressing student concerns

Teachers must avoid teaching tasks that fit only their own interests and goals and design activities that address the students' concerns. In order to do this, it is necessary to find out about students and to have a sense of *their* interests and goals. Teachers can do this by conducting student surveys and simply by questioning and listening to students. Once this information is obtained, the teacher can link students' interests with classroom tasks.

Teachers are learning the value of giving assignments that meet the individual abilities and needs of students. After instruction, discussion, questioning, and practice have been provided, rather than assigning one task to all students, teachers are asking students to generate tasks that will show their knowledge of the information presented. Students are given choices and thereby have the opportunity to demonstrate more effectively the skills, concepts, or topics that they as individuals have learned. It has been established that student choice increases student originality, intrinsic motivation, and higher mental processes.

> *It has been established that student choice increases student originality, intrinsic motivation, and higher mental processes.*

> **SKILL 13.5 Applies procedures for enhancing student interest and helping students find their own motivation** (e.g., *relates concepts presented in the classroom to students' everyday experiences; encourages students to ask questions, initiate activities, and pursue problems that are meaningful to them; highlighting connections between academic learning and the workplace*)

When students are interested in the lesson, their motivation for learning increases. Teachers should provide opportunities for students to work toward becoming self-directed and, therefore, self-motivated learners. Skill knowledge, strategy use, motivation, and personal interests are all factors that influence individual student success.

Develop a Plan for Progression from Directed to Self-Directed Activity

Learning progresses in stages from initial acquisition, when the student requires a lot of teacher guidance and instruction, to adaptation, where the student is able to apply what he has learned to new situations outside of the classroom. As students progress through the stages of learning, the teacher gradually decreases the amount of direct instruction and guidance. The teacher is slowly encouraging the student to function more independently.

The ultimate goal of the learning process is to teach students how to become independent and apply their knowledge. Here is a summary of these stages and their features:

> *The ultimate goal of the learning process is to teach students how to become independent and apply their knowledge.*

STAGES OF THE LEARNING PROCESS		
State	**Teacher Activity**	**Emphasis**
Initial Acquisition	Provide rationale Guidance demonstration Modeling Shaping Cueing	Errorless learning Backward chaining (working from the final product backward through the steps) Forward chaining (proceeding through the steps to a final product)
Advanced Acquisition	Feedback Error correction Specific directions	Criterion evaluation Reinforcement and reward for accuracy
Proficiency	Positive reinforcement Progress monitoring Teach self-management Increased teacher expectations	Increase speed or performance to the automatic level with accuracy Set goals Self-management
Maintenance	Withdraw direct reinforcement Retention and memory Overlearning Intermittent schedule of reinforcement	Maintain high level of performance Mnemonic techniques Social and intrinsic reinforcement

Continued on next page

Generalization	Corrective feedback	Perform skill in different times and places
Adaptation	Stress independent problem solving	Independent problem solving methods No direct guidance or direct instruction

See Skills 2.2, 2.4, and 2.6 for more information on linking lessons to students' interests.

SKILL 13.6 Recognizes the importance of encouragement in sustaining students' interest and cooperation in learning

Using Student Responses

Various studies have shown that learning is increased when the teacher acknowledges and amplifies the student responses. In addition, this can be even more effective if the teacher takes one student's response and directs it to another student for further comment. When this occurs, the students acquire greater subject matter knowledge because of several factors. One is that the student feels that she is a valuable contributor to the lesson. Another is that all students are forced to pay attention because they never know when they will be called on; this is known as **GROUP ALERT**. The teacher achieves group alert by stating the question, allowing for a pause for the students to process the question and formulate an answer, and then calling on someone to answer. If the teacher calls on someone before stating the question, the rest of the students tune-out because they know they are not responsible for the answer. Teachers are advised to also alert the nonperformers to pay attention because they may be called on to elaborate on the answer. (Nonperformers are defined as all the students not chosen to answer.)

Directing student comments

The idea of directing the student comment to another student is a valuable tool for engaging the lower-achieving student. If the teacher can elicit even part of an answer from a lower-achieving student and then move the spotlight off of that student onto another student, the lower-achieving student will be more likely to engage in the class discussion the next time. Because they were not put "on the spot" for very long and successfully contributed to the class discussion, they are more willing to participate.

> *Various studies have shown that learning is increased when the teacher acknowledges and amplifies the student responses.*

> **GROUP ALERT:** a strategy to increase student involvement that forces all students to pay attention because they never know when they will be called on

> *If the teacher can elicit even part of an answer from a lower-achieving student and then move the spotlight off of that student onto another student, the lower-achieving student will be more likely to engage in the class discussion the next time.*

Accepting student responses

In addition, the teacher shows acceptance and gives value to student responses by acknowledging, amplifying, discussing, or restating the comment or question. If you allow a student response, even if it is blurted out, you must acknowledge the student response and tell the student the quality of the response.

For example, the teacher asks, "Is chalk a noun?" During the pause time a student says, "Oh, so my bike is a noun." Without breaking the concentration of the class, the teacher looks to the student, nods, and then places his index finger to the lips as a signal for the student not to speak out of turn and then calls on someone to respond to the original question. If the blurted out response is incorrect or needs further elaboration, the teacher may just hold up his index finger as an indication to the student that the class will address that in a minute when the class is finished with the current question.

A teacher acknowledges a student response by commenting on it. For example, the teacher states the definition of a noun and then asks for examples of nouns in the classroom. A student responds, "My pencil is a noun." The teacher answers, "Okay, let us list that on the board." Through this response and the action of writing "pencil" on the board, the teacher has just incorporated the student's response into the lesson.

Redirecting responses

A teacher may also amplify the student response through another question directed to either the original student or to another student. For example, the teacher may say, "Okay," giving the student feedback on the quality of the answer, and then add, "What do you mean by 'run' when you say the battery runs the radio?"

Another way of showing acceptance and value of student response is to discuss the student response. For example, after a student responds, the teacher would say, "Class, let us think along that line. What is some evidence that proves what Susie just stated?"

And finally, the teacher may restate the response. For example, the teacher might say, "So you are saying that the seasons are caused by the tilt of the Earth. Is this what you said?"

Therefore, a teacher keeps students involved by using group alert. In addition, the teacher shows acceptance and value of student responses by acknowledging, amplifying, discussing, or restating the response. This response contributes to maintaining academic focus.

Positive reinforcement

Praise in the classroom increases the desirable and eliminates the undesirable in both conduct and academic focus. It further states that effective praise should be:

- Authentic

- Used in a variety of ways

- Low-key

Academic praise is a group of specific statements that give information about the value of the response or its implications. For example, a teacher using academic praise would respond, "That is an excellent analysis of Twain's use of the river in *Huckleberry Finn.*" Whereas a simple positive response to the same question would be, "That's correct."

> *Praise in the classroom increases the desirable and eliminates the undesirable in both conduct and academic focus.*

SKILL 13.7 Recognizes the important of utilizing peers *(e.g., as peer mentors, in group activities)* to benefit students' learning and to sustain their interest and cooperation

Students as Community

Flexible grouping, pair shares, small groups, base groups, etc.—these are all terms used to describe the ways in which students can learn in community-like settings. Much research has shown that students are highly successful learners when learning with peers primarily, because the social interaction helps stimulate ideas in natural contexts. Furthermore, students learning in group settings have additional opportunities to learn material successfully. Some ways this occurs include:

- By talking about concepts, students have to put ideas into words. By putting ideas into words, students will remember the ideas better and by articulating the ideas, they will begin to make better sense of those ideas.

- Students get to test ideas out in comfortable settings. In whole-group settings, students may be fearful to share ideas with the whole class. However, without sharing thoughts, students never get the chance to really think through complex ideas. Small groups are safer places to do this.

- Help is immediately available. Students can get assistance from those right next to them in a social, natural setting.

- When students help other students learn, they commit ideas to memory for themselves.

> *Much research has shown that students are highly successful learners when learning with peers primarily, because the social interaction helps stimulate ideas in natural contexts.*

How to group

Often, teachers consider grouping students by ability level. While this grouping can be productive some of the time, it is often best to mix and match students for various lesson purposes. Sometimes, it is important to have similar levels together; other times, it is good to have different levels together. It is always important to change groups often.

Grouping does not have to be highly structured or scientific all the time. Sometimes, it is helpful just to have students turn to their neighbors and discuss an idea.

Whatever the grouping method, it is important that students not just sit and listen to the teacher; rather, the more that students can interact and discuss knowledge, the more opportunity they will have to really understand it.

COMPETENCY 14

UNDERSTAND COMMUNICATION PRACTICES THAT ARE EFFECTIVE IN PROMOTING STUDENT LEARNING AND CREATING A CLIMATE OF TRUST AND SUPPORT IN THE CLASSROOM, AND HOW TO USE A VARIETY OF COMMUNICATION MODES TO SUPPORT INSTRUCTION

> **SKILL 14.1** **Analyzes how cultural, gender, and age differences affect communication in the classroom** *(e.g., eye contact, use of colloquialisms, interpretation of body language)*, **and recognizing effective methods for enhancing communication with all students, including being a thoughtful and responsive listener**

Communication in the Classroom

The effective teacher uses advanced communication skills as a means to facilitate communication. These include:

- Clarification
- Reflection
- Perception
- Summarization

Listening

Teachers who are effective communicators are also good listeners. Teachers who exhibit such behaviors as eye contact, focusing on student body language, clarifying students' statements, and using "I" messages are effective listeners. The ability to communicate with students, listen effectively, identify relevant and nonrelevant information, and summarize students' messages facilitates establishing and maintaining an optimum classroom learning environment.

Teachers who are effective communicators are also good listeners.

Body language

Body language can be defined as teachers' facial or other body behavior that express:

- Interest
- Excitement
- Joy
- Positive personal relations
- Boredom
- Sadness
- Dissatisfaction
- Negative personal relations
- No clear message at all

The effective teacher communicates nonverbally with students by using positive body language, expressing warmth, concern, acceptance, and enthusiasm. The energy and enthusiasm of the effective teacher can be amplified through positive body language.

Effective teachers augment their instructional presentations by using positive nonverbal communication such as smiles, open body posture, movement, and eye contact with students.

SKILL 14.2 **Applies strategies to promote effective classroom interactions that support learning, including teacher-student and student-student interactions**

Positive Classroom Climate

Student-student and teacher-student interactions play a significant role in a positive classroom climate. When interactions among classroom members are encouraging, learning becomes a more natural and genuine process. Cold or routine interactions discourage questioning, critical thinking, and useful discussion. Teachers should make every effort to be available to their students, as well as provide natural, collaborative opportunities for students in order to strengthen classroom interactions. Reflection, observations, and asking for feedback regarding one's classroom interactions (perhaps during a yearly observation) will help teachers to analyze the effectiveness of their classroom's interactions.

Trust

The most important component in probing for student understanding is trust. Only if students trust their teacher will the communications process yield such things as the level of understanding a student has attained on any topic. If that component is in place, then creative questioning, which requires planning ahead, can sometimes reveal what the teacher needs to know. So can writing exercises that focus not on correctness but on a recording of the student's thoughts on a topic. Sometimes assuring the student that only the teacher will see what is written is helpful in freeing students to reveal their own thoughts. When a new unit is introduced, including vocabulary lessons related to the unit can help students find the words they need to talk or write about the topic.

Nonjudgmental environment

If a teacher can help students to take responsibility for their own ideas and thoughts, much has been accomplished. They will only reach that level in a nonjudgmental environment—an environment that doesn't permit criticism of the ideas of others and that accepts any topic for discussion that is in the realm of appropriateness. Success in problem solving boosts students' confidence and makes them more willing to take risks; the teacher must provide those opportunities for success.

> **SKILL 14.3 Analyzes teacher-student interactions with regard to communication issues** (e.g., those relating to communicating expectations, providing feedback, building student self-esteem, modeling appropriate communication techniques for specific situations)

Possible Communication Issues

Communication between teachers and students is important, sometimes complex, and always necessary. First, even when secondary teachers, for example, see more than one hundred students each day, any communication from teacher to an individual student is prized. Therefore, students in especially large public schools sometimes feel lost and not cared about by teachers. When teachers go that extra mile to let students know they care and that they notice them, students feel welcome, important, and less "alone."

Understanding complexity

However, teacher-student interaction can often be complex. For example, on a busy day, teachers may accidentally say something to a student or to their classes that may get misinterpreted by students. Of particular concern is any message that conveys to students that they are:

- Not capable

- Not trustworthy

- Not smart enough

- Not important enough

We've all heard stories from people who say that they were told by a teacher that they would not amount to much. People carry negative sentiments about such comments through their entire lives. And in many cases, their teachers may not have even realized what they had said. The point is that teachers must speak carefully and considerately to ensure that their words are appropriate for all students.

Listening to students

It is particularly important in many circumstances that teachers listen carefully to what students are saying to them. Often, teachers may disregard cries for help. Whenever students talk to teachers, teachers must think specifically about potential messages of concern that students are trying to get across. However, do not constantly worry about this; often, students simply want an adult to talk with about random issues and observations. Teachers do quite often serve in the capacity of loving parent to many students who do not get much attention at home. Realize that students sometimes just want an adult friend to talk with about their lives.

Considering appropriateness of interactions

One important consideration, though, is ensuring that all interaction between teachers and students is appropriate. It is never a good idea to be in a classroom alone with one student. Typically, when such cases occur, it is a good idea to open the door to avoid miscommunication about intent of student or teacher.

In all, teachers in K–12 settings are more than providers of educational content. They serve in a strong social capacity for the healthy social and emotional development of all their students.

SKILL 14.4 Recognizes purposes for questioning *(e.g., encouraging risk taking and problem solving, maintaining student engagement, facilitating factual recall, assessing student understanding)*, **and selecting appropriate questioning techniques**

A Successful Teacher

Teachers who couple diversity in instructional practices with engaging and challenging curriculum and the latest advances in technology can create the ultimate learning environment for creative thinking and continuous learning for students. Teachers who are innovative and creative in instructional practices are able to model and foster creative thinking in their students. Encouraging students to maintain journals or portfolios of their valued work from projects and assignments will allow students to make conscious choices on including a diversity of their creative endeavors in a filing format that can be treasured throughout the educational journey.

> *Teachers who are innovative and creative in instructional practices are able to model and foster creative thinking in their students.*

Questioning

When teachers are very deliberate about the questions they use with their students, amazing things in the classroom can happen. Most of us remember questions at the end of the chapter in the textbook, or we remember quiz or test questions. While these things potentially have value, they are completely useless if the questions are not well crafted, the purposes for the questions are not defined, and the methods by which students will answer the questions are not engaging.

> *Good questioning usually implies that teachers are encouraging deep reflection and active thinking in students.*

Keep in mind that good questioning does not always imply that there are correct answers (by the way, yes or no questions in the classroom do not provide much in the way of stimulation and thought). Good questioning usually implies that teachers are encouraging deep reflection and active thinking in students. In general, we can say that through questioning, we want students to take risks, solve problems, recall facts, and demonstrate understanding.

Risk-taking questions

When we say that we want students to take risks, we mean that we want them to "try out" various answers and possibilities. By answering a risk-taking question, students experiment with their academic voices.

Problem-solving questions

Problem-solving questions provoke thought and encourage students to think of questions as entries into problems, not indicators that correct answers are always available in the world.

Factual recall questions

Even though factual recall questions should not be over-used, it is important to teach students how to comprehend reading, speech, film, or other media. It is also important that students remember certain facts—and questioning can bring on small levels of stress that potentially trigger memory. However, realize that stress may be very upsetting for some students and that such questions, particularly in public settings, may be inappropriate.

Finally, by questioning students, we see how much they know. All types of questioning can be done in a variety of formats. For example, we can question students out loud with a whole class. Teachers should refrain from calling on students too often, but occasionally it is an effective technique. Wait time is particularly important: When asking a question, a teacher should not assume that nobody will answer it if a couple seconds have elapsed. Often wait time encourages some students to answer, or it allows all students time to think about the question. Questioning can also take place in small groups or on paper.

SKILL **Applies strategies for adjusting communication to enhance student**
14.5 **understanding** (e.g., by providing examples, simplifying a complex problem, using verbal and nonverbal modes of communication, using audiovisual and technological tools of communication)

Communicating with Students

While teachers should never consider that all students' learning is based on a teacher's communication to students, much valuable information does occur in the transmission of words between teacher and student. The problem, however, is in dealing with the various types of learning difficulties that students have, as well as with other environmental factors and learning preferences.

> While teachers should never consider that all students' learning is based on teacher's communication to students, much valuable information does occur in the transmission of words between teacher and student.

Disabilities and communication

First, various disabilities, including hearing loss, Attention Deficit Hyperactivity Disorder, and others, can severely impact a student's ability to successfully listen to and comprehend what the teacher may be saying. In such cases, teachers should communicate with Special Education and other resource teachers about procedures and practices to follow. But teachers can also place these students in specific classroom locations, give them "partners" who can assist, and periodically walk near them to find out how they are doing.

Environment and communication

Environmental factors can inhibit a teacher's communication to students. Often, air conditioners and other room or building noises can impact students' understanding of course content. Students also have various preferences in how they best understand. Some need a lot of teacher explanation and assistance; others need very little. While a teacher can never judge how much students understand simply by looking at their expressions, the teacher may get a pretty good idea if the students are in need of a change of communication style, a new activity, or if they simply need further review.

> Environmental factors can inhibit a teacher's communication to students.

SKILL **Demonstrates knowledge of the limits of verbal understanding of**
14.6 **students at various ages and with different linguistic backgrounds**
and strategies for ensuring that these limitations do not become
barriers to learning *(e.g., by linking to known language; by saying things*
in more than one way; by supporting verbalization with gestures, physical
demonstrations, dramatizations, and media and manipulatives

Using Definitions and Examples

Research indicates that when students gain knowledge through instruction that
includes a combination of providing definitions, examples and nonexamples,
and identifying attributes, they are more likely to grasp complicated concepts
than by other instructional methods. Several studies have been carried out to
determine the effectiveness of giving examples as well as the difference in effectiveness of various types of examples. It was found conclusively that the most effective
method of concept presentation included giving a definition along with examples
and nonexamples and also providing an explanation of the examples and nonexamples. These same studies indicate that boring examples were just as effective
as interesting examples in promoting learning.

Using Critical/Classifying Attributes

Learning is further enhanced when critical attributes are listed along with a definition, examples, and nonexamples. Classifying attributes is an effective strategy
for both very young students and older students. According to Piaget's preoperational phase of development, children learn concepts informally
through experiences with objects just as they naturally acquire language. One of
the most effective learning experiences with objects is learning to classify objects
by a single obvious feature or attribute. Children classify objects typically, often
without any prompting or directions. This natural inclination to classify objects
carries over to classifying attributes of a particular concept and contributes to the
student's understanding of concepts.

The natural inclination to classify objects carries over to classifying attributes of a particular concept and contributes to the student's understanding of concepts.

Using Various Transmissions of Information

It is not always guaranteed that once a teacher instructs on a concept that students will automatically retain the information. It is often the case that students
may need to see or hear information in more than one manner (kinesthetically,
spatially, visually) before it is truly internalized. Therefore, teachers should present
information to benefit various learning styles (or multiple intelligences), and use
technologies (i.e., overhead projectors, related video clips, music, presentations) or
other resources to supplement student learning and retention.

It is often the case that students may need to see or hear information in more than one manner (kinesthetically, spatially, visually) before it is truly internalized.

COMPETENCY 15

UNDERSTAND USES OF TECHNOLOGY, INCLUDING INSTRUCTIONAL AND ASSISTIVE TECHNOLOGY, IN TEACHING AND LEARNING; AND APPLY THIS KNOWLEDGE TO USE TECHNOLOGY EFFECTIVELY AND TO TEACH STUDENTS HOW TO USE TECHNOLOGY TO ENHANCE THEIR LEARNING

SKILL 15.1 **Demonstrates knowledge of educational uses of various technology tools, such as calculators, software applications, input devices** (e.g., keyboard mouse, scanner, modem, CD-ROM), **and the Internet**

The Challenges of Computers in Schools

When dealing with large class sizes and at the same time trying to offer opportunities for students to use computers, it is often necessary to use a lot of ingenuity. If the number of computers available for student use is limited, the teacher must take a tip from elementary school teachers who are skilled at managing centers. Students can be rotated singly or in small groups to the computer centers as long as they are well oriented in advance to the task to be accomplished and with the rules to be observed. Rules for using the computer should be emphasized with the whole class before individual computer usage and then prominently posted.

Computer labs

If a computer lab is available for use by the curriculum teacher, the problem of how to give each student the opportunity to use the computer as an educational tool might be alleviated, but a whole new set of problems must be dealt with. Again, the rules to be observed in the computer lab should be discussed before the class ever enters the lab, and students should have a thorough understanding of the assignment. When a large group of students is visiting a computer lab, it is very easy for the expensive hardware to suffer from accidental or deliberate harm if the teacher is not aware of what is going on at all times. Students need to be aware of the consequences for not following the rules because it is so tempting to experiment and show off to their peers.

Rules for using computers should be emphasized with the whole class before individual computer usage and then prominently posted.

Preventing damage to computers

Unfortunately, students who have access to computers outside of school often feel like they know everything already and are reluctant to listen to instruction on lab etiquette or program usage. The teacher must be constantly on guard to prevent physical damage to the machines from things such as:

- Foreign objects finding their way into disk drives

- Key caps from disappearing from keyboards (or being rearranged)

- Stray pencil or pen marks appearing on computer systems

Experienced students also get a lot of enjoyment from saving games on hard drives, moving files into new directories or eliminating them altogether, creating passwords to prevent others from using machines, etc. At the same time, other students need a lot of assistance to prevent accidents caused by their inexperience. It is possible to pair inexperienced students with more capable ones to alleviate some of the problem. Teachers must constantly rotate around the room, and students must be prepared before their arrival in the lab so that they know exactly what to do when they get there to prevent them from exercising their creativity.

Choosing Educational Software

With a surplus of educational software on the market, it is important for an educator to be able to evaluate a program before purchasing it. Software can vary greatly in content, presentation, skill level, and objectives, and it is not always possible to believe everything that is advertised on the package. If a teacher is in the position of having to purchase a computer program for use in the classroom without any prior knowledge of the program itself, it is useful to have some guidelines to follow. Once a program has been purchased and the shrink-wrap has been removed, many vendors are reluctant to allow its return because of a possible violation of copyright laws or damage to the software medium. For this reason, previewing the software personally before buying it is important. If a vendor is reluctant to let the teacher preview a program before its purchase, it is sometimes possible to get a preview copy from the publisher.

Approved lists and evaluation forms

Many school districts have addressed this problem by publishing a list of approved software titles for each grade level in much the same way that they publish lists of approved textbooks and other classroom materials. In addition, most districts have developed a software evaluation form to be used by any instructor involved in the purchase of software that is not already on the "approved" list. Use of a software evaluation form can eliminate a lot of the risk involved when shopping for appropriate titles for the classroom. In many districts, all software is evaluated by the actual instructors who will use the software, and the completed evaluation forms are made available for the perusal of other prospective buyers.

Compatibility

The first thing that must be considered before purchasing software is its compatibility with the computer on which it is to be used. If the program will not run efficiently on the computer in the classroom because of hardware limitations, there is no need to continue the evaluation process. Some of the restrictions to consider are:

- The operating system (Windows, Macintosh, Linux) for which the particular software package was developed

- The recommended memory size

- The required hard drive space

- The medium type (CD-ROM, DVD)

- The type of monitor

- The need for any special input devices such as a mouse, joystick, or speech card

Steps to evaluate software

There are three general steps to follow when evaluating a software program:

1. One must read the instructions thoroughly to familiarize oneself with the program, its hardware requirements, and its installation.

2. Once the program is installed and ready to run, the evaluator should first run the program as it would be run by a successful student. This should be done without deliberate errors but making use of all the possibilities available to the student.

3. The program should be run making deliberate mistakes to test the handling of errors. One should try to make as many different kinds of mistakes as possible, including those for incorrect keyboard usage and the validity of user directions.

Filling out a form

Most software evaluation forms include the same types of information. There is usually a section for a general description of the program consisting of the:

- Intended grade level

- Additional support materials available

- Type of program (game, simulation, drill, etc.)
- Stated goals and objectives
- Clarity of instructions

Other sections will provide checklists for educational content, presentation, and type and quality of user interaction with the program.

Once a software package has been thoroughly tested, the teacher will be able to make an intelligent decision regarding its purchase.

SKILL 15.2 Recognizes purposes and uses of common types of assistive technology *(e.g., amplification devices, communication boards)*

Assistive Technology in the Classroom

Technology has advanced so rapidly in the last decade that many learning disabilities can be addressed, in part, with unique tools. Furthermore, in various situations, other technological tools can enhance and broaden students' exposure to concepts and modalities of learning.

Common examples of assistive technology

Some common tools for assisting students with disabilities are:

- Amplification devices that make computer content more clear
- Speech recognition devices that type in text as it is spoken by the student
- Large print keys for students who have trouble with hand-eye coordination
- Readers that read aloud alerts on screens

Other tools that have become very helpful for students are:

- Communication boards, which are asynchronous discussion or dialogue programs that allow students to post content in a discussion format. It is a particularly helpful way to encourage written discussion. It also is highly beneficial for students who have physical trouble getting to school.
- Wikis are tools that teachers are using more and more each day. Wikis are collaborative definitions, posted to computers, and often the Web. After units, teachers might ask students in groups to post a wiki on a particular topic.

- Even though they are thought of as a tool for journalists, **BLOGS** have become popular in the classroom. Teachers often ask students to maintain blogs, or Web logs, on particular topics. Often, blogs are used for students to respond to classroom novels as students progress through books.

Many additional tools are becoming available every day. It is a good idea to keep up-to-date on technological tools that can assist teachers in meeting all students' needs.

> **BLOGS:** short for web logs, are places where people can post thoughts and opinions on particular topics in a journal or log format

SKILL 15.3 **Recognizes issues related to the appropriate use of technology** *(e.g., privacy issues, security issues, copyright laws and issues, ethical issues regarding the acquisition and use of information from technology resources),* **and identifying procedures that ensure the legal and ethical use of technology resources**

Legal Responsibilities and Technology

In this technological age, it is important that teachers be aware of their legal responsibilities when using computers in the classroom. As public employees, teachers are particularly vulnerable to public scrutiny. Not only are teachers more likely to be caught if they are unethical in the use of computers in the classroom, but it is also the responsibility of educators to model, as well as teach, ethical computer behaviors.

Recent changes

In 1980, P. L.96-517, Section 117 of the copyright law was amended to cover the use of computers. The following changes were made:

1. The definition of a "computer program" was inserted and is defined now as "a set of statements or instructions to be used directly in a computer in order to bring about a certain result."

2. The owner of a copy of a computer program is not infringing on the copyright by making or authorizing the making of or adaptation of that program if the following criteria are met:

   - The new copy or adaptation must be created in order to be able to use the program in conjunction with the machine and is used in no other manner.

   - The new copy or adaptation must be for archival purpose only and all archival copies must be destroyed in the event that continued possession of the computer program should cease to be rightful.

   - Any copies prepared or adapted may not be leased, sold, or otherwise transferred without the authorization of the copyright owner.

Multiple copies of a program

The intent of this amendment to the copyright act is to allow an individual or institutional owner of a program to make "backup" copies in case of the destruction of the original program disk, while restricting the owner from making copies in order to use the program on more that one machine at a time or to share with other teachers. Under the Software Copyright Act of 1980, once a program is loaded into the memory of a computer, a temporary copy of that program is made. Multiple machine loading (moving from machine to machine and loading a single program into several computers for simultaneous use) constitutes making multiple copies, which is not permitted under the law.

Since the same is true of a networked program, it is necessary to obtain permission from the owner of the copyright or purchase a license agreement before multiple use of a program in a school setting.

Risks of ignoring the law

Infringement of copyright laws is a serious offense and can result in significant penalties if a teacher chooses to ignore the law.

Infringement of copyright laws is a serious offense and can result in significant penalties if a teacher chooses to ignore the law. Not only does the teacher risk losing all personal computer equipment, but she is also placing her job as an educator in jeopardy.

SKILL 15.4 Identifies and addresses equity issues related to the use of technology in the classroom *(e.g., equal access to technology for all students)*

Equity and Technology

There are two primary areas of equity issues related to technology. One is the level at which students come to school with proficiency in technology. The other is the fair distribution of technology exposure to all students in a class.

Student background with technology

The first area, the level at which students come to school with a background in technology, is particularly important. First, teachers will need to understand that they have a variety of ability levels in their classrooms. Second, a lack of technology proficiency may actually be an embarrassment to students. Usually, not having technology skill can indicate that the student does not have much money—or even that the student is living in poverty.

When students come to school with a wide variety of skills, teachers need to find unique ways to provide students who have fewer skills more opportunities to learn without compromising the ability of other students to still grow in their understanding of technology. Often, group-based work can be very helpful.

Fair distribution of technology opportunity

The second level is ensuring that all students have similar opportunities to use technology, particularly since the students with the least home exposure will need more time. Again, a good way of dealing with this is by having students work in groups. Specific rules should be put in place to ensure that students share actual keyboard and mouse control.

When students come to school with a wide variety of skills, teachers need to find unique ways to provide students who have fewer skills more opportunities to learn without compromising the ability of other students to still grow in their understanding of technology.

SKILL 15.5 **Identifies effective instructional uses of current technology in relation to communication** *(e.g., audio and visual recording and display devices)*

Technology and Communication

The number of tools that teachers have available to them to present information to students is always growing. Where just ten years ago teachers needed to only know how to use word processing programs, grading programs, and overhead projectors, today, electronic slideshows (most people think of PowerPoint) are becoming the new norm, and other methods of information distribution are expected by principals, parents, and students alike.

Videos

Many instructional programs include short video clips for students to help amplify ideas. For example, many science programs include very short clips to demonstrate scientific principles. Literature programs might include short dramatizations of stories or background information on a literature selection. These tools are particularly helpful to replace "prior knowledge" for students before embarking on new topics, and they are especially important for students who are strong visual learners.

Technology and communication with parents

In many schools, electronic and print information from teachers is necessary for communicating things to parents. For example, since many students' parents are at work all day long, it is more efficient for parents to look online for homework assignments rather than discuss certain homework issues. Many schools have instituted homework hotlines where teachers record homework assignments for parents or absent students to call in and access.

In general, we know that the more a teacher communicates with parents, the more likely parents will trust and assist the teacher in his methods and strategies. And parents are impressed by teachers who take the time to put together something in a professional manner. So, teachers will earn much more respect from families by providing information in a timely and professional manner.

Web sites

Many teachers now also have Web sites where they post:

- Assignments

- Exemplary student work

- Helpful links

- Other useful information

While this use of technology is good, teachers should double-check to ensure that sensitive student information is not included on the Web. Although most people would say that including a picture of the students at work in the classroom is acceptable, schools are finding that having *no* pictures of students—individually or in a group—is better for the protection of students.

Learning to use technology effectively

Teachers who do now know how to use these various tools have multiple learning options. Many community colleges specifically teach these skills, and many Web sites are available with video-based tutorials.

Incorporating technology effectively into a fully content- and skill-based curriculum requires a good understanding of lesson objectives and how those objectives can be met with the technology. While teachers should definitely consider technological integration as an important aspect of their work in any subject and at any grade level, teachers should not include technology simply for the sake of technology. The best approach, considering all subjects can in certain ways be enhanced with technology, is for the teacher to consider a variety of lessons and units and decide which focus areas can be enhanced with technological tools.

Technology and Group Situations

Using technology in collaborative student group situations is considered to be the most effective method for a few reasons. Practically, most teachers cannot assign one computer to each student in the class whenever the teacher would like to

> In general, we know that the more a teacher communicates with parents, the more likely parents will trust the teacher and assist the teacher in his methods and strategies.

utilize computers in the classroom. But that should not matter. As technological tools are complicated and complex, pair and small group work better facilitates stronger, social-based learning.

Groups and addressing skill disparity

Even though teachers may assume all students know how to use various technological tools, they need to remember two very important things:

1. Not *all* students are proficient. Even though some highly proficient students lead teachers to believe that the entire generation of kids in schools today already understands technology, many students actually never learned it at home. Some actually do not have the tools at home because of the high costs and, therefore, have no opportunity to practice.

2. Not all technology skills transfer. While one student may navigate the Web easily, she may not be able to use a word processing program with a similar level of expertise.

Social opportunities to learn technology will help students to engage in a more productive, friendly, and help-centered fashion. Learning together, particularly in technology, can indeed reduce any anxiety or fear a student may have.

Enhancing lessons through technology and groups

Teachers can consider technology learning as a method to also teach coopera-tion, decision-making skills, and problem-solving skills. For example, as a small group of students work together on a project on a computer, they must decide together how they will proceed and create. Teachers can instruct students in good cooperative decision-making skills to make the process easier. Students can also engage in activities where they are required to solve problems, build real-life solutions to situations, and create real-world products. Doing so will only enhance content-area instruction.

> Teachers can consider technology learning as a method to also teach co-operation, decision-making skills, and problem-solving skills.

Assessing appropriate technology

Finally, it is important to remember that, as with all other learning, technological learning must be developmentally appropriate. Realize that while very young students can perform various functions on the computer, by virtue of development level, the time required for a particular activity may be greatly increased. Also, various technological tools are simply too advanced, too fast, and too complex for very young students. It may be best to introduce basic elements of technology in the earlier grades.

SKILL 15.6 Applies strategies for helping students acquire, analyze, and evaluate electronic information *(e.g., locating specific information on the Internet and verifying its accuracy and validity)*

Evaluating Technologies for the Classroom

Many computer programs are available that enhance instruction in various curricula areas. Tutorials, educational programs, and games exist on almost every imaginable subject, but computers can also be used as a tool to enhance regular instruction.

Resources and materials for instruction are everywhere—in schools, on the Web, in bookstores, and in adopted school programs. How does one decide where to get materials for instruction? And how does one evaluate materials for use in instruction?

The Internet

The Internet and other research resources provide a wealth of information on thousands of interesting topics for students preparing presentations or projects. Using search engines like Google and Yahoo!, student can search multiple Internet resources on one subject search. Students should have an outline of the purpose of a project or research presentation, as shown in the table below.

THINGS TO ADDRESS WHEN USING THE INTERNET FOR A PROJECT	
Purpose	Identify the reason for the research information.
Objective	A clear thesis for a project will allow the students opportunities to be specific on Internet searches.
Preparation	When using resources or collecting data, students should create folders for sorting through the information. Providing labels for the folders will create a system of organization that will make construction of the final project or presentation easier and less time consuming.
Procedure	Organized folders and a procedural list of what the project or presentation needs to include will create A+ work for students and A+ grading for teachers.
Visuals or Artifacts	Choose data or visuals that are specific to the subject content or presentation. Make sure that poster boards or presentations can be visually seen from all areas of the classroom. Teachers can provide laptop computers for multimedia presentations.

When a teacher models and instructs students in the proper use of search techniques, the teacher can minimize wasted time in preparing projects and wasted paper from students who print every search. In some school districts, students are allowed a minimum number of printed pages per week. Since students have

Internet accounts for computer usage, the monitoring of printing is easily done by the school's librarian and teachers in classrooms.

Experts and guest speakers

Having the school's librarian or technology expert as a guest speaker in classrooms provides another method of sharing and modeling proper presentation preparation using technology. Teachers can also appoint technology experts from the students in a classroom to work with students on projects and presentations. In high schools, technology classes provide students with upper-class teacher assistants who fill the role of technology assistants.

The wealth of resources for teachers and students seeking to incorporate technology and structured planning for student presentations and projects is as diverse as the presentations. There is an expert in every classroom who is always willing to offer advice and instruction. In school communities, that expert may begin with the teacher.

Shared media and Internet resources

Many school districts have shared drives that contain multiple files of lesson and unit plans, curriculum maps, pacing guides, and assessment ideas. While these can be very beneficial, it is always a good idea to determine the intended use for such files and documents.

The best place to start is identifying the required materials that should be used in instruction. After that, many Web sites contain lesson plans and instructional ideas. Be careful, though, as some Web sites do not monitor the information placed on their servers. While a lesson may have a creative title and purpose, it may not always serve the best purpose for your instructional agenda. In fact, there is no guarantee that such lessons are any good. Consider the following:

- How you would adapt it

- If your students would get something out of it

- If it seems inappropriate for your particular group of students

When looking through shared drives, remote devices, and other online databases, it is important to understand who has posted information and for what the information is intended. Often, it might be for specialized programs within the district. It's always safest to ask.

> **SKILL 15.7** Evaluates students' technologically produced products using established criteria related to content, delivery, and the objective(s) of the assignment

When teachers ask students to produce something with technology, typically to practice—and then prove—proficiency with a particular content-based skill or area of knowledge, they are giving students the opportunity to be creative with new learning. Furthermore, they are giving students the chance to utilize knowledge in authentic situations.

Evaluating Technologically Produced Work

As with any open-ended assignment, teachers will be more objective in their evaluations, as well as be more specific about expectations to students, if they develop scoring criteria, rubrics, or other evaluation guides. Several elements should be considered.

Design

DESIGN: the format that the product takes

DESIGN is the format that the product takes. Teachers can (considering developmental level) expect that students will present information in a way that is organized, clear, and straightforward. However, with design, nonlanguage elements, such as graphics, pictures, sounds, video, etc., can demonstrate an added element of creativity. Furthermore, it can help to add a symbolic touch that conveys more than words are able. While clarity is important, even in this regard, the use of nonlinguistic material must not confuse the viewer.

Content delivery

CONTENT DELIVERY: the method of technology used

CONTENT DELIVERY refers to the method of technology used. Often, the teacher should make it clear to students what program should be used to complete an assignment (for example, an essay would be better completed in a word processing program, while a more creative piece should be done in a multimedia program format).

Teachers can evaluate the ways in which the tool is used. So, for example, if the teacher asks students to produce something in a multimedia program, content must be taught (let's say it's a history lesson). But the teacher would also have to teach students how to use the program itself. Students will end up demonstrating knowledge of the content (history), as well as the method of content delivery (the computer program).

Audience

When students focus on **AUDIENCE**, they consider what the audience will need to comprehend. So, while a very creative student may have fun with a program and use it to do very unusual things, the student will not be evaluated highly in this regard as it does not focus on presenting information in a clear manner to the anticipated audience. Teachers do not always have to be the audience. Teachers can either ask students to produce something for hypothetical situations, or they can suggest to students that their audience is the rest of the class.

> **AUDIENCE:** the intended recipients of the information contained in the project

Relevance

RELEVANCE could actually be the most important element. Students may demonstrate incredible proficiency with the technological tool, but if they do not demonstrate how it was used to prove proficiency on the content, then the activity was done for the sake of the technological tool only. We want to encourage students to view technology as a tool for learning, research, and presentation.

> **RELEVANCE:** how a project relates to the subject being taught and demonstrates learning

Presenting the Research

Once the research is completed, use of a desktop publishing program on the computer can produce professional quality documents enhanced by:

- Typeset text
- Graphs
- Clip art
- Photographs downloaded from the World Wide Web

Even primary grade students can use the computer to type and illustrate their stories on simple publishing programs like the *Children's Writing and Publishing Center* by The Learning Company. Spell check programs and other tools included in these publishing programs can assist students in producing top quality work.

Computers and Relevance to the Real World

Computers are as much a part of a child's life today as pencils and paper, and the capabilities of computers need to be thoroughly explored to enable students to see computers as much more than a glorified game machine. A major goal of education is to prepare students for their futures in business and the work place, and if they are not taught how to use the available technology to its fullest advantage, educators will have failed in at least part of that purpose.

> *The computer should not replace traditional research and writing skills taught to school-age children, but use of the computer as a tool must also be taught to children who live in a technological society.*

DOMAIN III
THE PROFESSIONAL ENVIRONMENT

PERSONALIZED STUDY PLAN

KNOWN MATERIAL/ SKIP IT

COMPETENCY 16
UNDERSTAND THE HISTORY, PHILOSOPHY, AND ROLE OF EDUCATION IN NEW YORK STATE AND THE BROADER SOCIETY

> **SKILL 16.1** **Analyzes relationships between education and society** *(e.g., schools reflecting and affecting social values, historical dimensions of the school-society relationship, the role of education in a democratic society, the role of education in promoting equity in society)*

Historical Foundations of Education

The relationship between education and society is ever evolving. Originally, schools were for the wealthy, as education was highly valued and also an expensive burden on local governments that were not equipped to educate every child. In poorer and more rural families, the children were needed to help the family either by working and bringing home a wage, or by helping to tend the house or farm. Large families might have older children watch the younger children—none of these children were typically able to get schooling or, if they did, it was intermittent. Thus, the schools reflected the social value of having a large, uneducated work force.

Integration of poor students

Around the time of the Great Depression, Franklin Roosevelt's New Deal increasingly helped keep young people in school while adults were given the menial tasks that children had once performed. While the primary reason for fuller schools was not education so much as a reorganization of workers—making room in the workforce for the out-of-work adults—the result was that poorer children began to be more evenly and regularly educated and this would eventually set the foundations for a middle class.

Integration of racially diverse students

After *Plessy v. Ferguson* in 1896 (but before *Brown v. The Board of Education* in 1954), "separate but equal" school facilities segregated the African-American children from the Caucasians. However, it was clear that African-American schools generally received less funding than schools for white children. *Brown v. Board of Education of Topeka* struck down segregation after the Supreme Court ruled that a separate but equal form of education would never truly give African-American children an equal foundation in learning. Society would begin to follow suit, albeit slowly, as segregated facilities began to fall away (in 1955, Rosa Parks would famously refuse to give up her seat on a bus for a white passenger).

Generally, schools and education are considered the great equalizer—giving each child a level start in life, the same tools to work with so that each might chisel out his future, regardless of class, color, religion, or other factors.

> Generally, schools and education are considered the great equalizer—giving each child a level start in life, the same tools to work with so that each might chisel out his future, regardless of class, color, religion, or other factors.

Federal, State, and Local Involvement in Education

However, because schools depend largely on local funding from city and state budgets, not all schools are created equal. The tax money in poorer towns does not stretch as far as the money in wealthier neighborhoods, and schools and their facilities often suffer for it. Recently, the federal government has begun to step in and attempt to make schools throughout the nation more equal in standards, so that every child gets a solid grounding in learning. One proposal has been for school vouchers, which would allow parents to choose which school their children attend. This idea is based on the principle that if the local school does not have desirable facilities, then children could attend one that does. Contesters of this plan say that vouchers would only cause poor schools to become even less desirable as students flee and less tax money comes in.

No Child Left Behind Act

In 2001, the federal government implemented the NO CHILD LEFT BEHIND ACT, which aims to improve schools by increasing educational standards and holding schools, school districts, and states accountable for performance and progress of students.

> **NO CHILD LEFT BEHIND ACT:** a federal act passed in 2001 that aims to improve schools by increasing educational standards and holding schools, school districts, and states accountable for performance and progress of students

Types of schools

Another issue in governance has been the debate between local, neighborhood, and choice schools. NEIGHBORHOOD SCHOOLS are those that students attend based on their home address. For the past few decades, some school districts have provided students with the option of attending MAGNET SCHOOLS, or schools that are available for any student within the district. Usually, these schools have themes, such as business academies or college preparatory curricula.

> **NEIGHBORHOOD SCHOOLS:** those that students attend based on their home address

> **MAGNET SCHOOLS:** schools that are available for any student within the district

In addition to magnet schools, money is now available for CHARTER SCHOOLS, which do not have to abide by the same policies as regular public schools. Charter schools do not have to be run by school districts, but they take money from the districts in which their students originate. So, for example, if the local public school gets $5,000 per student per school year from local property taxes and the

> **CHARTER SCHOOLS:** schools that do not have to abide by the same policies as regular public schools

VOUCHER MONEY: part or all of the money that would have been put into the local public district(s) that is given to parents so they can use it to send their children to private schools

state (or however the state finances schools), that $5,000 would instead go to the charter school if one student opted to go there.

Finally, in some states and cities, **VOUCHER MONEY** is available for students attending private schools; in this plan, the government gives parents part or all of the money that would have been put into the local public district(s) so that they can use it to send their children to private schools. None of these options is without controversy in this country.

The Ideal Classroom

Ideally, a school gives every child a solid base of learning so that each child can compete equally in life and society.

Ideally, a school gives every child a solid base of learning so that each child can compete equally in life and society. An ideal classroom has a fair mix of different types of students—different genders, different classes, and different races—so that the children in them learn to relate to all types of people, however different they may be. Unfortunately, this mix seldom happens in the classroom because people of different ethnicities, incomes, and religions typically live in different towns and neighborhoods; each neighborhood school reflects only the immediate area, which is typically a homogenous cross-section of society as a whole. No single plan (vouchers, No Child Left Behind) has managed to effect much change in this regard.

SKILL 16.2 Demonstrates knowledge of the historical foundations of education in the United States and of past and current philosophical issues in education *(e.g., teacher-directed versus child-centered instruction)*

To understand where we are today in American public education is to appreciate how politics, history, research, society, and the economy have all come together to develop a complex, sometimes bureaucratic, system of teaching and learning.

To understand where we are today in American public education is to appreciate how politics, history, research, society, and the economy have all come together to develop a complex, sometimes bureaucratic, system of teaching and learning.

Instructional Debates

Debates on instruction have typically focused on the role of the teacher. Some people argue that child-centered instruction is favorable, as it is more engaging for students. Others have advocated for more traditional methods, such as lecturing, note taking, and other teacher-centered activities.

Evolution of Education

Historically, public education has evolved from being something relegated to the wealthy. Education was usually private, tutor-based, and uneven. The concept of a free public education was developed in order to ensure that as many people in this country could participate in (and further develop) the nation's economy. Decades ago, a small one-room schoolhouse sufficed, but today, each neighborhood requires multiple schools to educate all of the local children. In these traditional settings, the teacher was the lecturer and leader of all instruction.

As the population has grown, the structure of public schooling has been shaped by bureaucracy. To accommodate all the children, the structures of public schools have changed so each child will have a similar, equal education no matter which school she attends. As classrooms and research grew and more beneficial instructional styles emerged, many classroom teachers began to incorporate cooperative learning, learning centers, reading and writing workshops, group projects (and other developmentally appropriate styles) into their classrooms.

> As the population has grown, the structure of public schooling has been shaped by bureaucracy.

SKILL 16.3 Applies procedures for working collaboratively and cooperatively with various members of the New York State educational system to accomplish a variety of educational goals

---

Suggestions for New York State Teachers

As a teacher in the state of New York, the goal of educating children is shared with not only other teachers but also with a wide-ranging staff of local and state administrators. Therefore, collaboration and cooperation can only help you achieve that goal.

Lesson plans

To ensure the students in the classroom are receiving the most benefit from the teaching efforts, the regular evaluating and updating of lesson plans and asking for suggestions and tips from other teachers can go a long way in providing new ideas to keep the lessons fresh and fun—for you as well as for your students.

Professional organizations

Joining a professional organization can also help by putting the teacher in touch with other educators outside of their own school, district, or system who they wouldn't otherwise meet. (For example, a math teacher might benefit from joining the National Council for Teachers of Mathematics). Again, being in touch with other teachers may provide new insights into ways of teaching.

New York State Department of Education

The New York State Department of Education also has resources on core curriculum and learning standards. Keeping up-to-date with these will help ensure that both teacher and students are able to meet the educational goals set forth by the state and federal governments.

SKILL 16.4 Analyzes differences between school-based and centralized models of decision making

---

Decision-Making Models

Centralized decision making

CENTRALIZED DECISION MAKING: when a large entity (the federal government or even the state government) makes the decisions that will affect all the smaller groups (local schools)

CENTRALIZED DECISION MAKING is when a large entity (the federal government or even the state government) makes the decisions that will affect all the smaller groups (local schools). Centralized decision making helps set one standard, everyone shares the same objectives, and the same content is used by everyone. The idea is that everything becomes equal and so the results should also be equal across the board—all the students should do equally well and because the teachers use the same content they can discuss it with one another at length and be on the same page.

Centralized decision making also helps reduce paperwork and administrative costs since everyone is doing the same thing; reporting should be streamlined and fewer administrators are needed. With centralized decision making, standardization is key, and it becomes easy to spot problems with a student, teacher, or district that is struggling or failing to meet those standards.

School-based decision making

SCHOOL-BASED DECISION MAKING: when a smaller, local entity makes the decisions that will affect local schools

SCHOOL-BASED DECISION MAKING is more costly because it requires more administration to handle the many different programs that might be occurring within each individual school. Also, the reporting system becomes more complicated as each school may be doing something different and so the central administration (state or federal) requires more time and more manpower to sift through the increased information from each school. It takes longer to spot problems.

However, school-based decision making has several benefits, including the school's ability to make changes when students or teachers are having difficulty. Schools can make their own decisions about what content to teach, which textbooks to use, and adjust as needed when something isn't working. School-based decision making also gives parents more ability to effect changes because their voices can be heard more immediately by the local school board, rather than having to fight the state or federal governments for changes to curriculum.

SKILL **Applies knowledge of the roles and responsibilities of different**
16.5 **components of the education system in New York** (e.g., local school boards, Board of Regents, district superintendents, school principals, Boards of Cooperative Educational Services [BOCES], higher education, unions, professional organizations, parent organizations)

Local School Boards

Local school boards are often charged with spending the public money on schools. They have the fiscal responsibility to manage the local schools' money in such a way that the schools are able to meet their educational goals and requirements (such as the standards set by No Child Left Behind). Local school boards are generally made up of locally elected officials.

The New York State Board of Regents

THE NEW YORK STATE BOARD OF REGENTS is made of sixteen members elected by the state legislature. There is a member for each of the twelve judicial districts and four members who serve at large. Each member serves a five-year term. The board of regents is responsible for the general supervision of all educational activities in the state and presides over the New York State Education Department. Various committees within the board handle such topics as:

- Developing guidelines for cultural education

- Creating and monitoring aid programs to cultural institutions

- Developing policy for standards of professional conduct and competence and disciplinary processes

THE NEW YORK STATE BOARD OF REGENTS: elected by the state legislature, this group is responsible for the general supervision of all educational activities in the state and presides over the New York State Education Department.

Superintendents and Principals

A DISTRICT SUPERINTENDENT is the chief officer of the school district. The superintendent's job is to implement the policies set by the board of regents and to advocate for his district when necessary.

DISTRICT SUPERINTEN-DENT: the chief officer of the school district who supervises and implements the policies set by the board of regents

SCHOOL PRINCIPAL: the head of the individual school

A **SCHOOL PRINCIPAL** is head of the individual school. He is under the supervision of the superintendent. The principal handles disciplinary actions for students in the school and may also discipline teachers for minor infractions. For major violations, the principal will consult with the superintendent, who may in turn go to the Board of Regents.

Boards of Cooperative Educational Services

BOARDS OF COOPERATIVE EDUCATIONAL SERVICES (BOCES): boards created under the Intermediate School District Act in 1948; they allow small school districts to combine their financial power to share costs

BOARDS OF COOPERATIVE EDUCATIONAL SERVICES (BOCES) were created under the Intermediate School District Act in 1948. BOCES allow small school districts to combine their financial power to share costs of services and programs that no one small district would be able to afford on its own. BOCES are voluntary. A district is free to buy their own services separate from others if it feels it can better serve its students in that manner.

Unions

UNIONS: collective bargaining units allow teachers to work together and develop professionally.

UNIONS, such as the New York State United Teachers and other collective bargaining organizations, allow teachers to work together and develop professionally. These organizations also help keep teachers up-to-date on current educational standards and developments. Unions in particular often work to make sure teachers receive fair wages and that when a teacher is facing charges for an alleged crime, he or she receives adequate legal counsel. Unions tend to be active in lobbying the legislature on behalf of the teaching community.

Parent Organizations

PARENT ORGANIZA-TIONS: groups that help parents to access to their children's schools and provide them a voice in school-based decisions

PARENT ORGANIZATIONS, such as the PTO or PTA, allow parents to have access to their children's schools and also provide them a voice in school-based decisions. These organizations also allow parents and teachers to work together on behalf of the students.

COMPETENCY 17

UNDERSTAND HOW TO REFLECT PRODUCTIVELY ON ONE'S OWN TEACHING PRACTICE AND HOW TO UPDATE ONE'S PROFESSIONAL KNOWLEDGE, SKILLS, AND EFFECTIVENESS

> SKILL 17.1 Assesses one's own teaching strengths and weaknesses

The Importance of Self Assessment

The very nature of the teaching profession—the yearly cycle of doing the same thing over and over again—creates the tendency to fossilize, to quit growing, to become complacent. Teachers who are truly successful are those who have built into their own approach safeguards against that tendency. They see themselves as constant learners. They believe that learning never ends. They are careful never to teach their classes the same as they did the last time. They build in a tendency to reflect on what is happening to the students under their care or what happened this year as compared to last year. They ask questions of themselves such as:

- What worked the best?

- What didn't work so well?

- What can be changed to improve success rates?

- What about continuing education?

- Should I go for another degree or should I enroll in more classes?

How to self asses

There are several avenues a teacher might take in order to assess his own teaching strengths and weaknesses. Having several students who are unable to understand a concept might be an early indicator of the need for a self-evaluation. In such a case, a teacher might want to go over her lesson plans to make sure the topic is being covered thoroughly and in a clear fashion. Brainstorming other ways to tackle the content might also help. Speaking to other teachers, asking how they teach a certain skill, might give new insight to one's own teaching tactics.

Any good teacher will understand that he needs to self-evaluate and adjust his lessons periodically. Signing up for professional courses or workshops can also help a teacher assess her abilities by opening one's eyes to new ways of teaching.

SKILL 17.2 Uses different types of resources and opportunities *(e.g., journals, in-service programs, continuing education, higher education, professional organizations, other educators)* to enhance one's teaching effectiveness

Professional Development

Professional development opportunities for teacher performance improvement or enhancement in instructional practices are essential for creating comprehensive learning communities.

In order to promote the vision, mission, and action plans of school communities, teachers must be given the toolkits to maximize instructional performances. The development of student-centered learning communities that foster the academic capacities and learning synthesis for all students should be the fundamental goal of professional development for teachers.

Professional development requirements

The level of professional development may include traditional district workshops that enhance instructional expectations for teachers or the more complicated multiple-day workshops given by national and state educational organizations. Most workshops on the national and state level provide clock hours that can be used to renew certifications for teachers every five years. Typically, 150 clock hours is the standard certification number needed to provide a five-year certification renewal, so teachers must attend and complete paperwork for a diversity of workshops that range from one to fifty clock hours according to the timeframe of the workshops.

Most districts and schools provide in-service professional development opportunities for teachers during the school year dealing with district objectives and expectations and relevant workshops or classes that can enhance the teaching practices for teachers.

Most districts and schools provide in-service professional development opportunities for teachers during the school year dealing with district objectives and expectations and relevant workshops or classes that can enhance the teaching practices for teachers. Clock hours are provided with each class or workshop and the type of professional development being offered to teachers determines clock hours. Each year, schools are required to report the number of workshops, along with the participants attending the workshops, to the superintendent's office for filing. Teachers collecting clock hour forms are required to file the forms to maintain certification eligibility and job eligibility.

Practices needed for professional development

The research by the National Association of Secondary Principals, *Breaking Ranks II: Strategies for Leading High School Reform,* created the following multiple listing of educational practices needed for expanding the professional development opportunities for teachers:

- Interdisciplinary instruction between subject areas

- Identification of individual learning styles to maximize student academic performance

- Training teachers in understanding and applying multiple assessment formats and implementations in curriculum and instruction

- Looking at multiple methods of classroom management strategies

- Providing teachers with national, federal, state, and district curriculum expectations and performance outcomes

- Identifying the school communities' action plan of student learning objectives and teacher instructional practices

- Helping teachers understand how to use data to impact student learning goals and objectives

- Teaching teachers on how to disaggregate student data in improving instruction and curriculum implementation for student academic equity and access

- Developing leadership opportunities for teachers to become school and district trainers to promote effective learning communities for student achievement and success

In promoting professional development opportunities for teachers that enhance student achievement, the bottom line is that teachers must be given the time to complete workshops at no or minimal costs. School and district budgets must include financial resources to support and encourage teachers to engage in mandatory and optional professional development opportunities that create a win-win learning experience for students.

In promoting professional development opportunities for teachers that enhance student achievement, the bottom line is that teachers must be given the time to complete workshops at no or minimal costs.

Using available data in professional development

Whether a teacher is using criterion-referenced, norm-referenced, or performance-based data to inform and impact student learning and achievement, the more important objective is ensuring that teachers know how to effectively use the data to improve and reflect upon existing teaching instructions. The goal of identifying ways for teachers to use the school data is simple: Is the teacher's instructional practice improving student learning goals and academic success?

School data can include:

- Demographic profiling

- Cultural and ethic academic trends

- State and national assessments

- Portfolios

- Academic subject pre- and post-assessment and weekly assessments

- Projects

- Disciplinary reports

By looking at trends and discrepancies in school data, teachers can ascertain whether they are meeting the goals and objectives of the state, national, and federal mandates for school improvement reform and curriculum implementation.

Assessments and professional development

Assessments can be used to motivate students to learn and shape the learning environment to provide learning stimulation that optimizes student access to learning. Butler and McMunn (2006) have shown that factors that help motivate students to learn are:

- Involving students in their own assessment

- Matching assessment strategies to student learning

- Considering thinking styles and using assessments to adjust the classroom environment in order to enhance student motivation to learn

Teachers can shape the way students learn by creating engaging learning opportunities that promote student achievement.

SKILL 17.3 Applies strategies for working effectively with members of the immediate school community (e.g., colleagues, mentor, supervisor, special needs professionals, principal, building staff) **to increase one's knowledge or skills in a given situation**

Mentors

Part of being an effective teacher is to not only have students grow educationally, but to allow oneself to also continue to grow as a teacher. Working with other members of the school community—peers, supervisors, and other staff—will give the teacher the necessary grounding needed to increase skills and knowledge sets. When identifying possible mentors, teachers should choose fellow teachers who are respected and who should be emulated. Searching out other teachers who have had an amount of success in the area needing growth is another step. Asking them questions and for advice on brushing up lesson plans or techniques for delivery of instruction can be helpful. Talk to the supervisor or the principal when you are having difficulties or when you want to learn more about a topic. They may know of development training seminars, books, journals, or other resources that might be available. Teachers should remember that they are part of a team of professionals and that their personal success is part of a greater success that everyone hopes to achieve.

SKILL 17.4 **Analyzes ways of evaluating and responding to feedback** *(e.g., from supervisors, students, parents, colleagues)*

Feedback

It has often been said that everyone is a critic, and this is certainly true when one is a teacher. Students, other teachers, supervisors, parents—all will have something to say about the way you handle any given situation or subject. If you are hearing the same critiques from many different sources, then there is probably some truth behind what is being said. Take a step back and examine the criticism. Putting personal feelings aside is important; look at the mechanics of the problem. Work with your supervisor, your mentor, and your colleagues to restructure your lesson plans or your way of interacting with the students.

Responding to feedback

Even when a piece of feedback seems spurious, a fair response is to thank the person for their thoughts and say that you will take them into consideration. Always give the critic the benefit of the doubt; chances are they have your and your students' best interests at heart. If a discussion becomes heated, everyone will lose sight of the goal—to make the classes the best they can be so that the students meet the standards they need to meet in order to progress, learn, and grow.

COMPETENCY 18
UNDERSTAND THE IMPORTANCE OF AND APPLY STRATEGIES FOR PROMOTING PRODUCTIVE RELATIONSHIPS AND INTERACTIONS AMONG THE SCHOOL, HOME, AND COMMUNITY TO ENHANCE STUDENT LEARNING

SKILL 18.1 **Identifies strategies for initiating and maintaining effective communication between the teacher and parents or other caregivers, and recognizes factors that may facilitate or impede communication in given situations** *(including parent-teacher conferences)*

Encouraging Parental and Family Involvement

Research proves that the more families are involved in a child's educational experience, the more that child will succeed academically. The problem is that often teachers assume that involvement in education simply means that the parents show up to help at school events or participate in parental activities on campus. In response, many teachers devise clever strategies to increase parental involvement at school. However, just because a parent shows up to school and assists with an activity does not mean that the child will learn more. Furthermore, many parents work during the day and cannot assist at the school. Teachers, therefore, have to think of different ways to encourage parental and family involvement in the educational process.

Newsletters

Quite often, teachers have great success involving families by just informing families of what is going on in the classroom. Newsletters are particularly effective for this purpose. Parents love to know what is going on in the classroom, and this way, they'll feel included. In newsletters, for example, teachers can provide suggestions on how parents can help with the educational goals of the school. Teachers can recommend that parents read with their children for twenty minutes per day or they can also provide suggestions on what to do when their children come across difficult words or when they ask a question about comprehension. These suggestions give parents practical strategies to use with their children.

Phone calls

Parents often equate phone calls from teachers with news about misbehaviors. Teachers can change that tone by calling parents with good news. Or they can send positive notes home with students. Thus, when they need to make negative phone calls, teachers will have greater success connecting with the parents.

Specific suggestions

Teachers can also provide very specific suggestions to individual parents. For example, let's say a student needs additional assistance in a particular subject. The teacher can provide tips to parents to encourage and increase deeper understandings in the subject outside of class.

Addressing Concerns with a Parent

When it is necessary to communicate (whether by phone, letter, or in person) with a parent regarding a concern about a student, the teacher should allow herself a "cooling off" period before making contact with the parent. It is important that the teacher remain professional and objective. The purpose for contacting the parent is to elicit support and additional information that may have a bearing on the student's behavior or performance. The teacher should be careful to not demean the child and not to appear antagonistic or confrontational. Be aware that the

The purpose for contacting the parent is to elicit support and additional information that may have a bearing on the student's behavior or performance.

parent is likely to be quite uncomfortable with the bad news and will respond best if you take a cooperative, problem-solving approach to the issue. It is also a nice courtesy to notify parents of positive occurrences with their children. The teacher's communication with parents should not be limited to negative items.

Parent conferences

The parent-teacher conference is generally for one of three purposes.

1. The teacher may wish to share information with the parents concerning the performance and behavior of the child

2. The teacher may be interested in obtaining information from the parents about the child; such information may help answer questions or concerns that the teacher has

3. The teacher may want to request parent support or involvement in specific activities or requirements; in many situations, more than one of the purposes may be involved

Planning the conference

When a conference is scheduled, whether at the request of the teacher or parent, the teacher should allow sufficient time to prepare thoroughly. Collect all relevant information, samples of student work, records of behavior, and other items needed to help the parent understand the circumstances surrounding the issue. It is also a good idea to compile a list of questions or concerns you wish to address. Arrange the time and location of the conference to provide privacy and to avoid interruptions.

Conducting the conference

Begin the conference by putting the parents as ease. Take the time to establish a comfortable mood, but do not waste time with unnecessary small talk. Begin your discussion with positive comments about the student. Identify strengths and desirable attributes, but do not exaggerate.

The teacher shoul address issues or areas of concern, being sure to focus on observable behaviors and concrete results or information. It is important to not make judgmental statements about parent or child. Sharing specific work samples, anecdotal records of behavior, etc., that clearly demonstrate the concerns is important as well. The teacher should be a good listener by hearing the parent's comments and explanations. Such background information can be invaluable in understanding the needs and motivations of the child.

Finally, end the conference with an agreed-upon plan of action between parents and teacher (and, when appropriate, the child). Bring the conference to a close politely but firmly, and thank the parents for their involvement.

After the conference

A day or two after the conference, it is a good idea to send a follow-up note to the parents. In this note, briefly and concisely reiterate the plan or step agreed to in the conference. Be polite and professional; avoid the temptation to be too informal or chatty. If the issue is a long-term, one such as the behavior or ongoing work performance of the student, make periodic follow-up contacts to keep the parents informed of the progress.

> **SKILL 18.2 Identifies a variety of strategies for working with parents, caregivers, and others to help students from diverse backgrounds reinforce in-school learning outside the school environment**

Dealing with Demographics

According to Campbell, Campbell, and Dickinson (1992), *Teaching and Learning Through Multiple Intelligences*, "The changing nature of demographics is one of the strongest rationales for multicultural education in the United States." The Census Bureau predicts a changing demographic for the American population and school communities that will include a forecast between 1990 and 2030, that "while the white population will increase by 25%, the African American population will increase by 68%, the Asian-American, Pacific Island, and American Indian by 79%, and the Hispanic-American population by 187%." Reinforcing that learning beyond the classroom must include a diversity of instructional and learning strategies for adult role models in a student's life.

Mentoring

Mentoring has become an instrumental tool in addressing student achievement and access to learning. Adult mentors work individually with identified students on specific subject areas to reinforce the learning through tutorial instruction and application of knowledge. Providing students with adult role models to reinforce the learning has become a crucial instructional strategy for teachers seeking to maximize student learning beyond the classroom. Students who work with adult mentors from culturally diverse backgrounds are given a multicultural aspect of learning that is cooperative and multimodal in personalized instruction.

Technology and the Classroom

The use of technology provides a mentoring tutorial support system and different conceptual learning modalities for students seeking to understand classroom material. Technology provides a networking opportunity for students to find study buddies and peer study groups, along with free academic support to problem-solve and develop critical thinking skills that are imperative in acquiring knowledge and conceptual learning.

DISTANCE LEARNING is a technological strategy that keeps students and teachers interactively communicating about issues in the classroom and beyond. Students will communicate more freely using technology to ask teacher or adult mentors clarity questions than they will in a classroom of peers.

Community Resources

Connecting with community resources will also provide viable avenues of support in helping students who need additional academic remediation to access learning. Diversity programs are offered through the local universities and community agencies that connect college students or working adults with subject areas and classrooms in need of additional student interns and adult volunteers to support the academic programs in school communities.

> *The use of technology provides a mentoring tutorial support system and different conceptual learning modalities for students seeking to understand classroom material.*

> **DISTANCE LEARNING:** a technological strategy that keeps students and teachers interactively communicating about issues in the classroom and beyond

---

> SKILL 18.3 **Applies strategies for using community resources to enrich learning experiences**

Utilizing Community Resources

The community is a vital link to increasing learning experiences for students. Community resources can supplement the minimized and marginal educational resources of school communities. With state and federal educational funding becoming increasingly subject to legislative budget cuts, school communities welcome the financial support that community resources can provide in terms of discounted prices on high end supplies (e.g., computers, printers, and technology supplies), along with providing free notebooks, backpacks, and student supplies for low-income students who may have difficulty obtaining the basic supplies for school.

Community stores can provide cash rebates and teacher discounts for educators in struggling school districts and compromised school communities. Both profes sionally and personally, communities can enrich the student learning experiences by including the following support strategies:

- Provide programs that support student learning outcomes and future educational goals

- Create mentoring opportunities that provide adult role models in various industries to students interested in studying in that industry

- Provide financial support for school communities to help low-income or homeless students begin the school year with the basic supplies

- Develop paid internships with local university students to provide tutorial services for identified students in school communities who are having academic and social difficulties processing various subject areas

- Providing parent-teen-community forums to create public voice of change in communities

- Offer parents who do not have computers or Internet connections, stipends to purchase technology to create equitable opportunities for students to do research and complete requirements

- Visit classrooms and ask teachers and students what's needed to promote academic progress and growth

Community resources are vital in providing the additional support to students, school communities, and families struggling to remain engaged in declining educational institutions competing for federal funding and limited district funding.

The commitment that a community shows to its educational communities is a valuable investment in the future. Community resources that are able to provide additional funding for tutors in marginalized classrooms or help schools reduce classrooms of students needing additional remedial instruction directly impact educational equity and facilitation of teaching and learning for both teachers and students.

> SKILL 18.4 **Recognizes various ways in which school personnel, local citizens, and community institutions** *(e.g., businesses, cultural institutions, colleges and universities, social agencies)* **can work together to promote a sense of neighborhood and community**

The Importance of Collaboration

The bridge to effective learning for students begins with a collaborative approach by all stakeholders that supports the educational needs of students. Underestimating the power and integral role of the community institutions in impacting the current and future goals of students can carry high stakes for students beyond the high school years who are competing for college access, student internships, and entry-level jobs in the community.

Researchers have shown that school involvement and connections with community institutions promote student retention rates, graduations, and higher education experiences. The current disconnect and autonomy that has become commonplace in today's society must be reevaluated in terms of promoting tomorrow's citizens.

Students as community liaisons

When community institutions provide students and teachers with meaningful connections and input, the commitment is apparent in terms of volunteering, loyalty, and professional promotion. Providing students with placements in leadership positions such as the Associated Student Body (ASB); the Parent Teacher Student Association (PTSA); school boards; neighborhood subcommittees addressing political or social issues; or government boards that impact and influence school communities creates an avenue for students to explore ethical, participatory, collaborative, transformational leadership that can be applied to all areas of a student's educational and personal life.

Community liaisons provide students with opportunities to experience accountability and responsibility. They also allow students to learn about life and how organizations work with effective communication and the ability of teams to work together to accomplish goals and objectives. Teaching students skills of inclusion and social and environmental responsibility and creating public forums that represent student voices and votes foster student interest and access in developing and reflecting on individual opinions and understanding the dynamics of the world around them.

When students see that various support systems are in place and consistently working as a team to effectively provide resources and avenues of academic promotion and accountability, they have no fear of taking risks to grow by, say, becoming a teen voice on a local committee about teen violence or volunteering in a local hospice for young children with terminal diseases. The linkages of community institutions provide role models of a world in which the student will soon become an integral and vital member, so being a part of that world as a student makes the transition easier as a young adult.

Researchers have shown that school involvement and connections with community institutions promote student retention rates, graduations, and higher education experiences.

Community liaisons provide students with opportunities to experience accountability and responsibility.

COMPETENCY 19

UNDERSTAND RECIPROCAL RIGHTS AND RESPONSIBILITIES IN SITUATIONS INVOLVING INTERACTIONS BETWEEN TEACHERS AND STUDENTS, PARENTS, GUARDIANS, COMMUNITY MEMBERS, COLLEAGUES, SCHOOL ADMINISTRATORS, AND OTHER SCHOOL PERSONNEL

> **SKILL 19.1** **Applies knowledge of laws related to students' rights in various situations** *(e.g., in relation to due process, discrimination, harassment, confidentiality, discipline, privacy)*

Resources for Students

One of the first things that a teacher learns is how to obtain resources and help for his or her students. All schools have guidelines for receiving this assistance especially since the implementation of the Americans with Disabilities Act. The first step in securing help is for the teacher to approach the school's administration or exceptional education department for direction in attaining special services or resources for qualifying students. Many schools have a committee designated for addressing these needs such as a Child Study Team or Core Team. These teams are made up of both regular and special education teachers, school psychologists, guidance counselors, and administrators. The particular student's classroom teacher usually has to complete some initial paper work and will need to complete some behavioral observations.

Inside the school system

The teacher will take this information to the appropriate committee for discussion and consideration. The committee will recommend the next step to be taken. Often, subsequent steps include a complete psychological evaluation along with certain physical examinations such as vision and hearing screening and a complete medical examination by a doctor.

The referral of students for this process is usually relatively simple for the classroom teacher and requires little more than some initial paper work and discussion. The services and resources the student receives as a result of the process typically prove to be invaluable to the student with a behavioral disorder.

Beyond the school system

At times, the teacher must go beyond the school system to meet the needs of some students. When the school system is unable to address the needs of a student, the teacher often must take the initiative and contact agencies within the community. Frequently, there is no special policy for finding resources. It is simply up to the individual teacher to be creative and resourceful and to find whatever help is available to meet the students' needs. Meeting the needs of all students is certainly a team effort that is most often spearheaded by the classroom teacher.

An awareness of special services and resources and how to obtain them is essential to all teachers and their students.

Family involvement

Under the IDEA, parent or guardian involvement in the development of the student's IEP is required and absolutely essential for the advocacy of the disabled student's educational needs. IEPs must be tailored to meet the student's needs, and no one knows those needs better than the parent or guardian and other significant family members. Optimal conditions for a disabled student's education exist when teachers, school administrators, special education professionals, and parents or guardians work together to design and execute the IEP.

Under the IDEA, parent or guardian involvement in the development of the student's IEP is required and absolutely essential for the advocacy of the disabled student's educational needs.

Due process

Under the IDEA, Congress provides safeguards for students against schools' actions, including the right to sue in court, and encourages states to develop hearing and mediation systems to resolve disputes. No student or their parents or guardians can be denied due process because of disability.

No student or their parents or guardians can be denied due process because of disability.

Inclusion, mainstreaming, and least restrictive environment

Inclusion, mainstreaming, and least restrictive environment are interrelated policies under the IDEA, with varying degrees of statutory imperatives.

Inclusion	The right of students with disabilities to be placed in the regular classroom
Least Restrictive Environment	The mandate that children be educated to the maximum extent appropriate with their nondisabled peers
Mainstreaming	A policy where disabled students can be placed in the regular classroom, as long as such placement does not interfere with the student's educational plan

Alcohol and Drug Abuse

There is a saying, *If you're going to be an alcoholic or drug addict in America, you will be.* Cynical but true, this comment implies that exposure to alcohol and drugs is 100 percent. We now have a widespread second generation of drug abusers in families. And alcohol is the oldest form of drug abuse known to humankind, with many families affected for three or more known generations. It's hard to tell youth to eschew drugs when even mom and dad, who grew up in the early illicit drug era, partake.

Dealing with student drug abuse

Educators, therefore, are not only likely to, but often do, face students who are high on something in school. Of course, they are not only a hazard to their own safety and those of others, but their ability to be productive learners is greatly diminished if not nonexistent. They show up instead of skip, because it's not always easy or practical for them to spend the day away from home but not in school. Unless they can stay inside they are at risk of being picked up for truancy. Some enjoy being high in school, getting a sense of satisfaction by putting something over on the system. Some just don't take drug use seriously enough to think use at school might be inappropriate.

Abuse Situations

The child who is undergoing abuse is the one whose needs must be served first. A suspected case gone unreported may not only destroy a child's life, but affect his ability to function as an adult. It is the duty of any citizen who suspects abuse and neglect to make a report, and it is especially important—and required—for state licensed and certified individuals to make a report. All reports can be kept confidential if required, but it is best to disclose your identity in case more information is required of you. This personal matter has no impact on qualifications for license or certification. Failure to make a report when abuse or neglect is suspected is punishable by revocation of certification and license, a fine, and criminal charges.

It is the right of any accused individual to have counsel and make a defense, as in any matter of law. The procedure for reporting makes clear the rights of the accused, who stands before the court innocent until proven guilty, with the right to representation, redress, and appeal, as in all matters of U. S. law. The state is cautious about receiving spurious reports, but investigates any that seem authentic. Some breaches of standards of decency are not reportable offenses, such as possession of pornography that is not hidden from children.

Reporting suspected abuse

There is no time limit on an acceptable or safe period of time to wait before reporting, so hesitation to report may be a cause for action against you. Do not wait once your suspicion is firm. All you need to have is a reasonable suspicion, not actual proof. It is the job of investigators to determine the facts.

Interventions

Many safe and helpful interventions are available to the classroom teacher when dealing with a student who is suffering from a serious emotional disturbance. First and foremost, the teacher must maintain open communication with the parents and other professionals who are involved with the student whenever overt behavior characteristics are exhibited. Students with behavior disorders need constant behavioral interventions, which may involve two-way communication between the home and school on a daily basis.

The teacher must establish an environment that promotes appropriate behavior for all students, as well as respect for one another. Classmates may need to be informed of a classmate's special needs to better understand behavioral interventions and outbursts that may occur in the classroom. The teacher should also initiate a behavior intervention program for any student who might demonstrate emotional or behavioral disorders. Such behavior modification plans can be an effective means of preventing deviant behavior. If deviant behavior does occur, the teacher needs to have previously arranged for a safe and secure time-out place where the student can go for a respite and an opportunity to regain self-control.

Program treatment

Often when a behavior disorder is more severe, the student must be involved in a more concentrated program aimed at alleviating deviant behavior, such as psychotherapy. In such instances, the school psychologist, guidance counselor, or behavior specialist should be directly involved with the student and provide counseling and therapy on a regular basis. Frequently, they are also involved with the student's family.

Drug therapy

As a last resort, many families are turning to drug therapy. Once viewed as a radical step, administering drugs to children to balance their emotions or to control their behavior has become a widely used form of therapy. Of course, only a medical doctor can recommend or prescribe such drugs. Great care must be exercised when giving pills to children in order to change their behavior, especially since so many medicines have undesirable side effects. It is important to know that these drugs relieve only the symptoms of behavior and do not always eliminate the underlying causes. Parents and teachers need to be educated as to the side effects of these medications.

> Do not wait once your suspicion is firm. All you need to have is a reasonable suspicion, not actual proof, which is the job for the investigators.

> **SKILL 19.2** **Applies knowledge of a teacher's rights and responsibilities in various situations** *(e.g., in relation to students with disabilities, potential abuse, safety issues)*

See Skill 19.1

> **SKILL 19.3** **Applies knowledge of parents' rights and responsibilities in various situations** *(e.g., in relation to student records, school attendance)*

Permanent Records

PERMANENT RECORD: a file of the student's cumulative educational history

The student **PERMANENT RECORD** is a file of the student's cumulative educational history. It contains a profile of the student's academic background as well as the student's behavioral and medical background. Other pertinent individual information contained in the permanent record includes the student's attendance, grade average, and schools attended. Personal information such as parents' names and addresses, immunization records, child's height and weight, and narrative information about the child's progress and physical and mental well-being is an important aspect of the permanent record. All information contained within the permanent record is strictly confidential and is only to be discussed with the student's parents or other involved school personnel.

The purpose of the permanent record is to provide applicable information about the student so that the student's individual educational needs can be met. If any specialized testing has been administered, the results are noted in the permanent record. Any special requirements that the student may have are indicated in the permanent record. Highly personal information, including court orders regarding custody, is filed in the permanent record as is appropriate. The importance and value of the permanent record cannot be underestimated. It offers a comprehensive knowledge of the student.

Teacher's responsibility

The current teacher is responsible for maintaining the student's permanent record. All substantive information in regard to testing, academic performance, the student's medical condition, and personal events are placed in the permanent record file. Updated information in regard to the student's grades, attendance, and behavior is added annually. These files are kept in a locked fireproof room or file cabinet and cannot be removed from this room unless the person removing them signs a form acknowledging full responsibility for the safe return of the complete file. Again, only the student's parents (or legal guardians), the teacher, or other involved school personnel may view the contents of the permanent record file.

The permanent record file follows the student as she moves through the school system, with information being added and updated along the way. Any time the student leaves a school, the permanent record is transferred with the student. The permanent record is regarded as legal documentation of a student's educational experience.

Intended contents

The content of any student records should be indicative of the student's academic aptitude and achievement. The information contained should never be derogatory or potentially damaging in any way. It is important to keep in mind that others who view the contents of the records may form an opinion of the student based on the information in the student's record or file. Anyone who places information in a student's record must make every effort to give an accurate reflection of the student's performance while maintaining a neutral position as to the student's potential for future success or failure.

Confidentiality

The most essential fact to remember in regard to students' records is that the information within is confidential. Although specific policies may vary from one school or district to another, confidentiality remains constant and universal. Teachers should never discuss any student and his or her progress with anyone other than the student's parents or essential school personnel.

> *Confidentiality applies to all student information whether it is a student's spelling test, portfolio, standardized test information, report card, or the contents of the permanent record file.*

Significance

The significance of the student's records is not to be taken lightly. In many instances, teachers have access to a student's records before she actually meets the student. It is important for the teacher to have helpful information about the student without developing any preconceived biases about the student. Careful regard must be given to all information that is added to a student's file without diluting the potential effectiveness of that information. It is also important to be cognizant of the fact that the primary function of student records is that they are intended to be used as a means of developing a better understanding of the students' needs and to generate a more effective plan for meeting these needs.

> **SKILL 19.4** Analyzes the appropriateness of a teacher's response to a parent, a community member, another educator, or a student in various situations *(e.g., when dealing with differences of opinion in regard to current or emerging policy)*

Dealing with Confrontation

A teacher does not want to lose his position over a difference of opinion; therefore, remaining level-headed when dealing with an argumentative person, be it a parent, student, or peer, is key. Passions—and tempers—tend to run high when people have very definite ideas and feelings about policies. For example, there has been much debate and argument about "zero tolerance" policies that give strict punishment at the first offense, no matter how small that offense might be. (A "zero tolerance" drug policy, for example, might expel a student if he or she is found with aspirin or ibuprofen.)

Addressing parents and getting support

Remind an argumentative parent that you did not write the policy they are contesting, but that as a teacher you are bound to uphold that policy. Have the school principal and superintendent advocate on your behalf in this situation. Parents, students, and even other teachers have avenues they can use to affect change in policy, but that avenue does not go directly through you. They should lodge complaints in the appropriate venue, and petition the school board or State Education Department for changes.

Witnesses

It is usually best to have witnesses to any discussion when there is a difference of opinion so that subsequent recounts do not become "he said, she said" or hearsay.

It is usually best to have witnesses to any discussion when there is a difference of opinion so that subsequent recounts do not become "he said, she said" or hearsay. Bringing up such topics during a meeting may be appropriate so that there is a record of the discussion in the minutes. In order to get a fair analysis of whether a teacher's response to an attack by a parent, educator, or student was appropriate, witnesses to that attack will be a key factor.

SAMPLE TEST

SAMPLE TEST

Student Development and Learning

Directions: Read each item and select the best response.

(Average) (Skill 1.1)

1. What developmental patterns should a professional teacher assess to meet the needs of the student?

    A. Academic, regional, and family background

    B. Social, physical, and academic

    C. Academic, physical, and family background

    D. Physical, family, and ethnic background

(Average) (Skill 1.3)

2. Louise is a first grade teacher. She is planning her instructional activities for the week. In considering her planning, she should keep in mind that activities for this age of child should change how often?

    A. 25–40 minutes

    B. 30–40 minutes

    C. 5–10 minutes

    D. 15–30 minutes

(Rigorous) (Skill 2.1)

3. What are the two types of performance that teaching entails?

    A. Classroom management and questioning techniques

    B. Skill-building and analysis of outcomes

    C. Interaction with students and manipulation of subject matter

    D. Management techniques and levels of questioning

(Easy) (Skill 2.2)

4. What are the two ways concepts can be taught?

    A. Factually and interpretively

    B. Inductively and deductively

    C. Conceptually and inductively

    D. Analytically and facilitatively

(Rigorous) (Skill 2.2)

5. What is one component of the instructional planning model that must be given careful evaluation?

    A. Students' prior knowledge and skills

    B. The script the teacher will use in instruction

    C. Future lesson plans

    D. Parent participation

(Rigorous) (Skill 2.3)

6. When using a kinesthetic approach, what would be an appropriate activity?

    A. List

    B. Match

    C. Define

    D. Debate

(Rigorous) (Skill 2.3)

7. Ms. Smith says, "Yes, exactly what do you mean by "It was the author's intention to mislead you." What does this illustrate?

A. Digression

B. Restates response

C. Probes a response

D. Amplifies a response

(Average) (Skill 2.4)

8. What are critical elements of instructional process?

A. Content, goals, teacher needs

B. Means of getting money to regulate instruction

C. Content, materials, activities, goals, learner needs

D. Materials, definitions, assignments

(Rigorous) (Skill 2.4)

9. According to Piaget, what stage is characterized by the ability to think abstractly and to use logic?

A. Concrete operations

B. Preoperational

C. Formal operations

D. Conservative operational

(Easy) (Skill 2.4)

10. How many stages of intellectual development does Piaget define?

A. Two

B. Four

C. Six

D. Eight

(Easy) (Skill 2.4)

11. Who developed the theory of multiple intelligences?

A. Bruner

B. Gardner

C. Kagan

D. Cooper

(Average) (Skill 2.4)

12. Students who can solve problems mentally have:

A. Reached maturity

B. Physically developed

C. Reached the preoperational stage of thought

D. Achieved the ability to manipulate objects symbolically

(Rigorous) (Skill 2.5)

13. Which description of the role of a teacher is no longer an accurate description?

A. Guide on the side

B. Authoritarian

C. Disciplinarian

D. Sage on the stage

(Rigorous) (Skill 2.5)

14. In the past, teaching has been viewed as _____ while in more current society it has been viewed as _____.

A. isolating, collaborative

B. collaborative, isolating

C. supportive, isolating

D. isolating, supportive

(Rigorous) (Skill 2.6)

15. The teacher states, "We will work on the first page of vocabulary words. On the second page we will work on the structure and meaning of the words. We will go over these together and then you will write out the answers to the exercises on your own. I will be circulating to give help if needed." What is this an example of?

A. Evaluation of instructional activity

B. Analysis of instructional activity

C. Identification of expected outcomes

D. Pacing of instructional activity

(Rigorous) (Skill 2.6)

16. If teachers attend to content, instructional materials, activities, learner needs, and goals in instructional planning, what could be an outcome?

A. Planning for the next year

B. Effective classroom performance

C. Elevated test scores on standardized tests

D. More student involvement

(Rigorous) (Skill 2.6)

17. When planning instruction, which of the following is an organizational tool to help ensure you are providing a well-balanced set of objectives?

A. Using a taxonomy to develop objectives

B. Determining prior knowledge skill levels

C. Determining readiness levels

D. Ensuring you meet the needs of diverse learners

(Average) (Skill 3.4)

18. What do cooperative learning methods all have in common?

A. Philosophy

B. Cooperative task/cooperative reward structures

C. Student roles and communication

D. Teacher roles

(Average) (Skill 3.5)

19. What is the definition of proactive classroom management?

A. Management that is constantly changing

B. Management that is downplayed

C. Management that gives clear and explicit instructions and rewarding compliance

D. Management that is designed by the students

(Rigorous) (Skill 3.7)

20. According to recent studies, what is the estimated number of adolescents that have physical, social, or emotional problems related to the abuse of alcohol?

A. Less that one million

B. 1–2 million

C. 2–3 million

D. More than four million

(Rigorous) (Skill 4.1)

21. Abigail has had intermittent hearing loss from the age of 1 through age 5 when she had tubes put in her ears. What is one area of development that may be affected by this?

   A. Math

   B. Language

   C. Social skills

   D. None

(Rigorous) (Skill 4.1)

22. Active listening is an important skill for teachers to utilize with both students and teachers. Active listening involves all of the following strategies except…

   A. Eye contact

   B. Restating what the speaker has said

   C. Clarification of speaker statements

   D. Open and receptive body language

(Rigorous) (Skill 4.3)

23. Students who are learning English as a second language often require which of the following to process new information?

   A. Translators

   B. Reading tutors

   C. Instruction in their native language

   D. Additional time and repetitions

(Easy) (Skill 4.3)

24. Many of the current ESOL approaches used in classrooms today are based on which approach?

   A. Social Learning Methods

   B. Native Tongue Methods

   C. ESOL Learning Methods

   D. Special Education Methods

(Easy) (Skill 4.3)

25. Which of the following is the last stage of second language acquisition according to the theories of Stephen Krashen?

   A. The affective filter hypothesis

   B. The input hypothesis

   C. The natural order hypothesis

   D. The monitor hypothesis

(Average) (Skill 4.4)

26. If a student has a poor vocabulary, the teacher should recommend that:

   A. The student read newspapers, magazines, and books on a regular basis

   B. The student enroll in a Latin class

   C. The student write the words repetitively after looking them up in the dictionary

   D. The student use a thesaurus to locate synonyms and incorporate them into her vocabulary

(Rigorous) (Skill 4.4)

27. **All of the following are true about phonological awareness EXCEPT:**

    A. It may involve print

    B. It is a prerequisite for spelling and phonics

    C. Activities can be done by the children with their eyes closed

    D. Starts before letter recognition is taught

(Easy) (Skill 4.4)

28. **The arrangement and relationship of words in sentences or sentence structure best describes:**

    A. Style

    B. Discourse

    C. Thesis

    D. Syntax

(Easy) (Skill 4.4)

29. **Which of the following is not a technique of prewriting?**

    A. Clustering

    B. Listing

    C. Brainstorming

    D. Proofreading

(Rigorous) (Skill 4.5)

30. **One of the many ways in which a child can demonstrate comprehension of a story is by:**

    A. Filling in a strategy sheet

    B. Retelling the story orally

    C. Retelling the story in writing

    D. All of the above

(Easy) (Skill 4.5)

31. **Greg Ball went to an author signing where Faith Ringgold gave a talk about one of her many books. He was so inspired by her presence and by his reading of her book *Tar Beach* that he used the book for his reading and writing workshop activities. His supervisor wrote in his plan book that he was pleased that Greg had used the book as an/a _____ book.**

    A. basic

    B. feature

    C. anchor

    D. focus

(Easy) (Skill 5.1)

32. **Which of the following is an example of a restriction within the affective domain?**

    A. Unable to think abstractly

    B. Inability to synthesize information

    C. Inability to concentrate

    D. Inability complete physical activities

(Average) (Skill 5.2)

33. **What is a good strategy for teaching ethnically diverse students?**

    A. Don't focus on the students' culture

    B. Expect them to assimilate easily into your classroom

    C. Imitate their speech patterns

    D. Include ethnic studies in the curriculum

(Easy) (Skill 5.2)

34. Which of the following is an accurate description of ESL students?

    A. Remedial students

    B. Exceptional education students

    C. Are not a homogeneous group

    D. Feel confident in communicating in English when with their peers

(Rigorous) (Skill 5.2)

35. What is an effective way to help a non-English speaking student succeed in class?

    A. Refer the child to a specialist

    B. Maintain an encouraging, success-oriented atmosphere

    C. Help them assimilate by making them use English exclusively

    D. Help them cope with the content materials you currently use

(Average) (Skill 5.2)

36. How can text be modified for low-level ESOL students?

    A. Add visuals and illustrations

    B. Let students write definitions

    C. Change text to a narrative form

    D. Have students write details out from the text

(Rigorous) (Skill 5.2)

37. Etienne is an ESOL student. He has begun to engage in conversation, which produces a connected narrative. In what developmental stage for second language acquisition is he?

    A. Early production

    B. Speech emergence

    C. Preproduction

    D. Intermediate fluency

(Rigorous) (Skill 5.2)

38. What is a roadblock to second language learning?

    A. Students are forced to speak

    B. Students speak only when ready

    C. Mistakes are considered a part of learning

    D. The focus is on oral communication

(Average) (Skill 5.2)

39. Why is praise for compliance important in classroom management?

    A. Students will continue deviant behavior

    B. Desirable conduct will be repeated

    C. It reflects simplicity and warmth

    D. Students will fulfill obligations

(Average) (Skill 5.4)

40. Which of the following is not a communication issue that is related to diversity within the classroom?

   A. Learning disorder

   B. Sensitive terminology

   C. Body language

   D. Discussing differing viewpoints and opinions

(Rigorous) (Skill 6.2)

41. Mr. Ryan has proposed to his classroom that the students may demonstrate understanding of the unit taught in a variety of ways including: taking a test, writing a paper, creating an oral presentation, or building a model or project. Which of the following areas of differentiation has Mr. Ryan demonstrated?

   A. Synthesis

   B. Product

   C. Content

   D. Product

(Average) (Skill 6.2)

42. When creating and selecting materials for instruction, teachers should complete which of the following steps:

   A. Make them relevant to the prior knowledge of the students

   B. Allow for a variation of learning styles

   C. Choose alternative teaching strategies

   D. All of the above

(Rigorous) (Skill 6.4)

43. Mr. Weiss understands that it is imperative that students who are struggling with acquiring concepts at a specific grade level can still benefit from participating in whole classroom discussions and lessons. In fact, such students should be required to be present for whole classroom lessons. Mr. Weiss's beliefs fall under which of the following principles?

   A. Self-fulfilling prophecy

   B. Partial participation

   C. Inclusion

   D. Heterogeneous grouping

Instruction and Assessment

(Rigorous) (Skill 7.1)

44. Reducing off-task time and maximizing the amount of time students spend attending to academic tasks is closely related to which of the following?

   A. Using whole class instruction only

   B. Business-like behaviors of the teacher

   C. Dealing only with major teaching functions

   D. Giving students a maximum of two minutes to come to order

(Easy) (Skill 7.1)

45. While teaching, three students cause separate disruptions. The teacher selects the major one and tells that student to desist. What is the teacher demonstrating?

    A. Deviancy spread

    B. Correct target desist

    C. Alternative behavior

    D. Desist major deviance

(Average) (Skill 7.2)

46. What must occur for seatwork to be effective?

    A. All seatwork is graded immediately

    B. All seatwork should be explained by another student for clarification

    C. The teacher should monitor and provide corrective feedback for seatwork

    D. Seatwork should be a review of the previous day's lesson

(Rigorous) (Skill 7.2)

47. Mrs. Peck wants to justify the use of personalized learning community to her principal. Which of the following reasons should she use?

    A. They build multiculturalism

    B. They provide a supportive environment to address academic and emotional needs

    C. They builds relationships between students that promote lifelong learning

    D. They are proactive in their nature

(Rigorous) (Skill 7.2)

48. Mrs. Potts has noticed an undercurrent of an unsettled nature in her classroom. She is in the middle of her math lesson but still notices that many of her students seem to be having some sort of difficulty. Mrs. Potts stops class and decides to have a class meeting. She understands that even though her math objectives are important, it is equally important to address whatever is troubling her classroom. What is it Mrs. Potts knows?

    A. Discipline is important

    B. Social issues can impact academic learning

    C. Maintaining order is important

    D. Social skills instruction is important

(Average) (Skill 7.2)

49. Which of the following could be an example of a situation that could have an effect on a student's learning and academic progress?

    A. Relocation

    B. Abuse

    C. Both of the above

    D. Neither of the above

(Rigorous) (Skill 7.2)

50. Mrs. Graham has taken the time to reflect, completed observations, and asked for feedback about the interactions between her and her students from her principal. It is obvious by seeking this information out that Mrs. Graham understands which of the following?

    A. The importance of clear communication with the principal

    B. She needs to analyze her effectiveness of classroom interactions

    C. She is clearly communicating with the principal

    D. She cares about her students

(Rigorous) (Skill 7.3)

51. What has been established to increase student originality, intrinsic motivation, and higher-order thinking skills?

    A. Classroom climate

    B. High expectations

    C. Student choice

    D. Use of authentic learning opportunities

(Easy) (Skill 7.3)

52. Which of the following can be measured utilizing the following types of assessments: direct observation, role playing, context observation, and teacher ratings?

    A. Social skills

    B. Reading skills

    C. Math skills

    D. Need for specialized instruction

(Average) (Skill 7.5)

53. What would improve planning for instruction?

    A. Describe the role of the teacher and student

    B. Evaluate the outcomes of instruction

    C. Rearrange the order of activities

    D. Give outside assignments

(Average) (Skill 7.5)

54. How can student misconduct be redirected at times?

    A. The teacher threatens the students

    B. The teacher assigns detention to the whole class

    C. The teacher stops the activity and stares at the students

    D. The teacher effectively handles changing from one activity to another

(Rigorous) (Skill 7.5)

55. What have recent studies regarding effective teachers concluded?

    A. Effective teachers let students establish rules

    B. Effective teachers establish routines by the sixth week of school

    C. Effective teachers state their own policies and establish consistent class rules and procedures on the first day of class

    D. Effective teachers establish flexible routines

(Average) (Skill 7.5)

56. To maintain the flow of events in the classroom, what should an effective teacher do?

    A. Work only in small groups

    B. Use only whole class activities

    C. Direct attention to content rather than focusing the class on misbehavior

    D. Follow lectures with written assignments

(Rigorous) (Skill 7.5)

57. The concept of efficient use of time includes which of the following?

    A. Daily review, seatwork, and recitation of concepts

    B. Lesson initiation, transition, and comprehension check

    C. Review, test, and review

    D. Punctuality, management transition, and wait time avoidance

(Average) (Skill 7.5)

58. What is a sample of an academic transition signal?

    A. How do clouds form?

    B. Today we are going to study clouds.

    C. We have completed today's lesson.

    D. That completes the description of cumulus clouds. Now we will look at the description of cirrus clouds.

(Average) (Skill 8.1)

59. When is utilization of instructional materials most effective?

    A. When the activities are sequenced

    B. When the materials are prepared ahead of time

    C. When the students choose the pages to work on

    D. When the students create the instructional materials

(Rigorous) (Skill 8.1)

60. When considering the development of the curriculum, which of the following accurately describes the four factors that need to be considered?

    A. Alignment, Scope, Sequence, and Design

    B. Assessment, Instruction, Design, and Sequence

    C. Data, Alignment, Correlation, and Score

    D. Alignment, Sequence, Design, and Assessment

(Average) (Skill 8.2)

61. What should be considered when evaluating textbooks for content?

    A. Type of print used

    B. Number of photos used

    C. Free of cultural stereotyping

    D. Outlines at the beginning of each chapter

(Easy) (Skill 9.1)

62. **Which of the following is a presentation modification?**

    A. Taking an assessment in an alternate room

    B. Providing an interpreter to give the test in American Sign Language

    C. Allowing dictation of written responses

    D. Extending the time limits on an assessment

(Average) (Skill 9.2)

63. **What should a teacher do when students have not responded well to an instructional activity?**

    A. Reevaluate learner needs

    B. Request administrative help

    C. Continue with the activity another day

    D. Assign homework on the concept

(Average) (Skill 9.2)

64. **What is the best definition for an achievement test?**

    A. It measures mechanical and practical abilities

    B. It measures broad areas of knowledge that are the result of cumulative learning experiences

    C. It measures the ability to learn to perform a task

    D. It measures performance related to specific, recently acquired information

(Average) (Skill 9.2)

65. **How are standardized tests useful in assessment?**

    A. For teacher evaluation

    B. For evaluation of the administration

    C. For comparison from school to school

    D. For comparison to the population on which the test was normed

(Rigorous) (Skill 9.2)

66. **Which of the following test items is not objective?**

    A. Multiple choice

    B. Essay

    C. Matching

    D. True or false

(Rigorous) (Skill 9.2)

67. **Which of the following is NOT used in evaluating test items?**

    A. Student feedback

    B. Content validity

    C. Reliability

    D. Ineffective coefficient

(Average) (Skill 9.2)

68. **Safeguards against bias and discrimination in the assessment of children include:**

    A. The testing of a child in standard English

    B. The requirement for the use of one standardized test

    C. The use of evaluative materials in the child's native language or other mode of communication

    D. All testing performed by a certified, licensed psychologist

(Average) (Skill 9.3)

69. On intelligence quotient scales, what is the average intelligence score?

    A. 100–120

    B. 60–80

    C. 90–110

    D. 80–100

(Easy) (Skill 9.3)

70. On what is evaluation of the instructional activity based?

    A. Student grades

    B. Teacher evaluation

    C. Student participation

    D. Specified criteria

(Average) (Skill 9.3)

71. What is an example of formative feedback?

    A. The results of an intelligence test

    B. Correcting the tests in small groups

    C. Verbal behavior that expresses approval of a student response to a test item

    D. Scheduling a discussion before the test

(Easy) (Skill 9.3)

72. What does the validity of a test refer to?

    A. Its consistency

    B. Its usefulness

    C. Its accuracy

    D. The degree of true scores it provides

(Rigorous) (Skill 9.3)

73. Which of the following describes why it is important and necessary for teachers to be able to analyze data on their students?

    A. To provide appropriate instruction

    B. To make instructional decisions

    C. To communicate and determine instructional progress

    D. All of the above

(Easy) (Skill 9.4)

74. When a teacher wants to utilize an assessment that is subjective in nature, which of the following is the most effective method for scoring?

    A. Rubric

    B. Checklist

    C. Alternative Assessment

    D. Subjective measures should not be utilized

(Rigorous) (Skill 9.5)

75. What steps are important in the review of subject matter in the classroom?

    A. A lesson-initiating review, topic, and a lesson-end review

    B. A preview of the subject matter, an in-depth discussion, and a lesson-end review

    C. A rehearsal of the subject matter and a topic summary within the lesson

    D. A short paragraph synopsis of the previous day's lesson and a written review at the end of the lesson

(Rigorous) (Skill 9.5)

76. The teacher states that the lesson the students will be engaged in will consist of a review of the material from the previous day, demonstration of the scientific of an electronic circuit, and small group work on setting up an electronic circuit. What has the teacher demonstrated?

    A. The importance of reviewing

    B. Giving the general framework for the lesson to facilitate learning

    C. Giving students the opportunity to leave if they are not interested in the lesson

    D. Providing momentum for the lesson

(Average) (Skill 9.5)

77. What is an effective way to prepare students for testing?

    A. Minimize the importance of the test

    B. Orient the students to the test by telling them of the purpose, how the results will be used, and how it is relevant to them

    C. Use the same format for every test are given

    D. Have them construct an outline to study from

(Average) (Skill 9.5)

78. How will students have a fair chance to demonstrate what they know on a test?

    A. When the examiner has strictly enforced rules for taking the test

    B. When the examiner provides a comfortable setting free of distractions and positively encourages the students

    C. When the examiner provides frequent stretch breaks to the students

    D. When the examiner stresses the importance of the test to the overall grade

(Rigorous) (Skill 9.5)

79. Which of the following is the correct term for the alignment of the curriculum across all grades K-12?

    A. Data-based decision making

    B. Curriculum mapping

    C. Vertical integration

    D. Curriculum alignment

(Average) (Skill 9.5)

80. Which of the following information can NOT be gained by examining school level data in an in-depth manner?

    A. Teacher effectiveness

    B. Educational trends within a school

    C. Student ability to meet state and national goals and objectives

    D. Ways to improve student learning goals and academic success

(Average) (Skill 10.1)

81. Which of following is NOT the role of the teacher in the instructional process:

    A. Instructor

    B. Coach

    C. Facilitator

    D. Follower

(Rigorous) (Skill 10.2)

82. Discovery learning is to inquiry as direct instruction is to…

    A. Scripted lessons

    B. Well-developed instructions

    C. Clear instructions that eliminate all misinterpretations

    D. Creativity of teaching

(Rigorous) (Skill 10.6)

83. When developing lessons it is imperative teachers provide equity in pedagogy so:

    A. Unfair labeling of students will not occur

    B. Student experiences will be positive

    C. Students will achieve academic success

    D. All of the above

(Average) (Skill 10.6)

84. Which of the following is a good reason to collaborate with a peer:

    A. To increase your knowledge in areas where you feel you are weak, but the peer is strong

    B. To increase your planning time and that of your peer by combining the classes and taking more breaks

    C. To have fewer lesson plans to write

    D. To teach fewer subjects

(Rigorous) (Skill 10.6)

85. Which of the following are ways a professional can assess her teaching strengths and weaknesses?

    A. Examining how many students were unable to understand a concept

    B. Asking peers for suggestions or ideas

    C. Self-evaluation/reflection of lessons taught

    D. All of the above

(Rigorous) (Skill 10.6)

86. Mr. German is a math coach. He is the only math coach in his building and, in fact, within his district. Mr. German believes it is imperative to seek out the support of colleagues to work in a more collaborative manner. Which of the following would be an appropriate step for him to take?

    A. Collaborating with other teachers in his building regardless of their skill level knowledge in his area

    B. Asking for the administration to find colleagues with whom he can collaborate

    C. Joining a professional organization such as the National Council of Teachers of Mathematics (NCTM)

    D. Searching the Internet for possible collaboration opportunities

(Average) (Skill 11.1)

87. **Why is it important for a teacher to pose a question before calling on students to answer?**

    A. It helps manage student conduct

    B. It keeps the students as a group focused on the class work

    C. It allows students time to collaborate

    D. It gives the teacher time to walk among the students

(Rigorous) (Skill 11.1)

88. **What is an example of a low order question?**

    A. Why is it important to recycle items in your home?

    B. Compare how glass and plastics are recycled.

    C. What items do we recycle in our county?

    D. Explain the importance of recycling in our county.

(Rigorous) (Skill 11.1)

89. **What would be espoused by Jerome Bruner?**

    A. Thought depends on the acquisition of operations

    B. Memory plays a significant role in cognitive growth

    C. Genetics is the most important factor for cognitive growth

    D. Enriched environments have significant effects on cognitive growth

(Easy) (Skill 11.1)

90. **When asking questions of students it is important to:**

    A. Ask questions the students can answer

    B. Provide numerous questions

    C. Provide questions at various levels

    D. Provide only a limited amount of questions

(Rigorous) (Skill 11.4)

91. **With the passage of the No Child Left Behind Act (NCLB), schools are required to develop action plans to improve student learning. Which of the following is not a part of this action plan?**

    A. Clearly defined goals for school improvement

    B. Clearly defined assessment plan

    C. Clearly defined timelines

    D. Clearly defined plans for addressing social skills improvement

(Rigorous) (Skill 12.1)

92. Mr. Smith is introducing the concept of photosynthesis to his class next week. In preparing for this lesson, he considers that this concept will be new to many of his students. Mr. Smith understands that his students' brains are like filing cabinets and that there is currently no file for photosynthesis in those cabinets. What does Mr. Smith need to do to ensure his students acquire the necessary knowledge?

   A. Help them create a new file

   B. Teach the students the information; they will organize it themselves in their own way

   C. Find a way to connect the new learning to other information they already know

   D. Provide many repetitions and social situations during the learning process

(Rigorous) (Skill 12.1)

93. Curriculum mapping is an effective strategy because it:

   A. Provides an orderly sequence to instruction

   B. Provides lesson plans for teachers to use and follow

   C. Ties the curriculum into instruction

   D. Provides a clear map so all students receive the same instruction across all classes

(Rigorous) (Skill 13.1)

94. Mrs. Grant is providing her students with many extrinsic motivators in order to increase their intrinsic motivation. Which of the best explains this relationship?

   A. This relationship is good and will increase intrinsic motivation

   B. The relationship builds animosity between the teacher and the students

   C. Extrinsic motivation does not in itself help to build intrinsic motivation

   D. There is no place for extrinsic motivation in the classroom

(Average) (Skill 13.5)

95. What is one way of effectively managing student conduct?

   A. State expectations about behavior

   B. Let students discipline their peers

   C. Let minor infractions of the rules go unnoticed

   D. Increase disapproving remarks

(Rigorous) (Skill 13.5)

96. How can mnemonic devices be used to increase achievement?

   A. They help the child rehearse the information

   B. They help the child visually imagine the information

   C. They help the child to code information

   D. They help the child reinforce concepts

(Rigorous) (Skill 13.5)

97. The success-oriented classroom is designed to ensure students are successful at attaining new skills. In addition, mistakes are viewed as _____ in this type of classroom.

   A. motivations to improve

   B. a natural part of the learning process

   C. ways to improve

   D. building blocks

(Easy) (Skill 13.6)

98. Which statement is an example of specific praise?

   A. John, you are the only person in class not paying attention.

   B. William, I thought we agreed that you would turn in all of your homework.

   C. Robert, you did a good job staying in line. See how it helped us get to music class on time?

   D. Class, you did a great job cleaning up the art room.

(Average) (Skill 13.6)

99. What is one way a teacher can supplement verbal praise?

   A. Help students evaluate their own performance and supply self-reinforcement

   B. Give verbal praise more frequently

   C. Give tangible rewards such as stickers or treats

   D. Have students practice giving verbal praise

(Average) (Skill 13.6)

100. What is a frequently used type of feedback to students?

   A. Correctives

   B. Simple praise–confirmation

   C. Correcting the response

   D. Explanations

(Rigorous) (Skill 13.6)

101. The teacher responds, "Yes, that is correct" to a student's answer. What is this an example of?

   A. Academic feedback

   B. Academic praise

   C. Simple positive response

   D. Simple negative response

(Average) (Skill 13.6)

102. Which of the following is not a characteristic of effective praise?

   A. Praise is delivered in front of the class so it will serve to motivate others

   B. Praise is low-key

   C. Praise provides information about student competence

   D. Praise is delivered contingently

(Average) (Skill 14.1)

103. What is NOT a way that teachers show acceptance and give value to a student response?

   A. Acknowledging

   B. Correcting

   C. Discussing

   D. Amplifying

(Average) (Skill 14.1)

104. **Which of the following is a definition of an intercultural communication model?**

    — A. Learning how different cultures engage in both verbal and nonverbal modes to communicate meaning

    B. Learning how classmates engage in both verbal and nonverbal modes to communicate meaning

    C. Learning how classmates engage in verbal dialogues

    D. Learning how different cultures engage in verbal modes to communicate meaning

(Average) (Skill 14.2)

105. **How can the teacher establish a positive climate in the classroom?**

    A. Help students see the unique contributions of individual differences

    B. Use whole group instruction for all content areas

    C. Help students divide into cooperative groups based on ability

    D. Eliminate teaching strategies that allow students to make choices

(Average) (Skill 14.4)

106. **Wait-time has what effect?**

    A. Gives structure to the class discourse

    — B. Fewer chain and low-level questions are asked with more higher-level questions included

    C. Gives the students time to evaluate, the response

    D. Gives the opportunity for in-depth discussion about the topic

(Rigorous) (Skill 14.4)

107. **When is optimal benefit reached when handling an incorrect student response?**

    A. When specific praise is used

    B. When the other students are allowed to correct that student

    — C. When the student is redirected to a better problem-solving approach

    D. When the teacher asks simple questions, provides cues to clarify, or gives assistance for working out the correct response

(Average) (Skill 14.4)

108. **What is an effective amount of "wait time?"**

    A. 1 second

    — B. 5 seconds

    C. 15 seconds

    D. 10 seconds

(Easy) (Skill 14.4)

109. **Which of the following can impact the desire of students to learn new material?**

    A. Assessments plan

    B. Lesson plans

    — C. Enthusiasm

    D. School community

(Average) (Skill 14.6)

110. **When are students more likely to under-stand complex ideas?**

   A. If they do outside research before coming to class

   B. Later when they write out the defini-tions of complex words

   C. When they attend a lecture on the subject

   — D. When they are clearly defined by the teacher and are given examples and nonexamples of the concept

(Easy) (Skill 15.1)

111. **How can DVDs be used in instruction?**

   A. Students can use the DVD to create pictures for reports

   B. Students can use the DVD to create a science experiment

   C. Students can use the DVD to record class activities

   —D. Students can use the DVD to review concepts studied

(Easy) (Skill 15.1)

112. **How can students use a computer desktop publishing center?**

   A. To set up a classroom budget

   B. To create student-made books

   C. To design a research project

   D. To create a classroom behavior management system

(Average) (Skill 15.1)

113. **Which of the following is NOT a part of the hardware of a computer system?**

   A. Storage device

   B. Input devices

   —C. Software

   D. Central processing unit

(Rigorous) (Skill 15.2)

114. **What is one benefit of amplifying a student's response?**

   A. It helps the student develop a positive self-image

   B. It is helpful to other students who are in the process of learning the reason-ing or steps in answering the question

   C. It allows the teacher to cover more content

   D. It helps to keep the information organized

(Average) (Skill 15.3)

115. **Which of the following statements is true about computers in the classroom?**

   A. Computers are simply a glorified game machine and just allow students to play games

   B. The computer should replace tra-ditional research and writing skills taught to school-age children

   C. Computers stifle the creativity of children

   D. Computers allow students to access information they may otherwise be unable to

(Average) (Skill 15.3)

116. While an asset to students, technology is also important for teachers. Which of the following can be taught using technology to students?

   A. Cooperation skills

   B. Decision-making skills

   C. Problem solving skills

   D. All of the above

(Easy) (Skill 15.3)

117. As a classroom teacher, you have data on all of your students that you must track over the remainder of the school year. You will need to keep copies of the scores students receive and then graph their results to share progress with the parents an administrators. Which of the following software programs will be most useful in this manner?

   A. Word processing program

   B. Spreadsheet

   C. Database

   D. Teacher utility and classroom management tools

(Average) (Skill 15.3)

118. Which of the following statements is NOT true?

   A. Printing and distributing material off of the Internet breaks the copyright law

   B. Articles are only copyrighted when there is a © in the article

   C. E-mail messages that are posted online are considered copyrighted

   D. It is not legal to scan magazine articles and place on your district Web site

(Easy) (Skill 15.5)

119. The use of technology in the classroom allows for:

   A. More complex lessons

   B. Better delivery of instruction

   C. Variety of instruction

   D. Better ability to meet more individual student needs

The Professional Environment

(Easy) (Skill 16.5)

120. A district superintendent's job is to:

   A. Supervise senior teachers in the district

   B. Develop plans for school improvement

   C. Allocate community resources to individual schools

   D. Implement policies set by the board of education

(Average) (Skill 16.5)

121. Teacher's unions are involved in all of the following EXCEPT:

   A. Updating teachers on current educational developments

   B. Advocating for teacher rights

   C. Matching teachers with suitable schools

   D. Developing professional codes and practices

(Average) (Skill 17.1)

122. **What is a benefit of frequent self-assessment?**

A. Opens new venues for professional development

B. Saves teachers the pressure of being observed by others

C. Reduces time spent on areas not needing attention

D. Offers a model for students to adopt in self-improvement

(Average) (Skill 17.1)

123. **Which of the following could be used to improve teaching skills?**

A. Developing a professional development plan

B. Use of self-evaluation and reflection

C. Building professional learning communities

D. All of the above

(Rigorous) (Skill 17.2)

124. **Which of the following is NOT a sound educational practice for expanding the professional development opportunities for teachers?**

A. Looking at multiple methods of classroom management strategies

B. Training teachers in understanding and applying multiple assessment formats and implementations in curriculum and instruction

C. Having the students complete professional development assessments on a regular basis

D. Teaching teachers how to disaggregate student data in improving instruction and curriculum implementation for student academic equity and access

(Rigorous) (Skill 17.3)

125. **What would happen if a school utilized an integrated approach to professional development?**

A. All stakeholders needs are addressed

B. Teachers and administrators are on the same page

C. High-quality programs for students are developed

D. Parents drive the curriculum and instruction

(Average) (Skill 17.4)

126. **What must be a consideration when a parent complains that he can't control a child's behavior?**

A. Consider whether the parent gives feedback to the child

B. Consider whether the parent's expectations for control are developmentally appropriate

C. Consider how much time the parent spends with the child

D. Consider how rigid the rules are that the parent sets

(Average) (Skill 18.1)

127. **Which of the following should NOT be a purpose of a parent-teacher conference?**

A. To involve the parent in their child's education

B. To establish a friendship with the child's parents

C. To resolve a concern about the child's performance

D. To inform parents of positive behaviors by the child

(Easy) (Skill 18.1)

128. Mr. Brown wishes to improve his parent communication skills. Which of the following is a strategy he can utilize to accomplish this goal?

A. Hold parent-teacher conferences

B. Send home positive notes

C. Have parent nights where the parents are invited into his classroom

D. All of the above

(Easy) (Skill 18.1)

129. Tommy is a student in your class, and his parents are deaf. Tommy is struggling with math and you want to contact the parents to discuss the issues. How should you proceed?

A. Limit contact because of the parents' inability to hear

B. Use a TTY phone to communicate with the parents

C. Talk to your administrator to find an appropriate interpreter to help you communicate with the parents personally

D. Both B and C

(Easy) (Skill 18.1)

130. When communicating with parents for whom English is not the primary language you should:

A. Provide materials whenever possible in their native language

B. Use an interpreter

C. Provide the same communication as you would to native English speaking parents

D. All of the above

(Rigorous) (Skill 19.1)

131. Which of the following increases appropriate behavior more than 80 percent?

A. Monitoring the halls

B. Having class rules

C. Having class rules, giving feedback, and having individual consequences

D. Having class rules and giving feedback

(Average) (Skill 19.1)

132. A 16-year-old girl who has been looking sad writes an essay in which the main protagonist commits suicide. You overhear her talking about suicide. What do you do?

A. Report this immediately to school administration, talk to the girl, letting her know you will talk to her parents about it

B. Report this immediately to authorities

C. Report this immediately to school administration, make your own report to authorities if required by protocol in your school, and do nothing else

D. Just give the child some extra attention, as it may just be that's all she's looking for

(Rigorous) (Skill 19.1)

133. Jeanne, a bright, attentive student is in her first hour English class. She is quiet, but very alert, often visually scanning the room in random patterns. Her pupils are dilated, and she has a slight but noticeable tremor in her hands. She fails to note a cue given from her teacher. At odd moments, she will act as if responding to stimuli that aren't there by suddenly changing her gaze. When spoken to directly, she has a limited response, but her teacher has a sense she is not herself. What should the teacher do?

A. Ask the student if she is all right, then let it go, as there are not enough signals to be alarmed

B. Meet with the student after class to get more information before making a referral

C. Send the student to the office to see the nurse

—D. Quietly call for administration, remain calm, and be careful not to alarm the class

(Average) (Skill 19.1)

134. Which is true of child protective services?

A. They have been forced to become more punitive in their attempts to treat and prevent child abuse and neglect

—B. They have become more a means for identifying cases of abuse and less an agent for rehabilitation because of the large volume of cases

C. They have become advocates for structured discipline within the school

D. They have become a strong advocate in the court system

(Average) (Skill 19.1)

135. In successful inclusion of students with disabilities:

A. A variety of instructional arrangements are available

B. School personnel shift the responsibility for learning outcomes to the student

C. The physical facilities are used as they are

D. Regular classroom teachers have sole responsibility for evaluating student progress

(Average) (Skill 19.1)

136. How may a teacher use a student's permanent record?

— A. To develop a better understanding of the needs of the student

B. To record all instances of student disruptive behavior

C. To brainstorm ideas for discussing with parents at parent-teacher conferences

D. To develop realistic expectations of the student's performance early in the year

(Rigorous) (Skill 19.1)

137. You receive a phone call from a person who indicates she is now tutoring a student in your class. She would like you to provide an overview of the academic areas which the student is having difficulties. What is the first thing you should do?

 A. Find a time and talk with the tutor about issues you see within the classroom

 B. Call the parents

 C. Put together a packet of information to share with the tutor

 D. Offer to invite the tutor in to have a discussion and observe the child

(Rigorous) (Skill 19.2)

138. Marcus is a first grade boy of good developmental attainment. His learning progress is good the first half of the year. He shows no indicators of emotional distress. After the holiday break, he returns much changed. He is quieter, sullen even, tending to play alone. He has moments of tearfulness, sometimes almost without cause. He avoids contact with adults as often as he can. Even play with his friends has become limited. He has episodes of wetting not seen before and often wants to sleep in school. What approach is appropriate for this sudden change in behavior?

 A. Give him some time to adjust; the holiday break was probably too much fun to come back to school from

 B. Report this change immediately to administration; do not call the parents until administration decides a course of action

 C. Document his daily behavior carefully as soon as you notice such a change, report to administration the next month or so in a meeting

 D. Make a courtesy call to the parents to let them know he is not acting like himself, being sure to tell them he is not making trouble for others

(Rigorous) (Skill 19.2)

139. Andy shows up to class abusive and irritable. He is often late, sleeps in class, sometimes slurs his speech, and has an odor of alcohol. What is the first intervention to take?

 A. Confront him, relying on a trusting relationship you think you have

 B. Do a lesson on alcohol abuse, making an example of him

 C. Do nothing; it is better to err on the side of failing to identify substance abuse

 D. Call administration, avoid conflict, and supervise others carefully

(Average) (Skill 19.4)

140. A parent has left an angry message on the teacher's voicemail. The message relates to a concern about a student and is directed at the teacher. The teacher should:

   A. Call back immediately and confront the parent

   B. Cool off, plan what to discuss with the parent, then call back

   C. Question the child to find out what set off the parent

   D. Ignore the message, since feelings of anger usually

Answer Key

ANSWER KEY								
1. B	18. B	35. B	52. A	69. C	86. C	103. B	120. D	137. B
2. D	19. C	36. A	53. B	70. D	87. B	104. A	121. C	138. B
3. C	20. D	37. D	54. D	71. C	88. C	105. A	122. A	139. D
4. B	21. B	38. A	55. C	72. B	89. D	106. B	123. D	140. B
5. A	22. B	39. B	56. C	73. D	90. C	107. C	124. C	
6. B	23. D	40. A	57. D	74. A	91. D	108. B	125. C	
7. C	24. A	41. B	58. D	75. A	92. C	109. C	126. B	
8. C	25. A	42. D	59. A	76. B	93. A	110. D	127. B	
9. C	26. A	43. B	60. A	77. B	94. C	111. D	128. D	
10. B	27. A	44. B	61. C	78. B	95. A	112. B	129. D	
11. B	28. D	45. D	62. B	79. C	96. B	113. C	130. D	
12. D	29. D	46. C	63. A	80. A	97. B	114. B	131. C	
13. D	30. D	47. B	64. B	81. D	98. C	115. D	132. C	
14. A	31. C	48. B	65. D	82. C	99. A	116. D	133. D	
15. B	32. C	49. C	66. B	83. D	100. B	117. B	134. B	
16. B	33. D	50. B	67. D	84. A	101. C	118. B	135. A	
17. A	34. C	51. C	68. C	85. D	102. A	119. D	136. A	

Rigor Table

RIGOR TABLE	
Rigor level	**Questions**
Easy 20%	4, 10, 11, 24, 25, 28, 29, 31, 32, 34, 45, 52, 62, 70, 72, 74, 90, 98, 109, 111, 112, 117, 119, 120, 128, 129, 130
Average 40%	1, 2, 8, 12, 18, 19, 26, 33, 36, 39, 40, 42, 46, 49, 53, 54, 56, 58, 59, 61, 63, 64, 65, 68, 69, 71, 77, 78, 80, 81, 84, 87, 95, 99, 100, 102, 103, 104, 105, 106, 108, 110, 113, 115, 116, 118, 121, 122, 123, 126, 127, 132, 134, 135, 136, 140
Rigorous 40%	3, 5, 6, 7, 9, 13, 14, 15, 16, 17, 20, 21, 22, 23, 27, 30, 35, 37, 38, 41, 43, 44, 47, 48, 50, 51, 55, 57, 60, 66, 67, 73, 75, 76, 79, 82, 83, 85, 86, 88, 89, 91, 92, 93, 94, 96, 97, 101, 104, 107, 114, 124, 125, 131, 133, 137, 138, 139

Sample Test with Rationales: Student Development and Learning

Directions: Read each item and select the best response.

(Average) (Skill 1.1)

1. What developmental patterns should a professional teacher assess to meet the needs of the student?

    A. Academic, regional, and family background

    B. Social, physical, and academic

    C. Academic, physical, and family background

    D. Physical, family, and ethnic background

    Answer: B. Social, physical, and academic

    The effective teacher applies knowledge of physical, social, and academic developmental patterns and individual differences to meet the instructional needs of all students in the classroom. The most important premise of child development is that all domains of development (physical, social, and academic) are integrated. The teacher has a broad knowledge and thorough understanding of the development that typically occurs during the student's current period of life. More important, the teacher understands how children learn best during each period of development. An examination of the student's file coupled with ongoing evaluation assures a successful educational experience for both teacher and students.

(Average) (Skill 1.3)

2. Louise is a first grade teacher. She is planning her instructional activities for the week. In considering her planning, she should keep in mind that activities for this age of child should change how often?

    A. 25–40 minutes

    B. 30–40 minutes

    C. 5–10 minutes

    D. 15–30 minutes

    Answer: D. 15–30 minutes

    For young children, average activities should change about every twenty minutes.

(Rigorous) (Skill 2.1)

3. What are the two types of performance that teaching entails?

    A. Classroom management and questioning techniques

    B. Skill-building and analysis of outcomes

    C. Interaction with students and manipulation of subject matter

    D. Management techniques and levels of questioning

    Answer: C. Interaction with students and manipulation of subject matter

    The effective teacher develops her skills in both areas. Manipulation of subject matter begins with planning but is constantly tested and adjusted in the classroom. Even if she is very good at that, if she does not develop her skills for interacting with students successfully, she will not be successful.

(Easy) (Skill 2.2)

4. **What are the two ways concepts can be taught?**

   A. Factually and interpretively

   B. Inductively and deductively

   C. Conceptually and inductively

   D. Analytically and facilitatively

   Answer: B. Inductively and deductively

   Induction is reasoning from the particular to the general—that is, looking at a feature that exists in several examples and drawing a conclusion about that feature. Deduction is the reverse; it's the statement of the generality and then supporting it with specific examples.

(Rigorous) (Skill 2.2)

5. **What is one component of the instructional planning model that must be given careful evaluation?**

   A. Students' prior knowledge and skills

   B. The script the teacher will use in instruction

   C. Future lesson plans

   D. Parent participation

   Answer: A. Students' prior knowledge and skills

   The teacher will, of course, have certain expectations regarding where the students will be physically and intellectually when he plans for a new class. However, there will be wide variations in the actual classroom. If he doesn't make the extra effort to understand where there are deficiencies and where there are strengths in the individual students, the planning will probably miss the mark, at least for some members of the class. This information can be obtained through a review of student records, by observation, and by testing.

(Rigorous) (Skill 2.3)

6. **When using a kinesthetic approach, what would be an appropriate activity?**

   A. List

   B. Match

   C. Define

   D. Debate

   Answer: B. Match

   Brain lateralization theory emerged in the 1970s and demonstrated that the left hemisphere appeared to be associated with verbal and sequential abilities, whereas the right hemisphere appeared to be associated with emotions and with spatial, holistic processing. Although those particular conclusions continue to be challenged, it is clear that people concentrate, process, and remember new and difficult information under very different conditions. For example, auditory and visual perceptual strengths, passivity, and self-oriented or authority-oriented motivation often correlate with high academic achievement, whereas tactual and kinesthetic strengths, a need for mobility, nonconformity, and peer motivation often correlate with school underachievement (Dunn & Dunn, 1992, 1993). Understanding how students perceive the task of learning new information differently is often helpful in tailoring the classroom experience for optimal success.

(Rigorous) (Skill 2.3)

7. **Ms. Smith says, "Yes, exactly what do you mean by "It was the author's intention to mislead you." What does this illustrate?**

   A. Digression

   B. Restates response

   C. Probes a response

   D. Amplifies a response

Answer: C. Probes a response

From ancient times, notable teachers such as Socrates and Jesus have employed oral-questioning to enhance their discourse, stimulate thinking, and stir emotion among their audiences. Educational researchers and practitioners virtually all agree that teachers' effective use of questioning promotes student learning. Effective teachers continually develop their questioning skills.

(Average) (Skill 2.4)

8. **What are critical elements of instructional process?**

   A. Content, goals, teacher needs

   B. Means of getting money to regulate instruction

   C. Content, materials, activities, goals, learner needs

   D. Materials, definitions, assignments

Answer: C. Content, materials, activities, goals, learner needs

Goal setting is a vital component of the instructional process. The teacher will, of course, have overall goals for her class, both short-term and long-term. However, perhaps even more important than that is the setting of goals that take into account the individual learner's needs, background, and stage of development. Making an educational program child-centered involves building on the natural curiosity children bring to school and asking children what they want to learn. Student-centered classrooms contain not only textbooks, workbooks, and literature, but they also rely heavily on a variety of audiovisual equipment and computers. There are tape recorders, language masters, filmstrip projectors, and DVD players to help meet the learning styles of the students. Planning for instructional activities entails identification or selection of the activities the teacher and students will engage in during a period of instruction.

(Rigorous) (Skill 2.4)

9. **According to Piaget, what stage is characterized by the ability to think abstractly and to use logic?**

   A. Concrete operations

   B. Preoperational

   C. Formal operations

   D. Conservative operational

Answer: C. Formal operations

The four development stages are described in Piaget's theory:

1. *Sensorimotor* stage: from birth to age 2 years (children experience the world through movement and senses)

2. *Preoperational stage*: from ages 2 to 7 (acquisition of motor skills)

3. *Concrete operational stage*: from ages 7 to 11 (children begin to think logically about concrete events)

4. *Formal operational stage*: after age 11 (development of abstract reasoning)

These chronological periods are approximate and, in light of the fact that studies have demonstrated great variation between children, cannot be seen as rigid norms. Furthermore, these stages occur at different ages, depending upon the domain of knowledge under consideration. The ages normally given for the stages reflect when each stage tends to predominate even though one might elicit examples of two, three, or even all four stages of thinking at the same time from one individual, depending upon the domain of knowledge and the means used to elicit it.

(Easy) (Skill 2.4)

10. **How many stages of intellectual development does Piaget define?**

    A. Two

    B. Four

    C. Six

    D. Eight

Answer: B. Four

The stages are:

1. *Sensorimotor stage*: from birth to age 2 years (children experience the world through movement and senses)

2. *Preoperational stage*: from ages 2 to 7 (acquisition of motor skills)

3. *Concrete operational stage*: from ages 7 to 11 (children begin to think logically about concrete events)

4. *Formal operational stage*: after age 11 (development of abstract reasoning)

(Easy) (Skill 2.4)

11. **Who developed the theory of multiple intelligences?**

    A. Bruner

    B. Gardner

    C. Kagan

    D. Cooper

Answer: B. Gardner

Howard Gardner's most famous work is probably *Frames of Mind*, which details seven dimensions of intelligence (visual/spatial intelligence, musical intelligence, verbal intelligence, logical/mathematical intelligence, interpersonal intelligence, intrapersonal intelligence, and bodily/kinesthetic intelligence). Gardner's claim that pencil and paper IQ tests do not capture the full range of human intelligences has garnered much praise within the field of education but has also been met with criticism, largely from psychometricians. Since the publication of *Frames of Mind*, Gardner has additionally identified the eighth dimension of intelligence, naturalist intelligence, and is still considering a possible ninth—existentialist intelligence.

(Average) (Skill 2.4)

12. **Students who can solve problems mentally have:**

    A. Reached maturity

    B. Physically developed

    C. Reached the preoperational stage of thought

    D. Achieved the ability to manipulate objects symbolically

Answer: D. Achieved the ability to manipulate objects symbolically

When students are able to solve mental problems, it is an indication to the teacher that they have achieved the ability to manipulate objects symbolically and should be instructed to continue to develop their cognitive and academic skills.

(Rigorous) (Skill 2.5)

13. **Which description of the role of a teacher is no longer an accurate description?**

    A. Guide on the side

    B. Authoritarian

    C. Disciplinarian

    D. Sage on the stage

Answer: D. Sage on the stage

The old phrase of describing a teacher as a sage on the stage is no longer accurate. It is not the responsibility of the teacher to impart his or her knowledge on students. Teachers do not, nor should it be thought that they, have all of the answers. In contrast, it is the responsibility of the teacher to guide students through the learning process.

(Rigorous) (Skill 2.5)

14. **In the past, teaching has been viewed as _____ while in more current society it has been viewed as _____.**

    A. isolating, collaborative

    B. collaborative, isolating

    C. supportive, isolating

    D. isolating, supportive

Answer: A. isolating, collaborative

In the past, teachers often walked into their own classrooms and closed the door. They were not involved in any form of collaboration and were responsible for only the students within their classrooms. However, in today's more modern schools, teachers work in collaborative teams and are responsible for all of the children in a school setting.

(Rigorous) (Skill 2.6)

15. The teacher states, "We will work on the first page of vocabulary words. On the second page we will work on the structure and meaning of the words. We will go over these together and then you will write out the answers to the exercises on your own. I will be circulating to give help if needed." What is this an example of?

   A. Evaluation of instructional activity

   B. Analysis of instructional activity

   C. Identification of expected outcomes

   D. Pacing of instructional activity

Answer: B. Analysis of instructional activity

The successful teacher carefully plans all activities to foresee any difficulties in executing the plan. This planning also ensures that the directions being given to students will be clear, avoiding any misunderstanding.

(Rigorous) (Skill 2.6)

16. If teachers attend to content, instructional materials, activities, learner needs, and goals in instructional planning, what could be an outcome?

   A. Planning for the next year

   B. Effective classroom performance

   C. Elevated test scores on standardized tests

   D. More student involvement

Answer: B. Effective classroom performance

Another outcome will be teacher satisfaction in a job well done and in the performance of her students. Her days will have far fewer disruptions and her classroom will be easy to manage.

(Rigorous) (Skill 2.6)

17. When planning instruction, which of the following is an organizational tool to help ensure you are providing a well-balanced set of objectives?

   A. Using a taxonomy to develop objectives

   B. Determining prior knowledge skill levels

   C. Determining readiness levels

   D. Ensuring you meet the needs of diverse learners

Answer: A. Using a taxonomy to develop objectives

The use of a taxonomy, such as Bloom's, allows teachers to ensure that the students are receiving instruction at a variety of different levels. It is important that students are able to demonstrate skills and knowledge at a variety of different levels.

(Average) (Skill 3.4)

18. **What do cooperative learning methods all have in common?**

    A. Philosophy

    B. Cooperative task/cooperative reward structures

    C. Student roles and communication

    D. Teacher roles

    Answer: B. Cooperative task/cooperative reward structures.

    Cooperative learning situations, as practiced in today's classrooms, grew out of searches conducted by several groups in the early 1970s. Cooperative learning situations can range from very formal applications such as STAD (Student Teams-Achievement Divisions) and CIRC (Cooperative Integrated Reading and Composition) to less formal groupings known variously as "group investigation," "learning together," and "discovery groups." Cooperative learning as a general term is now firmly recognized and established as a teaching and learning technique in American schools. Because cooperative learning techniques are so widely diffused in the schools, it is necessary to orient students in the skills by which cooperative learning groups can operate smoothly and thereby enhance learning. Students who cannot interact constructively with other students will not be able to take advantage of the learning opportunities provided by the cooperative learning situations and will furthermore deprive their fellow students of the opportunity for cooperative learning.

(Average) (Skill 3.5)

19. **What is the definition of proactive classroom management?**

    A. Management that is constantly changing

    B. Management that is downplayed

    C. Management that gives clear and explicit instructions and rewarding compliance

    D. Management that is designed by the students

    Answer: C. Management that gives clear and explicit instructions and rewards compliance

    Classroom management plans should be in place when the school year begins. Developing a management plan takes a proactive approach—that is, decide what behaviors will be expected of the class as a whole, anticipate possible problems, and teach the behaviors early in the school year. Involving the students in the development of the classroom rules lets the students know the rationale for the rules and allows them to assume responsibility in the rules because they had a part in developing them.

(Rigorous) (Skill 3.7)

20. **According to recent studies, what is the estimated number of adolescents that have physical, social, or emotional problems related to the abuse of alcohol?**

    A. Less that one million

    B. 1–2 million

    C. 2–3 million

    D. More than four million

Answer: D. More than four million

Because of the egregious behavioral problems encountered in the teenage world today that have nothing to do with substance abuse but mimic its traits, discrimination is difficult. Predisposing behaviors indicating a tendency toward the use of drugs and alcohol usually are behaviors that suggest low self-esteem and as such might be indicated by academic failure, social maladaptation, antisocial behavior, truancy, disrespect, chronic rule breaking, aggression and anger, and depression. The student tending toward the use of drugs and alcohol will exhibit losses in social and academic functional levels that were previously attained. He may begin to experiment with substances.

(Rigorous) (Skill 4.1)

21. **Abigail has had intermittent hearing loss from the age of 1 through age 5 when she had tubes put in her ears. What is one area of development that may be affected by this?**

    A. Math

    B. Language

    C. Social skills

    D. None

Answer: B. Language

Frequent ear infections and intermittent hearing loss can significantly impair the development of language skills.

(Rigorous) (Skill 4.1)

22. **Active listening is an important skill for teachers to utilize with both students and teachers. Active listening involves all of the following strategies except…**

    A. Eye contact

    B. Restating what the speaker has said

    C. Clarification of speaker statements

    D. Open and receptive body language

Answer: B. Restating what the speaker has said

While it is often taught that it is important to restate conversations during meetings, when you are active listening it is more appropriate to seek clarification rather than simply restating.

(Rigorous) (Skill 4.3)

23. **Students who are learning English as a second language often require which of the following to process new information?**

    A. Translators

    B. Reading tutors

    C. Instruction in their native language

    D. Additional time and repetitions

Answer: D. Additional time and repetitions

While there are varying thoughts and theories on the most appropriate instruction for ESOL students, much ground can be gained by simply providing additional repetitions and time for new concepts. It is important to include visuals and the other senses into every aspect of this instruction.

(Easy) (Skill 4.3)

24. **Many of the current ESOL approaches used in classrooms today are based on which approach?**

    A. Social Learning Methods

    B. Native Tongue Methods

    C. ESOL Learning Methods

    D. Special Education Methods

    Answer: A. Social Learning Methods

    Placing students in mixed groups and pairing them with native speakers, ESOL students are given the opportunities to practice English in a more natural setting.

(Easy) (Skill 4.3)

25. **Which of the following is the last stage of second language acquisition according to the theories of Stephen Krashen?**

    A. The affective filter hypothesis

    B. The input hypothesis

    C. The natural order hypothesis

    D. The monitor hypothesis

    Answer: A. The affective filter hypothesis

    According to Stephen Krashen's theories the five principles are:

    1. The acquisition-learning hypothesis

    2. The monitor hypothesis

    3. The natural order hypothesis

    4. The input hypothesis

    5. The affective filter hypothesis

(Average) (Skill 4.4)

26. **If a student has a poor vocabulary, the teacher should recommend that:**

    A. The student read newspapers, magazines, and books on a regular basis

    B. The student enroll in a Latin class

    C. The student write the words repetitively after looking them up in the dictionary

    D. The student use a thesaurus to locate synonyms and incorporate them into her vocabulary

    Answer: A. The student read newspapers, magazines, and books on a regular basis

    It is up to the teacher to help the student choose reading material, but the student must be able to choose where she will search for the reading pleasure indispensable for enriching vocabulary.

(Rigorous) (Skill 4.4)

27. **All of the following are true about phonological awareness EXCEPT:**

    A. It may involve print

    B. It is a prerequisite for spelling and phonics

    C. Activities can be done by the children with their eyes closed

    D. Starts before letter recognition is taught

    Answer: A. It may involve print

    The key word here is EXCEPT, which will be highlighted in upper case on the test as well. All of the options are correct aspects of phonological awareness except the first one, because phonological awareness *does not* involve print.

(Easy) (Skill 4.4)

28. **The arrangement and relationship of words in sentences or sentence structure best describes:**

    A. Style

    B. Discourse

    C. Thesis

    D. Syntax

    Answer: D. Syntax

    Syntax is the grammatical structure of sentences.

(Easy) (Skill 4.4)

29. **Which of the following is not a technique of prewriting?**

    A. Clustering

    B. Listing

    C. Brainstorming

    D. Proofreading

    Answer: D. Proofreading

    Proofreading cannot be a method of prewriting, because it is done on already written texts only.

(Rigorous) (Skill 4.5)

30. **One of the many ways in which a child can demonstrate comprehension of a story is by:**

    A. Filling in a strategy sheet

    B. Retelling the story orally

    C. Retelling the story in writing

    D. All of the above

Answer: D. All of the above

All of the choices provided show different ways in which students can demonstrate the comprehension of a story.

(Easy) (Skill 4.5)

31. **Greg Ball went to an author signing where Faith Ringgold gave a talk about one of her many books. He was so inspired by her presence and by his reading of her book *Tar Beach* that he used the book for his reading and writing workshop activities. His supervisor wrote in his plan book that he was pleased that Greg had used the book as an/a _____ book.**

    A. basic

    B. feature

    C. anchor

    D. focus

    Answer: C. anchor

    A book that is used to teach reading and writing is called an anchor book.

(Easy) (Skill 5.1)

32. **Which of the following is an example of a restriction within the affective domain?**

    A. Unable to think abstractly

    B. Inability to synthesize information

    C. Inability to concentrate

    D. Inability complete physical activities

Answer: C. Inability to concentrate

The affective domain refers to such things as concentration, focus, lack of participation, inability to express one's self, and inconsistent behavior. Areas of the affective domain may affect other domains such as the cognitive or physical.

(Average) (Skill 5.2)

33. **What is a good strategy for teaching ethnically diverse students?**

    A. Don't focus on the students' culture

    B. Expect them to assimilate easily into your classroom

    C. Imitate their speech patterns

    D. Include ethnic studies in the curriculum

Answer: D. Include ethnic studies in the curriculum

Exploring a student's own cultures increases their confidence levels in the group. It is also a very useful tool when students are struggling to develop identities that they can feel comfortable with. The bonus is that this is good training for living in the world.

(Easy) (Skill 5.2)

34. **Which of the following is an accurate description of ESL students?**

    A. Remedial students

    B. Exceptional education students

    C. Are not a homogeneous group

    D. Feel confident in communicating in English when with their peers

Answer: C. Are not a homogeneous group

Because ESL students are often grouped in classes that take a different approach to teaching English than those for native speakers, it's easy to assume that they all present with the same needs and characteristics. Nothing could be further from the truth, even in what they need when it comes to learning English. It's important that their backgrounds and personalities be observed just as with native speakers. It was very surprising several years ago when Vietnamese children began arriving in American schools with little training in English and went on to excel in their classes, often even beyond their American counterparts. In many schools, there were Vietnamese merit scholars in the graduating classes.

(Rigorous) (Skill 5.2)

35. **What is an effective way to help a non-English speaking student succeed in class?**

    A. Refer the child to a specialist

    B. Maintain an encouraging, success-oriented atmosphere

    C. Help them assimilate by making them use English exclusively

    D. Help them cope with the content materials you currently use

Answer: B. Maintain an encouraging, success-oriented atmosphere

Anyone who is in an environment where his language is not the standard is likely to feel embarrassed and inferior. The student who is in that situation expects to fail. Encouragement is even more important for these students. They need many opportunities to succeed.

(Average) (Skill 5.2)

36. **How can text be modified for low-level ESOL students?**

    A. Add visuals and illustrations

    B. Let students write definitions

    C. Change text to a narrative form

    D. Have students write details out from the text

Answer: A. Add visuals and illustrations

No matter what name we put on it, a book is a book. If students can see the object, not only will they be able to compare their own word for it, a useful tool in learning a new language, but the object can serve as a mnemonic device. The teacher might use actual objects in a classroom to facilitate learning the new language.

(Rigorous) (Skill 5.2)

37. **Etienne is an ESOL student. He has begun to engage in conversation, which produces a connected narrative. In what developmental stage for second language acquisition is he?**

    A. Early production

    B. Speech emergence

    C. Preproduction

    D. Intermediate fluency

Answer: D. Intermediate fluency

Attaining total fluency usually takes several years, although the younger the learner, the shorter the time it takes.

(Rigorous) (Skill 5.2)

38. **What is a roadblock to second language learning?**

    A. Students are forced to speak

    B. Students speak only when ready

    C. Mistakes are considered a part of learning

    D. The focus is on oral communication

Answer: A. Students are forced to speak

It's embarrassing for anyone who is in a foreign language environment to be forced to expose his inability to use that language before she is ready. Being flexible with these students until they're ready to try their wings will shorten the time it will take to approach fluency.

(Average) (Skill 5.2)

39. **Why is praise for compliance important in classroom management?**

    A. Students will continue deviant behavior

    B. Desirable conduct will be repeated

    C. It reflects simplicity and warmth

    D. Students will fulfill obligations

Answer: B. Desirable conduct will be repeated

The tried-and-true principle that behavior that is rewarded will be repeated is demonstrated here. If other students laugh at a child's misbehavior, that child will repeat it. On the other hand, if the teacher rewards the behaviors she wants to see repeated, it is likely to happen.

(Average) (Skill 5.4)

40. Which of the following is not a communication issue that is related to diversity within the classroom?

   A. Learning disorder

   B. Sensitive terminology

   C. Body language

   D. Discussing differing viewpoints and opinions

   Answer: A. Learning disorders

   Learning disorders, while they may have a foundation in the specific communication skills of a student, are not in and of themselves a communication issue related to diversity within the classroom.

(Rigorous) (Skill 6.2)

41. Mr. Ryan has proposed to his classroom that the students may demonstrate understanding of the unit taught in a variety of ways including: taking a test, writing a paper, creating an oral presentation, or building a model or project. Which of the following areas of differentiation has Mr. Ryan demonstrated?

   A. Synthesis

   B. Product

   C. Content

   D. Product

   Answer: B. Product

   There are three ways to differentiate instruction: content, process, and product. In the described case, Mr. Ryan has chosen to provide the students with alternate opportunities to produce knowledge; therefore, the product is the area being differentiated.

(Average) (Skill 6.2)

42. When creating and selecting materials for instruction, teachers should complete which of the following steps:

   A. Make them relevant to the prior knowledge of the students

   B. Allow for a variation of learning styles

   C. Choose alternative teaching strategies

   D. All of the above

   Answer: D. All of the above

   It is imperative that when creating and selecting materials for instruction that teachers consider many different factors; this makes the planning for instruction a difficult and somewhat time consuming process. Numerous factors must be balanced in order to deliver the most appropriate and beneficial instruction to students.

(Rigorous) (Skill 6.4)

43. Mr. Weiss understands that it is imperative that students who are struggling with acquiring concepts at a specific grade level can still benefit from participating in whole classroom discussions and lessons. In fact, such students should be required to be present for whole classroom lessons. Mr. Weiss's beliefs fall under which of the following principles?

   A. Self-fulfilling prophecy

   B. Partial participation

   C. Inclusion

   D. Heterogeneous grouping

Answer: B. Partial participation

The concept of partial participation indicates that children, even those struggling, can participate in complex concepts at least to a partial degree. While they may not be able to complete all of the requirements of a lesson objective, they may be able complete portions of the objective and will benefit from that additional learning in a positive manner.

Sample Test with Rationales: Instruction and Assessment

(Rigorous) (Skill 7.1)

44. **Reducing off-task time and maximizing the amount of time students spend attending to academic tasks is closely related to which of the following?**

    A. Using whole class instruction only

    B. Business-like behaviors of the teacher

    C. Dealing only with major teaching functions

    D. Giving students a maximum of two minutes to come to order

Answer: B. Business-like behaviors of the teacher

The effective teacher continually evaluates his own physical/mental/social/emotional well-being with regard to the students in his classroom. There is always the tendency to satisfy social and emotional needs through relationships with the students. A good teacher genuinely likes his students, and that's a positive thing. However, if students are not convinced that the teacher's purpose for being there is to get a job done, the atmosphere in the classroom becomes difficult to control. This is the job of the teacher. Maintaining a business-like approach in the classroom yields many positive results. It's similar to a benevolent boss.

(Easy) (Skill 7.1)

45. **While teaching, three students cause separate disruptions. The teacher selects the major one and tells that student to desist. What is the teacher demonstrating?**

    A. Deviancy spread

    B. Correct target desist

    C. Alternative behavior

    D. Desist major deviance

Answer: D. Desist major deviance

When the teacher attempts to desist a deviancy, what she says and how it is said directly influence the probability of stopping the misbehavior. The effective teacher demonstrates awareness of what the entire class is doing and is in control of the behavior of all students even when she is working with only a small group of children. In an attempt to prevent student misbehaviors, the teacher makes clear, concise statements about what is happening in the classroom, directing attention to content and the students' accountability for their work rather than focusing the class on the misbehavior. It is also effective for the teacher to make a positive statement about the appropriate behavior that is observed. If deviant behavior does occur, the effective teacher will specify who the deviant is, what the student is doing wrong, and why this is unacceptable conduct or what the proper conduct would be. When more than one student is disrupting the class, it is wise to focus on the one that is causing the greatest problem. This is usually sufficient to bring the others into line. This can be a difficult task to accomplish, as the teacher must maintain academic focus and flow while addressing and desisting misbehavior. The teacher must make clear, brief statements about the expectations without raising her voice and without disrupting instruction.

(Average) (Skill 7.2)

46. **What must occur for seatwork to be effective?**

    A. All seatwork is graded immediately

    B. All seatwork should be explained by another student for clarification

    C. The teacher should monitor and provide corrective feedback for seatwork

    D. Seatwork should be a review of the previous day's lesson

Answer: C. The teacher should monitor and provide corrective feedback for seatwork

This period should not be seen as free time for the teacher when she can plan tomorrow's class or grade papers. She should be circulating among the students, observing what they are doing, and commenting in positive ways so that the time is spent profitably by the class in achieving the goals for that particular lesson.

(Rigorous) (Skill 7.2)

47. **Mrs. Peck wants to justify the use of personalized learning community to her principal. Which of the following reasons should she use?**

    A. They build multiculturalism

    B. They provide a supportive environment to address academic and emotional needs

    C. They builds relationships between students that promote lifelong learning

    D. They are proactive in their nature

Answer: B. They provide a supportive environment to address academic and emotional needs

While professional learning communities do provide all of the choices, this question asks for a justification statement. The best justification of those choices provided for implementing a personalized learning community in a classroom is to provide a supportive environment to help address the academic and emotional needs of her students.

(Rigorous) (Skill 7.2)

48. Mrs. Potts has noticed an undercurrent of an unsettled nature in her classroom. She is in the middle of her math lesson but still notices that many of her students seem to be having some sort of difficulty. Mrs. Potts stops class and decides to have a class meeting. She understands that even though her math objectives are important, it is equally important to address whatever is troubling her classroom. What is it Mrs. Potts knows?

A. Discipline is important

B. Social issues can impact academic learning

C. Maintaining order is important

D. Social skills instruction is important

Answer: B. Social issues can impact academic learning

Mrs. Potts understands that as long as there is a social situation or issue in the classroom, it is unlikely that any academics she presents will be learned. All of those areas instructed are important; however, it is this understanding of the fact that the academics will be impacted that is important in this particular situation as she is interrupting her math instruction.

(Average) (Skill 7.2)

49. Which of the following could be an example of a situation that could have an effect on a student's learning and academic progress?

A. Relocation

B. Abuse

C. Both of the above

D. Neither of the above

Answer: C. Both of the above

An unlimited number of situations can affect a student's learning. Teachers need to keep these situations in mind when teaching. Students are whole people and, just as stress affects us as adults, children experience the same feelings. They usually do not have the same toolbox that adults have to deal with the feelings and may require some additional guidance.

(Rigorous) (Skill 7.2)

50. Mrs. Graham has taken the time to reflect, completed observations, and asked for feedback about the interactions between her and her students from her principal. It is obvious by seeking this information out that Mrs. Graham understands which of the following?

A. The importance of clear communication with the principal

B. She needs to analyze her effectiveness of classroom interactions

C. She is clearly communicating with the principal

D. She cares about her students

Answer: B. She needs to analyze her effectiveness of classroom interactions

Utilizing reflection, observations, and feedback from peers or supervisors, teachers can help to build their own understanding of how they interact with students. In this way, they can better analyze their effectiveness at building appropriate relationships with students.

(Rigorous) (Skill 7.3)

51. What has been established to increase student originality, intrinsic motivation, and higher-order thinking skills?

A. Classroom climate

B. High expectations

C. Student choice

D. Use of authentic learning opportunities

Answer: C. Student choice

While all of the descriptors are good attributes for students to demonstrate, research has shown that providing student choice can increase all of the described factors.

(Easy) (Skill 7.3)

52. Which of the following can be measured utilizing the following types of assessments: direct observation, role playing, context observation, and teacher ratings?

A. Social skills

B. Reading skills

C. Math skills

D. Need for specialized instruction

Answer: A. Social skills

Social skills can be measured using the listed types of assessments. They can also be measured using sociometric measures including peer nomination, peer rating, and paired-comparison.

(Average) (Skill 7.5)

53. What would improve planning for instruction?

A. Describe the role of the teacher and student

B. Evaluate the outcomes of instruction

C. Rearrange the order of activities

D. Give outside assignments

Answer: B. Evaluate the outcomes of instruction

Important as it is to plan content, materials, activities, and goals and then taking into account learner needs in order to base what goes on in the classroom on the results of that planning, it makes no difference if students are not able to demonstrate improvement in the skills being taught. An important part of the planning process is for the teacher to constantly adapt all aspects of the curriculum to what is actually happening in the classroom. Planning frequently misses the mark or fails to allow for unexpected factors. Evaluating the outcomes of instruction regularly and making adjustments accordingly will have a positive impact on the overall success of a teaching methodology.

(Average) (Skill 7.5)

54. **How can student misconduct be redirected at times?**

    A. The teacher threatens the students

    B. The teacher assigns detention to the whole class

    C. The teacher stops the activity and stares at the students

    D. The teacher effectively handles changing from one activity to another

Answer: D. The teacher effectively handles changing from one activity to another

Appropriate verbal techniques include a soft nonthreatening voice void of undue roughness, anger, or impatience regardless of whether the teacher is instructing, providing student alerts, or giving a behavior reprimand. Verbal techniques that may be effective in modifying student behavior include simply stating the student's name and explaining briefly and succinctly what the student is doing that is inappropriate and what the student should be doing. Verbal techniques for reinforcing behavior include both encouragement and praise delivered by the teacher. In addition, for verbal techniques to positively affect student behavior and learning, the teacher must give clear, concise directives while implying her warmth toward the students.

(Rigorous) (Skill 7.5)

55. **What have recent studies regarding effective teachers concluded?**

    A. Effective teachers let students establish rules

    B. Effective teachers establish routines by the sixth week of school

    C. Effective teachers state their own policies and establish consistent class rules and procedures on the first day of class

    D. Effective teachers establish flexible routines

Answer: C. Effective teachers state their own policies and establish consistent class rules and procedures on the first day of class

The teacher can get ahead of the game by stating clearly, on the first day of school, exactly what the rules are. These should be stated firmly but unemotionally. When one of those rules is broken, he can then refer to the rules, rendering enforcement much easier to achieve. It's extremely difficult to achieve goals with students who are out of control. Establishing limits early and consistently enforcing them enhances learning. It is also helpful for the teacher to prominently display the classroom rules. This will serve as a visual reminder of the students' expected behaviors. In a study of classroom management procedures, it was established that the combination of conspicuously displayed rules, frequent verbal references to the rules, and appropriate consequences for appropriate behaviors led to increased levels of on-task behavior.

(Average) (Skill 7.5)
56. **To maintain the flow of events in the classroom, what should an effective teacher do?**

    A. Work only in small groups

    B. Use only whole class activities

    C. Direct attention to content rather than focusing the class on misbehavior

    D. Follow lectures with written assignments

Answer: C. Direct attention to content rather than focusing the class on misbehavior

Students who misbehave often do so to attract attention. Focusing the attention of the misbehaver as well as the rest of the class on the real purpose of the classroom sends the message that misbehaving will not be rewarded with class attention to the misbehaver. Engaging students in content by using the various tools available to the creative teacher goes a long way in ensuring a peaceful classroom.

(Rigorous) (Skill 7.5)
57. **The concept of efficient use of time includes which of the following?**

    A. Daily review, seatwork, and recitation of concepts

    B. Lesson initiation, transition, and comprehension check

    C. Review, test, and review

    D. Punctuality, management transition, and wait time avoidance

Answer: D. Punctuality, management transition, and wait time avoidance

The "benevolent boss" applies here. One who succeeds in managing a business follows these rules; so does the successful teacher.

(Average) (Skill 7.5)

58. **What is a sample of an academic transition signal?**

    A. How do clouds form?

    B. Today we are going to study clouds.

    C. We have completed today's lesson.

    D. That completes the description of cumulus clouds. Now we will look at the description of cirrus clouds.

Answer: D. That completes the description of cumulus clouds. Now we will look at the description of cirrus clouds.

Transitions are language bridges between one topic and another. The teacher should thoughtfully plan transitions when several topics are going to be presented in one lesson to be sure that students are carried along. Without transitions, sometimes students are still focused on a previous topic and are lost in the discussion.

(Average) (Skill 8.1)

59. **When is utilization of instructional materials most effective?**

    A. When the activities are sequenced

    B. When the materials are prepared ahead of time

    C. When the students choose the pages to work on

    D. When the students create the instructional materials

Answer: A. When the activities are sequenced

Most assignments will require more than one educational principle. It is helpful to explain to students the proper order in which these principles must be applied to complete the assignment successfully. Subsequently, students should also be informed of the nature of the assignment (i.e., cooperative learning, group project, individual assignment). This is often done at the start of the assignment.

(Rigorous) (Skill 8.1)

60. **When considering the development of the curriculum, which of the following accurately describes the four factors that need to be considered?**

    A. Alignment, Scope, Sequence, and Design

    B. Assessment, Instruction, Design, and Sequence

    C. Data, Alignment, Correlation, and Score

    D. Alignment, Sequence, Design, and Assessment

Answer: A. Alignment, Scope, Sequence, and Design

When developing curriculum, it is important to first start with alignment. Alignment to state, national, or other standards is the first step. Next, the scope of the curriculum involves looking at the amount of material covered within a grade level or subject. Next, the sequence of material needs to be considered. Finally, it is important to look at the design of the units individually from beginning to end.

(Average) (Skill 8.2)

61. **What should be considered when evaluating textbooks for content?**

    A. Type of print used

    B. Number of photos used

    C. Free of cultural stereotyping

    D. Outlines at the beginning of each chapter

Answer: C. Free of cultural stereotyping

While textbook writers and publishers have responded to the need to be culturally diverse in recent years, a few texts are still being offered that don't meet these standards. When teachers have an opportunity to be involved in choosing textbooks, they can be watchdogs for the community in keeping the curriculum free of matter that reinforces bigotry and discrimination.

(Easy) (Skill 9.1)

62. **Which of the following is a presentation modification?**

    A. Taking an assessment in an alternate room

    B. Providing an interpreter to give the test in American Sign Language

    C. Allowing dictation of written responses

    D. Extending the time limits on an assessment

Answer: B. Providing an interpreter to give the test in American Sign Language

There are numerous types of modifications that can be provided to students in the classroom and for assessments. All of the described choices are appropriate modifications, but the only one that affects the presentation of the items is the one related to providing an interpreter.

(Average) (Skill 9.2)

63. **What should a teacher do when students have not responded well to an instructional activity?**

    A. Reevaluate learner needs

    B. Request administrative help

    C. Continue with the activity another day

    D. Assign homework on the concept

Answer: A. Reevaluate learner needs

The value of teacher observations cannot be underestimated. It is through the use of observations that the teacher is able to informally assess the needs of the students during instruction. These observations will drive the lesson and determine the direction that the lesson will take based on student activity and behavior. After a lesson is carefully planned, teacher observation is the single most important component of an instructional presentation. If the teacher observes that a particular student is not on-task, she will change the method of instruction accordingly. She may change from a teacher-directed approach to a more interactive approach. Questioning will increase in order to increase the participation of the students. If appropriate, the teacher will introduce manipulative materials to the lesson. In addition, teachers may switch to a cooperative group activity, thereby removing the responsibility of instruction from the teacher and putting it on the students.

(Average) (Skill 9.2)

64. **What is the best definition for an achievement test?**

    A. It measures mechanical and practical abilities

    B. It measures broad areas of knowledge that are the result of cumulative learning experiences

    C. It measures the ability to learn to perform a task

    D. It measures performance related to specific, recently acquired information

Answer: B. It measures broad areas of knowledge that are the result of cumulative learning experiences

The ways that a teacher uses test data is a meaningful aspect of instruction and may increase the motivation level of the students especially when this information is available in the form of feedback to the students. This feedback should indicate to the students what they need to do in order to improve their achievement. Frequent testing and feedback is most often an effective way to increase achievement.

(Average) (Skill 9.2)

65. **How are standardized tests useful in assessment?**

    A. For teacher evaluation

    B. For evaluation of the administration

    C. For comparison from school to school

    D. For comparison to the population on which the test was normed

Answer: D. For comparison to the population on which the test was normed.

While the efficacy of the standardized tests that are being used nationally has come under attack recently, they are actually the only device for comparing where an individual student stands with a wide range of peers. They also provide a measure for a program or a school to evaluate how their own students are doing as compared to the populace at large. Even so, they should not be the only measure upon which decisions are made or evaluations drawn. There are many other instruments for measuring student achievement that the teacher needs to consult and take into account.

(Rigorous) (Skill 9.2)

66. Which of the following test items is not objective?

    A. Multiple choice

    B. Essay

    C. Matching

    D. True or false

Answer: B: Essay

Because you need to use a rubric and there are various interpretations of this type of assessment, it is not objective.

(Rigorous) (Skill 9.2)

67. Which of the following is NOT used in evaluating test items?

    A. Student feedback

    B. Content validity

    C. Reliability

    D. Ineffective coefficient

Answer: D. Ineffective coefficient

The purpose for testing the students is to determine the extent to which the instructional objectives have been met. Therefore, the test items must be constructed to achieve the desired outcome from the students. Gronlund and Linn advise that effective tests begin with a test plan that includes the instructional objectives and subject matter to be tested, as well as the emphasis each item should have. Having a test plan will result in valid interpretation of student achievement.

(Average) (Skill 9.2)

68. Safeguards against bias and discrimination in the assessment of children include:

    A. The testing of a child in standard English

    B. The requirement for the use of one standardized test

    C. The use of evaluative materials in the child's native language or other mode of communication

    D. All testing performed by a certified, licensed psychologist

Answer: C. The use of evaluative materials in the child's native language or other mode of communication

The law requires that the child be evaluated in his native language or mode of communication. The idea that a licensed psychologist evaluate the child does not meet the criteria if it is not done in the child's normal mode of communication.

(Average) (Skill 9.3)

69. On intelligence quotient scales, what is the average intelligence score?

    A. 100–120

    B. 60–80

    C. 90–110

    D. 80–100

Answer: C. 90–110

The use of a general index of cognitive ability raises technical issues that have attracted the attention of developmental researchers for many years. These issues are:

1. Whether IQ is an important developmental construct that is predictive of significant life outcomes

2. Whether IQ is changeable and whether changes in IQ are meaningful

3. Whether these changes are due primarily to error or are systematic

4. The degree, if any, to which there is continuity or discontinuity in IQ during different developmental stages

5. Whether other individual-difference variables are predictive of those life-quality indicators that are traditionally linked to IQ

These issues are relevant for the teacher, who should be cautioned to pay attention to the reported IQs of her students but not to take them as the final word for a particular student's capabilities. As we all know, tests can often err badly for all kinds of reasons, not the least of which is the state of mind of the subject at the time of the test. The teacher's own observations are more important in determining where to start with a particular student.

(Easy) (Skill 9.3)

70. **On what is evaluation of the instructional activity based?**

    A. Student grades

    B. Teacher evaluation

    C. Student participation

    D. Specified criteria

Answer: D. Specified criteria

The way that a teacher uses test data is a meaningful aspect of instruction and may increase the motivation level of the students, especially when this information takes the form of feedback to the students. However, in order for a test to be an accurate measurement of student progress, the teacher must know how to plan and construct tests. Perhaps the most important caveat in creating and using tests for classroom purposes is the old adage to test what you teach. Actually, it is better stated that you should teach what you plan to test. This second phrasing more clearly reflects the need for thorough planning of the entire instructional program. Before you begin instruction, you should have the assessment planned and defined. One common method of matching the test to the instruction is to develop a table of specifications, a two-way grid in which the objectives of instruction are listed on one axis and the content that has been presented is listed on the other axis. Then the individual cells are assigned percentages that reflect the focus and extent of instruction in each area. The final step is to distribute the number of questions to be used on the test among the cells of the table in proportion to the identified percentages.

(Average) (Skill 9.3)

71. **What is an example of formative feedback?**

    A. The results of an intelligence test

    B. Correcting the tests in small groups

    C. Verbal behavior that expresses approval of a student response to a test item

    D. Scheduling a discussion before the test

    Answer: C. Verbal behavior that expresses approval of a student response to a test item

    Standardized testing is currently under great scrutiny, but educators agree that any test that serves as a means of gathering and interpreting information about children's learning and that can provide accurate, helpful input for nurturing children's further growth is acceptable. All testing must be formative in nature. Formative evaluation is the basic, everyday kind of assessment that teachers continually do to understand students' growth and to help them learn further.

(Easy) (Skill 9.3)

72. **What does the validity of a test refer to?**

    A. Its consistency

    B. Its usefulness

    C. Its accuracy

    D. The degree of true scores it provides

Answer: B. Its usefulness

The joint technical standards for educational and psychological testing (APA, AERA, NCME, 1985) states: "Validity is the most important consideration in test evaluation. The concept refers to the appropriateness, meaningfulness, and usefulness of the specific inferences made from test scores. Test validation is the process of accumulating evidence to support such inferences. A variety of inferences may be made from scores produced by a given test, and there are many ways of accumulating evidence to support any particular inference. Validity, however, is a unitary concept. Although evidence may be accumulated in many ways, validity always refers to the degree to which that evidence supports the inferences that are made from test scores."

(Rigorous) (Skill 9.3)

73. **Which of the following describes why it is important and necessary for teachers to be able to analyze data on their students?**

    A. To provide appropriate instruction

    B. To make instructional decisions

    C. To communicate and determine instructional progress

    D. All of the above

Answer: D. All of the above

Especially in today's high stakes environment, it is critical teachers have a complete understanding of the process involved in examining student data in order to make instructional decisions, prepare lessons, determine progress, and report progress to stakeholders.

(Easy) (Skill 9.4)

74. **When a teacher wants to utilize an assessment that is subjective in nature, which of the following is the most effective method for scoring?**

   A. Rubric

   B. Checklist

   C. Alternative Assessment

   D. Subjective measures should not be utilized

Answer: A. Rubric

Rubrics are the most effective tool for assessing items that can be considered subjective. They provide the students with a clearer picture of teacher expectations and provide the teacher with a more consistent method of comparing this type of assignment.

(Rigorous) (Skill 9.5)

75. **What steps are important in the review of subject matter in the classroom?**

   A. A lesson-initiating review, topic, and a lesson-end review

   B. A preview of the subject matter, an in-depth discussion, and a lesson-end review

   C. A rehearsal of the subject matter and a topic summary within the lesson

   D. A short paragraph synopsis of the previous day's lesson and a written review at the end of the lesson

Answer: A. A lesson-initiating review, topic, and a lesson-end review

The effective teacher utilizes all three of these together with comprehension checks to make sure the students are processing the information. Lesson-end reviews are restatements (by the teacher or teacher and students) of the content of discussion at the end of a lesson. Subject matter retention increases when lessons include an outline at the beginning of the lesson and a summary at the end of the lesson. This type of structure is used in successful classrooms. Moreover, when students know what is coming next, and what is expected of them, they feel more a part of their learning environment and deviant behavior is lessened.

(Rigorous) (Skill 9.5)

76. The teacher states that the lesson the students will be engaged in will consist of a review of the material from the previous day, demonstration of the scientific of an electronic circuit, and small group work on setting up an electronic circuit. What has the teacher demonstrated?

   A. The importance of reviewing

   B. Giving the general framework for the lesson to facilitate learning

   C. Giving students the opportunity to leave if they are not interested in the lesson

   D. Providing momentum for the lesson

Answer: B. Giving the general framework for the lesson to facilitate learning

If children know where they're going, they're more likely to be engaged in getting there. It's important to give them a road map whenever possible for what is coming in their classes.

(Average) (Skill 9.5)

77. What is an effective way to prepare students for testing?

   A. Minimize the importance of the test

   B. Orient the students to the test by telling them of the purpose, how the results will be used, and how it is relevant to them

   C. Use the same format for every test are given

   D. Have them construct an outline to study from

Answer: B. Orient the students to the test by telling them of the purpose, how the results will be used, and how it is relevant to them

If a test is to be an accurate measure of achievement, it must test the information, not the format of the test itself. If students know ahead of time what the test will be like, why they are taking it, what the teacher will do with the results, and what it has to do with them, the exercise is more likely to result in a true measure of what they've learned.

(Average) (Skill 9.5)

78. How will students have a fair chance to demonstrate what they know on a test?

   A. When the examiner has strictly enforced rules for taking the test

   B. When the examiner provides a comfortable setting free of distractions and positively encourages the students

   C. When the examiner provides frequent stretch breaks to the students

   D. When the examiner stresses the importance of the test to the overall grade

Answer: B. When the examiner provides a comfortable setting free of distractions and positively encourages the students

Taking a test is intimidating to students at best. In addition, some students are unable to focus when there are distractions. Feeling that the teacher is on their side helps students relax and truly demonstrate what they have learned on a test.

(Rigorous) (Skill 9.5)

79. **Which of the following is the correct term for the alignment of the curriculum across all grades K-12?**

    A. Data-based decision making

    B. Curriculum mapping

    C. Vertical integration

    D. Curriculum alignment

Answer: C. Vertical integration

Curriculum mapping is the process of taking the curriculum and deciding when the information needs to be taught throughout the school year. Curriculum alignment involves the process of connecting the curriculum to something else (typically standards) to ensure that all areas are being taught. Vertical integration is the process of ensuring that the curriculum flows in an appropriate manner from the lowest levels to the highest levels in a logical and responsible manner.

(Average) (Skill 9.5)

80. **Which of the following information can NOT be gained by examining school level data in an in-depth manner?**

    A. Teacher effectiveness

    B. Educational trends within a school

    C. Student ability to meet state and national goals and objectives

    D. Ways to improve student learning goals and academic success

Answer: A. Teacher effectiveness

While to some degree student progress can provide information on the effectiveness of a teacher, looking only at statistical information may not provide a clear and accurate representation of the effectiveness of a teacher. For example, data showing that 75 percent of the students achieved the state goals may indicate that the teacher was not very effective. However, if in the previous year, only 10 percent of these same students achieved the state goals, the same data would provide a completely different picture on the effectiveness of this teacher.

(Average) (Skill 10.1)

81. **Which of following is NOT the role of the teacher in the instructional process:**

    A. Instructor

    B. Coach

    C. Facilitator

    D. Follower

Answer: D. Follower

The teacher demonstrates a variety of roles within the classroom. Teachers, however, should not be followers. They must balance all of their roles in an efficient way to ensure that instruction is delivered to meet the needs of his or her students.

(Rigorous) (Skill 10.2)

82. **Discovery learning is to inquiry as direct instruction is to…**

    A. Scripted lessons

    B. Well-developed instructions

    C. Clear instructions that eliminate all misinterpretations

    D. Creativity of teaching

    Answer: C. Clear instructions that eliminate all misinterpretations

    Direct instruction is a technique that relies on carefully, well-developed instructions and lessons that eliminate misinterpretations. In this manner, all students have the opportunity to acquire and learn the skills presented to the students. This approach limits teacher creativity to some extent, but has a good solid research-based following with much ability to replicate its results.

(Rigorous) (Skill 10.6)

83. **When developing lessons it is imperative teachers provide equity in pedagogy so:**

    A. Unfair labeling of students will not occur

    B. Student experiences will be positive

    C. Students will achieve academic success

    D. All of the above

    Answer: D. All of the above

    Providing equity of pedagogy allows for students to have positive learning experiences, achieve academic success, and helps to prevent the labeling of students in an unfair manner.

(Average) (Skill 10.6)

84. **Which of the following is a good reason to collaborate with a peer:**

    A. To increase your knowledge in areas where you feel you are weak, but the peer is strong

    B. To increase your planning time and that of your peer by combining the classes and taking more breaks

    C. To have fewer lesson plans to write

    D. To teach fewer subjects

    Answer: A. To increase your knowledge in areas where you feel you are weak, but the peer is strong

    Collaboration with a peer allows teachers to share ideas and information. In this way, the teacher is able to improve his skills and share additional information.

(Rigorous) (Skill 10.6)

85. **Which of the following are ways a professional can assess her teaching strengths and weaknesses?**

    A. Examining how many students were unable to understand a concept

    B. Asking peers for suggestions or ideas

    C. Self-evaluation/reflection of lessons taught

    D. All of the above

    Answer: D. All of the above

    It is important for teachers to involve themselves in constant periods of reflection and self-reflection to ensure they are meeting the needs of the students.

(Rigorous) (Skill 10.6)

86. Mr. German is a math coach. He is the only math coach in his building and, in fact, within his district. Mr. German believes it is imperative to seek out the support of colleagues to work in a more collaborative manner. Which of the following would be an appropriate step for him to take?

   A. Collaborating with other teachers in his building regardless of their skill level knowledge in his area

   B. Asking for the administration to find colleagues with whom he can collaborate

   C. Joining a professional organization such as the National Council of Teachers of Mathematics (NCTM)

   D. Searching the Internet for possible collaboration opportunities

Answer: C. Joining a professional organization such as the National Council of Teachers of Mathematics (NCTM)

Joining a professional organization, such as NCTM, would provide Mr. German with the ability to learn and update his own knowledge specifically in his field of study and also open up the opportunity for him to interact with colleagues in his field from across the country.

(Average) (Skill 11.1)

87. Why is it important for a teacher to pose a question before calling on students to answer?

   A. It helps manage student conduct

   B. It keeps the students as a group focused on the class work

   C. It allows students time to collaborate

   D. It gives the teacher time to walk among the students

Answer: B. It keeps the students as a group focused on the class work

It doesn't take much distraction for a class's attention to become diffused. Once this happens, effectively teaching a principle or a skill is very difficult. The teacher should plan presentations that will keep students focused on the lesson. A very useful tool is to use effective, well thought-out, pointed questions.

(Rigorous) (Skill 11.1)

88. What is an example of a low order question?

   A. Why is it important to recycle items in your home?

   B. Compare how glass and plastics are recycled.

   C. What items do we recycle in our county?

   D. Explain the importance of recycling in our county.

Answer: C. What items do we recycle in our county?

Remember that the difference between specificity and abstractness is a continuum. The most specific is something that is concrete and can be seen, heard, smelled, tasted, or felt, such as cans, bottles, and newspapers. At the other end of the spectrum is an abstraction, such as importance. Lower-order questions are on the concrete end of the continuum; higher-order questions are on the abstract end.

(Rigorous) (Skill 11.1)

89. **What would be espoused by Jerome Bruner?**

   A. Thought depends on the acquisition of operations

   B. Memory plays a significant role in cognitive growth

   C. Genetics is the most important factor for cognitive growth

   D. Enriched environments have significant effects on cognitive growth

Answer: D. Enriched environments have significant effects on cognitive growth

In "Selecting and Applying Learning Theory to Classroom Teaching Strategies," by Donald R. Coker and Jane White in *Education* (1993), they write: "Jerome Bruner poises the ultimate question for teachers when he asked, 'How do you teach something to a child, arrange a child's environment if you will, in such a way that he can learn something with some assurance that he will use the material that he has learned appropriately in a variety of situations?' When presented with this query, most teachers have difficulty responding even though their days are spent trying to accomplish this very purpose. Why do those of us who teach have such an apparent inability to define the nature of our instructional activities in terms of lasting benefit to the learner? Perhaps this dilemma results from confusion regarding basic concepts of how children learn.

When we honestly examine our own learning, the information we crammed into our heads for Friday's spelling test or Wednesday's history quiz is long gone.

What remains with us is typically learning we personally wanted or learning that actively involved us in the process, i.e., typing, sewing, woodworking, drama, acting, drafting, computers, writing, etc. A reflection on our own learning allows us to see what made the process work:

- Being taught by a teacher who knew more than we,

- Being interested and active in the learning process

- Learning to focus on ideas, concepts, and being encouraged to generalize

- Being teased into new areas of insight by teachers who encouraged risks, making mistakes, and learning from them

- Seeing connections between the new information and what we already knew

- Being taught by a mentor who expected us to succeed

- Being taught in an atmosphere of support, not anxiety and fear

- Seeing, talking, and doing made the task easier, while sitting quietly and listening was difficult

- Being allowed to choose from a variety of appropriate classroom activities

- Being responsible for our own learning

As teachers, we should examine our own teaching strategies and check them against criteria such as these in an effort to answer the question, 'Does my classroom allow for all of these conditions?'"

(Easy) (Skill 11.1)

90. **When asking questions of students it is important to:**

    A. Ask questions the students can answer

    B. Provide numerous questions

    C. Provide questions at various levels

    D. Provide only a limited amount of questions

    Answer: C. Provide questions at various levels

    Providing questions at various levels is essential to encourage deeper thinking and reflective thought processes.

(Rigorous) (Skill 11.4)

91. **With the passage of the No Child Left Behind Act (NCLB), schools are required to develop action plans to improve student learning. Which of the following is not a part of this action plan?**

    A. Clearly defined goals for school improvement

    B. Clearly defined assessment plan

    C. Clearly defined timelines

    D. Clearly defined plans for addressing social skills improvement

    Answer: D. Clearly defined plans for addressing social skills improvement

    The school action plan as related to NCLB should address all of the following areas:

    - Clearly defined goals and objectives for student learning and school improvement

    - Clear alignment of goals and objectives

    - Developing clear timelines and accountability for goal implementation steps

    - Constructing an effective evaluation plan for assessing data around student performance and established objectives for student learning outcomes

    - Defining a plan B in case plan A falls short of meeting the goals and objectives for student achievement and school improvement

(Rigorous) (Skill 12.1)

92. **Mr. Smith is introducing the concept of photosynthesis to his class next week. In preparing for this lesson, he considers that this concept will be new to many of his students. Mr. Smith understands that his students' brains are like filing cabinets and that there is currently no file for photosynthesis in those cabinets. What does Mr. Smith need to do to ensure his students acquire the necessary knowledge?**

    A. Help them create a new file

    B. Teach the students the information; they will organize it themselves in their own way

    C. Find a way to connect the new learning to other information they already know

    D. Provide many repetitions and social situations during the learning process

Answer: C. Find a way to connect the new learning to other information they already know

While behavioral theories indicate that it is through socialization and multiple repetitions that students acquire new information, new research into the brain and how it works indicates that students learn best by making connections Therefore, it is imperative when teaching new concepts that teachers find a way to connect new information to previously learned material.

(Rigorous) (Skill 12.1)

93. **Curriculum mapping is an effective strategy because it:**

A. Provides an orderly sequence to instruction

B. Provides lesson plans for teachers to use and follow

C. Ties the curriculum into instruction

D. Provides a clear map so all students receive the same instruction across all classes

Answer: A. Provides an orderly sequence to instruction

Curriculum mapping is a strategy used to tie the actual curriculum with the support materials (textbooks) being utilized to support the teaching of said curriculum. Mapping is usually done to the month or quarter and provides a logical sequence to instruction so that all necessary skills and topics are covered in an appropriate fashion.

(Rigorous) (Skill 13.1)

94. **Mrs. Grant is providing her students with many extrinsic motivators in order to increase their intrinsic motivation. Which of the best explains this relationship?**

A. This relationship is good and will increase intrinsic motivation

B. The relationship builds animosity between the teacher and the students

C. Extrinsic motivation does not in itself help to build intrinsic motivation

D. There is no place for extrinsic motivation in the classroom

Answer: C. Extrinsic motivation does not in itself help to build intrinsic motivation

There are some cases where it is necessary to utilize extrinsic motivation; however, the use of extrinsic motivation is not alone a strategy to use to build intrinsic motivation. Intrinsic motivation comes from within the student themselves, while extrinsic motivation comes from outside parties.

(Average) (Skill 13.5)

95. **What is one way of effectively managing student conduct?**

A. State expectations about behavior

B. Let students discipline their peers

C. Let minor infractions of the rules go unnoticed

D. Increase disapproving remarks

Answer: A. State expectations about behavior

The effective teacher demonstrates awareness of what the entire class is doing and is in control of the behavior of all students even when the teacher is working with only a small group of children. In an attempt to prevent student misbehaviors, the teacher makes clear, concise statements about what is happening in the classroom, directing attention to content and the students' accountability for their work rather than focusing the class on the misbehavior. It is also effective for the teacher to make a positive statement about the appropriate behavior that is observed. If deviant behavior does occur, the effective teacher will specify who the deviant is, what he or she is doing wrong, and why this conduct is unacceptable or what the proper conduct would be. This task can be difficult to accomplish because the teacher must maintain academic focus and flow while addressing and desisting misbehavior. The teacher must make clear, brief statements about the expectations without raising his voice and without disrupting instruction.

(Rigorous) (Skill 13.5)

96. **How can mnemonic devices be used to increase achievement?**

    A. They help the child rehearse the information

    B. They help the child visually imagine the information

    C. They help the child to code information

    D. They help the child reinforce concepts

Answer: B. They help the child visually imagine the information

Mnemonics are verbal cues, something such as a very short poem or a special word used to help a person remember something, particularly lists. Mnemonics rely not only on repetition to remember facts but also on associations between easy-to-remember constructs and lists of data, based on the principle that the humanistic mind much more easily remembers insignificant data attached to spatial, personal, or otherwise meaningful information than that occurring in meaningless sequences. The sequences must make sense, though. If a random mnemonic is made up, it is not necessarily a memory aid.

(Rigorous) (Skill 13.5)

97. **The success-oriented classroom is designed to ensure students are successful at attaining new skills. In addition, mistakes are viewed as _____ in this type of classroom.**

    A. motivations to improve

    B. a natural part of the learning process

    C. ways to improve

    D. building blocks

Answer: B. a natural part of the learning process

In the success-oriented classroom, mistakes are viewed as a natural part of learning. In this way, mistakes continue the learning. Students have the ability to continually improve their grades or learning by correcting mistakes, rather than the mistake being a penalty.

(Easy) (Skill 13.6)

98. **Which statement is an example of specific praise?**

    A. John, you are the only person in class not paying attention.

    B. William, I thought we agreed that you would turn in all of your homework.

    C. Robert, you did a good job staying in line. See how it helped us get to music class on time?

    D. Class, you did a great job cleaning up the art room.

    Answer: C. Robert, you did a good job staying in line. See how it helped us get to music class on time?

    Praise is a powerful tool in obtaining and maintaining order in a classroom. In addition, it is an effective motivator. It is even more effective if the positive results of good behavior are included.

(Average) (Skill 13.6)

99. **What is one way a teacher can supplement verbal praise?**

    A. Help students evaluate their own performance and supply self-reinforcement

    B. Give verbal praise more frequently

    C. Give tangible rewards such as stickers or treats

    D. Have students practice giving verbal praise

Answer: A. Help students evaluate their own performance and supply self-reinforcement

While praise is useful in maintaining order in a classroom and in motivating students, it's important for the teacher to remember at all times that one major educational objective is that of preparing students to succeed in the world once the supports of the classroom are gone. Self-esteem and lack of it are often barriers to success. An important lesson and skill for students to learn is how to bolster one's own self-esteem and confidence.

(Average) (Skill 13.6)

100. **What is a frequently used type of feedback to students?**

    A. Correctives

    B. Simple praise–confirmation

    C. Correcting the response

    D. Explanations

Answer: B. Simple praise–confirmation

Even if the student's answer is not perfect, there are always ways to praise her and to make use of her answer unless, of course, she was deliberately answering wrongly. When a behavior is praised, it is likely to be repeated.

(Rigorous) (Skill 13.6)

101. The teacher responds, "Yes, that is correct" to a student's answer. What is this an example of?

    A. Academic feedback

    B. Academic praise

    C. Simple positive response

    D. Simple negative response

Answer: C. Simple positive response

Academic praise is a group of specific statements that give information about the value of the response or its implications. For example, a teacher using academic praise would respond, "That is an excellent analysis of Twain's use of the river in *Huckleberry Finn*." Whereas a simple positive response to the same question would be:"That's correct."

(Average) (Skill 13.6)

102. Which of the following is not a characteristic of effective praise?

    A. Praise is delivered in front of the class so it will serve to motivate others

    B. Praise is low-key

    C. Praise provides information about student competence

    D. Praise is delivered contingently

Answer: A. Praise is delivered in front of the class so it will serve to motivate others

The reason for praise in the classroom is to increase the desirable in order to eliminate the undesirable in both conduct and academic focus. It further states that effective praise should be authentic, it should be used in a variety of ways, and it should be low-key.

(Average) (Skill 14.1)

103. What is NOT a way that teachers show acceptance and give value to a student response?

    A. Acknowledging

    B. Correcting

    C. Discussing

    D. Amplifying

Answer: B. Correcting

There are ways to treat every answer as worthwhile even if it happens to be wrong. The objective is to keep students involved in the dialogue. If their efforts to participate are "rewarded" with what seems to them to be a rebuke or that leads to embarrassment, they will be less willing to respond the next time.

(Average) (Skill 14.1)

104. Which of the following is a definition of an intercultural communication model?

    A. Learning how different cultures engage in both verbal and nonverbal modes to communicate meaning

    B. Learning how classmates engage in both verbal and nonverbal modes to communicate meaning

    C. Learning how classmates engage in verbal dialogues

    D. Learning how different cultures engage in verbal modes to communicate meaning

Answer: A. Learning how different cultures engage in both verbal and non-verbal modes to communicate meaning

This process lets students begin to understand the process of communicating with each other in a multicultural manner, which helps them better understand their own learning. It provides for a more global learning process for all students.

(Average) (Skill 14.2)

105. **How can the teacher establish a positive climate in the classroom?**

    A. Help students see the unique contributions of individual differences

    B. Use whole group instruction for all content areas

    C. Help students divide into cooperative groups based on ability

    D. Eliminate teaching strategies that allow students to make choices

Answer: A. Help students see the unique contributions of individual differences

In the first place, an important purpose of education is to prepare students to live successfully in the real world, and this is an important insight and understanding for them to take into that world. In the second place, the most fertile learning environment is one in which all viewpoints and backgrounds are respected and where everyone has equal respect.

(Average) (Skill 14.4)

106. **Wait-time has what effect?**

    A. Gives structure to the class discourse

    B. Fewer chain and low-level questions are asked with more higher-level questions included

    C. Gives the students time to evaluate the response

    D. Gives the opportunity for in-depth discussion about the topic

Answer: B. Fewer chain and low-level questions are asked with more higher-level questions included

One part of the questioning process for the successful teacher is wait time: the time between the question and either the student response or your follow-up. Many teachers vaguely recommend some general amount of wait-time (until the student starts to get uncomfortable or is clearly perplexed), but we focus here on wait-time as a specific and powerful communicative tool that speaks through its structured silences. Embedded in wait-time are subtle clues about your judgments of a student's abilities and your expectations of individuals and groups. For example, the more time you allow a student to mull through a question, the more you trust his or her ability to answer that question without getting flustered. As a rule, the practice of prompting is not a problem. Giving support and helping students reason through difficult conundrums is part of being an effective teacher.

(Rigorous) (Skill 14.4)

107. **When is optimal benefit reached when handling an incorrect student response?**

    A. When specific praise is used

    B. When the other students are allowed to correct that student

    C. When the student is redirected to a better problem-solving approach

    D. When the teacher asks simple questions, provides cues to clarify, or gives assistance for working out the correct response

Answer: C. When the student is redirected to a better problem-solving approach

It's important that students feel confident and comfortable in making responses, knowing that even if they give a wrong answer, they will not be embarrassed. If a student is ridiculed or embarrassed by an incorrect response, the student my shut down and not participate thereafter in classroom discussion. One way to respond to the incorrect answer is to ask the child, "Show me from your book why you think that." This gives the student a chance to correct the answer and redeem himself or herself. Another possible response from the teacher is to use the answer as a nonexample. For example, after discussing the characteristics of warm-blooded and cold-blooded animals, the teacher asks for some examples of warm-blooded animals. A student raises his or her hand and responds, "A snake." The teacher could then say, "Remember, snakes lay eggs; they do not have live births. However, a snake is a good nonexample of a mammal." The teacher then draws a line down the board and

under a heading of "nonexample" writes "snake." This action conveys to the child that even though the answer was wrong, it still contributed positively to the class discussion. Notice how the teacher did not digress from the task of listing warm-blooded animals, which in other words is maintaining academic focus, and at the same time allowed the student to maintain dignity.

(Average) (Skill 14.4)

108. **What is an effective amount of "wait time?"**

    A. 1 second

    B. 5 seconds

    C. 15 seconds

    D. 10 seconds

Answer: B. 5 seconds

In formal training, most preservice teachers are taught the art of questioning. One part of the questioning process is wait time: the time between the question and either the student response or your follow-up. Many teachers vaguely recommend some general amount of wait-time (until the student starts to get uncomfortable or is clearly perplexed), but we focus here on wait-time as a specific and powerful communicative tool that speaks through its structured silences. Embedded in wait-time are subtle clues about your judgments of a student's abilities and your expectations of individuals and groups. For example, the more time you allow a student to mull through a question, the more you trust his or her ability to answer that question without getting flustered. As a rule, the practice of prompting is not a problem. Giving support and helping students reason through difficult conundrums is part of being an effective teacher.

(Easy) (Skill 14.4)

109. **Which of the following can impact the desire of students to learn new material?**

   A. Assessments plan

   B. Lesson plans

   C. Enthusiasm

   D. School community

Answer: C. Enthusiasm

The enthusiasm a teacher exhibits can have positive effects on students' desire to learn, as well as on on-task behaviors.

(Average) (Skill 14.6)

110. **When are students more likely to understand complex ideas?**

   A. If they do outside research before coming to class

   B. Later when they write out the definitions of complex words

   C. When they attend a lecture on the subject

   D. When they are clearly defined by the teacher and are given examples and nonexamples of the concept

Answer: D. When they are clearly defined by the teacher and are given examples and nonexamples of the concept

Several studies have been carried out to determine the effectiveness of giving examples as well as the difference in effectiveness of various types of examples. It was found conclusively that the most effective method of concept presentation included giving a definition along with examples and nonexamples and also providing an explanation of them. These same studies indicate that boring examples were just as effective as interesting examples in promoting learning. Additional studies have been conducted to determine the most effective number of examples that will result in maximum student learning. These studies concluded that a few thoughtfully selected examples are just as effective as many examples. It was determined that the actual number of examples necessary to promote student learning was relative to the learning characteristics of the learners. It was again ascertained that learning is facilitated when examples are provided along with the definition.

(Easy) (Skill 15.1)

111. **How can DVDs be used in instruction?**

   A. Students can use the DVD to create pictures for reports

   B. Students can use the DVD to create a science experiment

   C. Students can use the DVD to record class activities

   D. Students can use the DVD to review concepts studied

Answer: D: Students can use the DVD to review concepts studied

The teacher's arms are never long enough to render all the help that is needed when students are learning new concepts and practicing skills. Audiovisual aids such as the DVD extend her arms. Students who need more time to master a skill can have that without the teacher having to work one-on-one with a single student or with a classroom of students.

(Easy) (Skill 15.1)

112. How can students use a computer desktop publishing center?

A. To set up a classroom budget

B. To create student-made books

C. To design a research project

D. To create a classroom behavior management system

Answer: B. To create student-made books

By creating a book, students gain new insights into how communication works. Suddenly, the concept of audience for what they write and create becomes real. They also have an opportunity to be introduced to graphic arts, an exploding field. In addition, just as computers are a vital part of the world they will be entering as adults, so is desktop publishing. It is universally used by businesses of all kinds.

(Average) (Skill 15.1)

113. Which of the following is NOT a part of the hardware of a computer system?

A. Storage device

B. Input devices

C. Software

D. Central processing unit

Answer: C. Software

Software is not a part of the hardware of a computer, but instead consists of all of the programs that allow the computer to run. Software is either an operating system or an application program.

(Rigorous) (Skill 15.2)

114. What is one benefit of amplifying a student's response?

A. It helps the student develop a positive self-image

B. It is helpful to other students who are in the process of learning the reasoning or steps in answering the question

C. It allows the teacher to cover more content

D. It helps to keep the information organized

Answer: B. It is helpful to other students who are in the process of learning the reasoning or steps in answering the question

Not only does the teacher show acceptance and give value to student responses by acknowledging, amplifying, discussing, or restating the comment or question, she also helps the rest of the class learn to reason. If a student response is allowed, even if it is blurted out, it must be acknowledged and the student made aware of the quality of the response. A teacher acknowledges a student response by commenting on it. For example, the teacher states the definition of a noun and then asks for examples of nouns in the classroom. A student responds, "My pencil is a noun." The teacher answers, "Okay, let us list that on the board." By this response and the action of writing "pencil" on the board, the teacher has just incorporated the student's response into the lesson. A teacher may also amplify the student response through another question directed to either the original student or to another student. For example, the teacher may say, "Okay," giving the student feedback on the quality of the answer, and then add, "What do you mean by 'run' when you say the battery runs the radio?" Another way of showing acceptance and value of student response is to discuss the student response. For example, after a student responds, the teacher would say, "Class, let us think along that line. What is some evidence that proves what Susie just stated?" The teacher may also restate the response. For example, the teacher might say, "So you are saying the seasons are caused by the tilt of the earth. Is this what you said?"

(Average) (Skill 15.3)
115. Which of the following statements is true about computers in the classroom?

A. Computers are simply a glorified game machine and just allow students to play games

B. The computer should replace traditional research and writing skills taught to school-age children

C. Computers stifle the creativity of children

D. Computers allow students to access information they may otherwise be unable to

Answer: D. Computers allow students to access information they may otherwise be unable to

Computers, particularly those connected to the Internet, provide students with the ability to research information school libraries might otherwise be unable to provide because of funding issues. It opens the doors and pathways for students to increase the amount of information they acquire in school.

(Average) (Skill 15.3)
116. While an asset to students, technology is also important for teachers. Which of the following can be taught using technology to students?

A. Cooperation skills

B. Decision-making skills

C. Problem solving skills

D. All of the above

Answer: D. All of the above

Having students work together on a project using the technology available to you within your school not only teaches the content you wish them to learn but can also provide them with skills in cooperation, decision making, and problem solving.

(Easy) (Skill 15.3)

117. **As a classroom teacher, you have data on all of your students that you must track over the remainder of the school year. You will need to keep copies of the scores students receive and then graph their results to share progress with the parents an administrators. Which of the following software programs will be most useful in this manner?**

    A. Word processing program

    B. Spreadsheet

    C. Database

    D. Teacher utility and classroom management tools

Answer: B. Spreadsheet

Spreadsheets help a teacher to organize numeric information and can easily take that data and transfer it into a graph for a visual representation to administrators or parents.

(Average) (Skill 15.3)

118. **Which of the following statements is NOT true?**

    A. Printing and distributing material off of the Internet breaks the copyright law

    B. Articles are only copyrighted when there is a © in the article

    C. E-mail messages that are posted online are considered copyrighted

    D. It is not legal to scan magazine articles and place on your district Web site

Answer: B. Articles are only copyrighted when there is a © in the article

Articles, even without the symbol, are considered copyrighted material. This includes articles from newspapers, magazines, or even posted online.

(Easy) (Skill 15.5)

119. **The use of technology in the classroom allows for:**

    A. More complex lessons

    B. Better delivery of instruction

    C. Variety of instruction

    D. Better ability to meet more individual student needs

Answer: D. Better ability to meet more individual student needs

The utilization of technology provides the teacher with the opportunity to incorporate more than one learning style into a lesson. In this way, the teacher is better able to meet the individual needs of his or her students.

Sample Test with Rationales: The Professional Environment

(Easy) (Skill 16.5)

120. **A district superintendent's job is to:**

   A. Supervise senior teachers in the district

   B. Develop plans for school improvement

   C. Allocate community resources to individual schools

   D. Implement policies set by the board of education

Answer: D. Implement policies set by the board of education

A district superintendent is the chief officer of the school district and has the responsibility of overseeing that the policies set forth by the Board of Education are implemented by the schools in the district. He does not have the responsibility of directly supervising teachers or students or developing individual school improvement plans.

(Average) (Skill 16.5)

121. **Teacher's unions are involved in all of the following EXCEPT:**

   A. Updating teachers on current educational developments

   B. Advocating for teacher rights

   C. Matching teachers with suitable schools

   D. Developing professional codes and practices

Answer: C. Matching teachers with suitable schools

The role of teacher's unions is to work with teachers to develop and improve the profession of teaching by advocating for higher wages and improved conditions for teachers, developing professional codes and practices, and keeping teachers up to date on current educational developments. It is not the role of unions to find suitable employment for teachers.

(Average) (Skill 17.1)

122. **What is a benefit of frequent self-assessment?**

   A. Opens new venues for professional development

   B. Saves teachers the pressure of being observed by others

   C. Reduces time spent on areas not needing attention

   D. Offers a model for students to adopt in self-improvement

Answer: A. Opens new venues for professional development

When a teacher is involved in the process of self-reflection and self-assessment, one of the common outcomes is that the teacher comes to identify areas of skill or knowledge that require more research or improvement on her part. She may become interested in overcoming a particular weakness in her performance or may decide to attend a workshop or consult with a mentor to learn more about a particular area of concern.

(Average) (Skill 17.1)

123. **Which of the following could be used to improve teaching skills?**

   A. Developing a professional development plan

   B. Use of self-evaluation and reflection

   C. Building professional learning communities

   D. All of the above

Answer: D. All of the above

Creating a personalized plan for increasing your professional development, using self reflection, and working with other teachers in a professional learning community are all excellent strategies for improving ones teaching skills.

(Rigorous) (Skill 17.2)

124. **Which of the following is NOT a sound educational practice for expanding the professional development opportunities for teachers?**

   A. Looking at multiple methods of classroom management strategies

   B. Training teachers in understanding and applying multiple assessment formats and implementations in curriculum and instruction

   C. Having the students complete professional development assessments on a regular basis

   D. Teaching teachers how to disaggregate student data in improving instruction and curriculum implementation for student academic equity and access

Answer: C. Having the students complete professional development assessments on a regular basis

Giving teachers tests on a regular basis, while providing information on what knowledge they may have, does not expand the professional development opportunities for teachers.

(Rigorous) (Skill 17.3)

125. **What would happen if a school utilized an integrated approach to professional development?**

   A. All stakeholders needs are addressed

   B. Teachers and administrators are on the same page

   C. High-quality programs for students are developed

   D. Parents drive the curriculum and instruction

Answer: C. High-quality programs for students are developed

The implementation of an integrated approach to professional development is a critical component to ensuring success of programs for students. It involves teachers, parents, and other community members working together to develop appropriate programs to ensure students are receiving the necessary instruction to be successful in the future workforce.

(Average) (Skill 17.4)

126. What must be a consideration when a parent complains that he can't control a child's behavior?

   A. Consider whether the parent gives feedback to the child

   B. Consider whether the parent's expectations for control are developmentally appropriate

   C. Consider how much time the parent spends with the child

   D. Consider how rigid the rules are that the parent sets

Answer: B. Consider whether the parent's expectations for control are developmentally appropriate

The teacher is the expert when it comes to developmental expectations. This is one area where a concerned and helpful teacher can be invaluable in helping a family through a crisis. Parents often have unrealistic expectations about their children's behavior simply because they don't know what is normal and what is not. Some stages tend to be annoying, especially if they are not understood. A teacher can help to defuse the conflicts in these cases.

(Average) (Skill 18.1)

127. Which of the following should NOT be a purpose of a parent-teacher conference?

   A. To involve the parent in their child's education

   B. To establish a friendship with the child's parents

   C. To resolve a concern about the child's performance

   D. To inform parents of positive behaviors by the child

Answer: B. To establish a friendship with the child's parents

The purpose of a parent teacher conference is to involve parents in their child's education, address concerns about the child's performance, and share positive aspects of the student's learning with the parents. It would be unprofessional to allow the conference to degenerate into a social visit to establish friendships.

(Easy) (Skill 18.1)

128. Mr. Brown wishes to improve his parent communication skills. Which of the following is a strategy he can utilize to accomplish this goal?

   A. Hold parent-teacher conferences

   B. Send home positive notes

   C. Have parent nights where the parents are invited into his classroom

   D. All of the above

Answer: D. All of the above

Increasing parent communication skills is important for teachers. All of the listed strategies are methods a teacher can utilize to increase his skills.

(Easy) (Skill 18.1)

129. Tommy is a student in your class, and his parents are deaf. Tommy is struggling with math and you want to contact the parents to discuss the issues. How should you proceed?

    A. Limit contact because of the parents' inability to hear

    B. Use a TTY phone to communicate with the parents

    C. Talk to your administrator to find an appropriate interpreter to help you communicate with the parents personally

    D. Both B and C

Answer: D. Both B and C

You should never avoid communicating with parents for any reason; instead you should find strategies to find an effective way to communicate in various methods, just as you would with any other student in your classroom.

(Easy) (Skill 18.1)

130. When communicating with parents for whom English is not the primary language you should:

    A. Provide materials whenever possible in their native language

    B. Use an interpreter

    C. Provide the same communication as you would to native English speaking parents

    D. All of the above

Answer: D. All of the above

When communicating with non-English speaking parents, it is important to treat them as you would any other parent and utilize any means necessary to ensure they have the ability to participate in their child's educational process.

(Rigorous) (Skill 19.1)

131. Which of the following increases appropriate behavior more than 80 percent?

    A. Monitoring the halls

    B. Having class rules

    C. Having class rules, giving feedback, and having individual consequences

    D. Having class rules and giving feedback

Answer: C. Having class rules, giving feedback, and having individual consequences

Clear, consistent class rules go a long way to preventing inappropriate behavior. Effective teachers give immediate feedback to students regarding their behavior or misbehavior. If there are consequences, they should be as close as possible to those they would receive in the outside world, especially for adolescents. Consistency, especially with adolescents, reduces the occurrence of power struggles and teaches them that predictable consequences follow for their choice of actions.

(Average) (Skill 19.1)

132. A 16-year-old girl who has been looking sad writes an essay in which the main protagonist commits suicide. You overhear her talking about suicide. What do you do?

    A. Report this immediately to school administration, talk to the girl, letting her know you will talk to her parents about it

    B. Report this immediately to authorities

    C. Report this immediately to school administration, make your own report to authorities if required by protocol in your school, and do nothing else

    D. Just give the child some extra attention, as it may just be that's all she's looking for

Answer: C. Report this immediately to school administration, make your own report to authorities if required by protocol in your school, and do nothing else

A child who is suicidal is beyond any help that can be offered in a classroom. The first step is to report the situation to administration. If your school protocol calls for it, the situation should also be reported to authorities.

(Rigorous) (Skill 19.1)

133. Jeanne, a bright, attentive student is in her first hour English class. She is quiet, but very alert, often visually scanning the room in random patterns. Her pupils are dilated, and she has a slight but noticeable tremor in her hands. She fails to note a cue given from her teacher. At odd moments, she will act as if responding to stimuli that aren't there by suddenly changing her gaze. When spoken to directly, she has a limited response, but her teacher has a sense she is not herself. What should the teacher do?

    A. Ask the student if she is all right, then let it go, as there are not enough signals to be alarmed

    B. Meet with the student after class to get more information before making a referral

    C. Send the student to the office to see the nurse

    D. Quietly call for administration, remain calm, and be careful not to alarm the class

Answer: D. Quietly call for administration, remain calm, and be careful not to alarm the class

These behaviors are indicative of drug use. The best thing a teacher can do in this case is call for help from administration.

(Average) (Skill 19.1)

134. **Which is true of child protective services?**

   A. They have been forced to become more punitive in their attempts to treat and prevent child abuse and neglect

   B. They have become more a means for identifying cases of abuse and less an agent for rehabilitation because of the large volume of cases

   C. They have become advocates for structured discipline within the school

   D. They have become a strong advocate in the court system

Answer: B. They have become more a means for identifying cases of abuse and less an agent for rehabilitation because of the large volume of cases

Nina Bernstein, who wrote *The Lost Children of Wilder*, told of a long-running lawsuit in New York City that attempted to hold the city and its child-care services responsible for meeting the needs of abused children. Unfortunately, while it is an extreme case, it is not atypical of the plight of children all across the country. The only thing a teacher can do is attempt to provide a refuge of concern and stability during the time such children are in her care, hoping that they will, somehow, survive.

(Average) (Skill 19.1)

135. **In successful inclusion of students with disabilities:**

   A. A variety of instructional arrangements are available

   B. School personnel shift the responsibility for learning outcomes to the student

   C. The physical facilities are used as they are

   D. Regular classroom teachers have sole responsibility for evaluating student progress

Answer: A. A variety of instructional arrangements are available

Here are some support systems and activities that are in evidence where successful inclusion has occurred:

Attitudes and beliefs

- The regular teacher believes the student can succeed

- School personnel are committed to accepting responsibility for the learning outcomes of students with disabilities

- School personnel and the students in the class have been prepared to receive a student with disabilities

Services and physical accommodations

- Services needed by the student are available (e.g., health, physical, occupational, or speech therapy)

- Accommodations to the physical plant and equipment are adequate to meet the students' needs (e.g., toys, building and playground facilities, learning materials, or assistive devices)

School support

- The principal understands the needs of students with disabilities

- Adequate numbers of personnel, including aides and support personnel, are available

- Adequate staff development and technical assistance, based on the needs of the school personnel, are being provided (e.g., information on disabilities, instructional methods, awareness and acceptance activities for students and team-building skills)

- Appropriate policies and procedures for monitoring individual student progress, including grading and testing are in place

Collaboration

- Special educators are part of the instructional or planning team

- Teaming approaches are used for program implementation and problem solving

- Regular teachers, special education teachers, and other specialists collaborate (e.g., co-teach, team teach, or work together on teacher assistance teams)

Instructional methods

- Teachers have the knowledge and skills needed to select and adapt curricular and instructional methods according to individual student needs

- A variety of instructional arrangements is available (e.g., team teaching, cross-grade grouping, peer tutoring, or teacher assistance teams)

- Teachers foster a cooperative learning environment and promote socialization

(Average) (Skill 19.1)

136. How may a teacher use a student's permanent record?

- **A.** To develop a better understanding of the needs of the student

- **B.** To record all instances of student disruptive behavior

- **C.** To brainstorm ideas for discussing with parents at parent-teacher conferences

- **D.** To develop realistic expectations of the student's performance early in the year

Answer: A. To develop a better understanding of the needs of the student

The purpose of a student's permanent record is to give the teacher a better understanding of the student's educational history and provide him with relevant information to support the student's learning. Permanent records may not be used to arrive at preconceived judgments or to build a case against the student. Above all, the contents of a student's permanent record are confidential.

(Rigorous) (Skill 19.1)

137. You receive a phone call from a person who indicates she is now tutoring a student in your class. She would like you to provide an overview of the academic areas which the student is having difficulties. What is the first thing you should do?

   A. Find a time and talk with the tutor about issues you see within the classroom

   B. Call the parents

   C. Put together a packet of information to share with the tutor

   D. Offer to invite the tutor in to have a discussion and observe the child

Answer: B. Call the parents

Before you share any information with anyone about a student, you should always secure parental permission in writing.

(Rigorous) (Skill 19.2)

138. Marcus is a first grade boy of good developmental attainment. His learning progress is good the first half of the year. He shows no indicators of emotional distress. After the holiday break, he returns much changed. He is quieter, sullen even, tending to play alone. He has moments of tearfulness, sometimes almost without cause. He avoids contact with adults as often as he can. Even play with his friends has become limited. He has episodes of wetting not seen before and often wants to sleep in school. What approach is appropriate for this sudden change in behavior?

   A. Give him some time to adjust; the holiday break was probably too much fun to come back to school from

   B. Report this change immediately to administration; do not call the parents until administration decides a course of action

   C. Document his daily behavior carefully as soon as you notice such a change, report to administration the next month or so in a meeting

   D. Make a courtesy call to the parents to let them know he is not acting like himself, being sure to tell them he is not making trouble for others

Answer: B. Report this change immediately to administration; do not call the parents until administration decides a course of action

Anytime a child's disposition, attitude, or habits change significantly, teachers and parents need to seriously consider the existence of emotional difficulties. Emotional disturbances in childhood are not uncommon and take a variety of forms. Usually these problems show up in the form of uncharacteristic behaviors. Most of the time, children respond favorably to brief treatment programs of psychotherapy. At other times, disturbances may need more intensive therapy and are harder to resolve. All stressful behaviors need to be addressed, and any type of chronic antisocial behavior needs to be examined as a possible symptom of deep-seated emotional upset. In a case where the change is sudden and dramatic, administration needs to become involved.

(Rigorous) (Skill 19.2)

139. Andy shows up to class abusive and irritable. He is often late, sleeps in class, sometimes slurs his speech, and has an odor of alcohol. What is the first intervention to take?

   A. Confront him, relying on a trusting relationship you think you have

   B. Do a lesson on alcohol abuse, making an example of him

   C. Do nothing; it is better to err on the side of failing to identify substance abuse

   D. Call administration, avoid conflict, and supervise others carefully

Answer: D. Call administration, avoid conflict, and supervise others carefully

Educators are not only likely to, but often do, face students who are high on something. Of course, they are not only a hazard to their own safety and those of others, but their ability to be productive learners is greatly diminished, if not nonexistent. They show up instead of skip, because it's not always easy or practical for them to spend the day away from home but not in school. Unless they can stay inside, they are at risk of being picked up for truancy. Some enjoy being high in school, getting a sense of satisfaction by putting something over on the system. Some just don't take drug use seriously enough to think usage at school might be inappropriate. The first responsibility of the teacher is to assure the safety of all of the children. Avoiding conflict with the student who is high and obtaining help from administration is the best course of action.

(Average) (Skill 19.4)

140. A parent has left an angry message on the teacher's voicemail. The message relates to a concern about a student and is directed at the teacher. The teacher should:

   A. Call back immediately and confront the parent

   B. Cool off, plan what to discuss with the parent, then call back

   C. Question the child to find out what set off the parent

   D. Ignore the message, since feelings of anger usually

Answer: B. Cool off, plan what to discuss with the parent, then call back

It is professional for a teacher to keep her head in the face of emotion and respond to an angry parent in a calm and objective manner. The teacher should give herself time to cool off and plan the conversation with the parent with the purpose of understanding the concern and resolving it, rather than putting the parent in their place. Above all, the teacher should remember that parent-teacher interactions should aim to benefit the student.

Sample Written Assignment

Instructions: Write an answer of 300–600 words that addresses the topic described below.

- You need to identify the grade level involved and provide information about the purpose of your approach, the strategies you would employ, and the rationale or reasoning behind your plan of action.

- Imagine the intended reader of this essay to be another educator.

- Take your time and think through what you want to write before you start.

- You may want to outline the essay before you actually start writing.

YOUR ASSIGNMENT

Your school district is barely meeting the AYP standards of No Child Left Behind in several areas. Although there are no official external goals that must be met, the faculty, administration, and parents want to improve student achievement across the board and prevent any difficulties with AYP scores. A joint task force has been formed to identify methods to help all students improve their performance. To this end, they have asked teachers to submit ideas for consideration. **Describe a plan that you believe would positively impact student achievement in multiple subject areas.**

A good response by an elementary teacher

This plan is designed for third graders.

Student achievement is affected by many factors. These include the teacher's style and attitude, the curriculum and instructional methods, the atmosphere of the classroom and the school, the home environment from which students come, students' unique learning styles, individual student needs and/or limitations, cultural and linguistic diversity, and prior learning experiences. In spite of individual differences and needs, all students can be supported to learn and grow in the academic environment with the right attention and approach. A commitment to an inclusive classroom, where students of all achievement levels work together and diversity is honored and supported, goes a long way to ensuring student success. Attending to students' individual academic and psychosocial needs and working collaboratively with parents and community supports are also essential in helping to ameliorate or remove obstacles to student achievement.

Another major element in student achievement is student motivation. My plan is to implement instructional approaches that will increase student motivation, thereby raising student achievement. I would recommend focusing on two areas: child-centered learning methodologies and an integrated curriculum. The advantages of the integrated curriculum is that it mirrors the real world, where learning crosses "subject" lines such as reading, science, the arts, math, social studies, and language arts. This is especially effective for young children as their worldview is not broken down into discrete "subjects." An integrated curriculum feels familiar to them and engages their natural curiosity, enhancing their motivation to learn.

Using child-centered instructional techniques increase the likelihood that students will enjoy learning. When they enjoy the process of learning, they are more highly motivated to complete tasks, to take risks to learn new things, and to consider new ideas. By capitalizing on young children's innate urge to discover and explore, as well as their use of play to attain mastery, child-centered approaches for young children can yield a high level of engagement and motivation to learn.

Specific child-centered learning methodologies could include the following:

- Generating a list of questions that students want to answer on a specific topic; these questions can be posted in the classroom with space for the answers to be added as the class learns about the topic. The teacher will develop activities across subjects to help student address these questions.

- Using integrated subject learning stations that the students can choose from, as long as they complete three out of five within a given time frame.

- Incorporating play activities into the classroom that access content-related material across subject areas. An example might be to put on a play about the animals that live in the forests and the fields.

- Being attuned to and utilizing teachable moments as they occur in classroom activities as well as on the playground.

- Creating small group activities where the students have the chance to make choices as a group about what and how they are going to study. For example, in groups of three or four, students have a worksheet with five key words related to the topic under study. The task is to learn three things about each of the key words. They can ask their parents/guardians for information, go to the library and ask for help, look in books in the classroom, or share information they already know. They may use the Internet, draw a picture of the key word, or create a pantomime. Each group can then share or post their information for the entire class.

A good response by a secondary teacher
This plan is designed for eleventh graders.

Student achievement is affected by many factors. These include the teacher's style and attitude, the curriculum and instructional methods, the atmosphere of the classroom and the school, the home environment from which students come, students' unique learning styles, individual student needs and/or limitations, cultural and linguistic diversity, and prior learning experiences. In spite of individual differences and needs, all students can be supported to learn and grow in the academic environment with the right attention and approach. A commitment to an inclusive classroom, where students of all achievement levels work together and diversity is honored and supported, goes a long way to ensuring student success. Attending to students' individual academic and psychosocial needs and working collaboratively with parents and community supports are also essential in helping to ameliorate or remove obstacles to student achievement.

Another major element in student achievement is student motivation. My plan is to implement instructional approaches that will increase student motivation by engaging them in self-chosen topics, thereby raising student achievement. I would use two strategies to improve student achievement with eleventh graders: using self-directed study and informational interviewing. These could be incorporated in various subject courses, such as English, social studies, science, and the arts. The intent behind both of these strategies is to engage students in active exploration of topics relevant to them and to help them to take responsibility for their learning process in and out of the classroom.

In both of these strategies, I would provide some guidelines and a rubric for assessment. The specific goals to be evaluated by the rubric would be part of the student's process of determining their topic and the learning approaches they will employ.

Self-directed study involves students picking a topic among those included in a specific curriculum and determining what they want to learn about that topic. They establish goals, learning strategies, and intended outcomes. There are checkpoints built in so they can receive feedback as they work on their project to ensure that they have crafted a workable plan and benefit from the teacher's input. They can utilize a wide range of methods (such as using the arts to describe scientific ideas or concepts) and sources (creative nonfiction, the Internet, professionals in the field, as well as textbooks). Outcomes can be equally varied.

Informational interviewing can be incorporated into a self-directed study project or can stand on its own as a strategy to engage students. The key is to generate interest in students to find a topic or profession about which they are curious. It can be a particular job, a scientific theory, a method of manufacture, or a form of artistic expression. The goal is for students to identify key questions that need to be asked in order to answer their general inquiry, identify informants (e.g., someone who performs a certain job or someone who works in the field of study), conduct the interview(s), and then create a report about the topic. The report must meet certain criteria per the teacher-derived rubric, but students have a lot of freedom in how the report is created (e.g., written text, artistic expression, multimedia presentation).

Both of these approaches can be part of a larger strategy to engage students in learning by drawing on interactions with real-world information and to take learning beyond the classroom. This learning can be brought back into the classroom through "poster sessions" (as is used at professional conferences) or in discussion groups or public speaking activities. All of these activities provide opportunities for the student to develop self-responsibility and a positive self-concept, also factors in increasing student motivation and achievement.

Guidelines for Crisis Management and Emergency Response

Increasingly, teachers are faced with emergency and crisis situations that demand careful, coordinated, and immediate response. These situations are challenging for many reasons. These guidelines address some of these reasons as well as the core concepts involved in effective crisis management, including the importance of preparedness.

Emergency response planning

To ensure student and personnel safety, various levels of planning must be implemented in an effort to anticipate a range of situations. At their most basic, plans must exist for ensuring safety in different scenarios. Local natural disasters must be accounted for, as should plans for ensuring safety when, for example, the police are searching for a loose criminal in the surrounding neighborhood or the community is faced with a health crisis such as a flu pandemic. Many schools may even have to consider safety plans for local terrorist attacks, particularly if the school is located near a strategic or popular site.

Plans should include methods for getting students to a safe area, as well as for communication among everyone involved. Strategies for dealing with crisis reactions also need to be in place. (Communication and intervention strategies are addressed in the next section.)

In planning for evacuation, routes should be drawn so that each hallway has the least amount of students walking through it as possible, with no student having to walk too far. The quickest route out of a building may clog a hallway, thereby making the route much slower. However, it would also be unwise to have a whole classroom full of students walk far around a particular hallway and still be in a potentially dangerous location. Often, fire departments or safety consultants can assist in designing solid, quality evaluation plans.

A lockdown plan is the opposite of an evacuation plan and consists of various rules and procedures for getting or keeping all students in a secure location, such as a classroom. Often communication suffers during a lockdown, so many schools now insist that school personnel look at their e-mail accounts as soon as a lock-down occurs, to give the administration an efficient way to communicate to many people quickly.

The next level of ensuring safety concerns communicating those plans to staff, parents, students, and the district. Clear directions should be posted all over campus for clarification when events occur. Directions and procedures should be mailed home to parents annually, as well.

Crisis Management and Intervention Planning

Crisis and emergency situations are events beyond the realm of every day life. They always involve some degree of surprise, shock, loss, and emotion. Crises include death, natural disasters such as earthquakes and hurricanes, vehicular and other accidents, health concerns such as flu pandemics, school shootings, and other forms of extreme violence. The unpredictability of crises, the experience of loss that invariably accompanies such situations, and the strong feelings that are evoked all make crisis and emergency events particularly potent and challenging for everyone involved.

The value of being prepared

As noted, preplanning is essential. Equally important, specialized training in crisis management skills can be extremely helpful in responding effectively. Although the events themselves may be unpredictable, there is a body of information about how people react to crisis and what responders can do to ameliorate and manage the aftermath of crisis. This is important in school settings, where there are a large number of people congregated in one place and contagion is a concern. Anxiety and misinformation can spread like wildfire, exacerbating the short- and long-term effects of traumatic events.

Designating and training a crisis response team is essential in well-functioning schools. Ideally, the crisis response team includes some administrators, counselors, teachers, and the school nurse. Comprehensive crisis management training and ongoing refresher courses are necessary for a team to function well. A clearly defined leader (not the principal or assistant principal, as he or she will have enough to do in any crisis situation) facilitates the work of the crisis team. The leader may be a teacher or other member of the team. The important skills the leader must possess are the ability to remain calm, think clearly, and have excellent communication skills. He or she will be responsible for "thinking on one's feet" with some decisions, although the larger decisions will be made by administrators.

In addition to a crisis team, school districts need to have clearly defined crisis response plans, including the evacuation and lockdown plans discussed previously. They should include as much detail as possible, with specific recommendations for different situations as needed, although a general plan is applicable in many circumstances. At minimum, the plan should incorporate the following:

- Delineate the school's goals in crisis situations (such as maintaining as normal a school day as possible, or providing timely information)

- Identify key players on the crisis response team, including a team leader and a backup leader

- Specify how communication will be handled

- Discuss how decisions will be made regarding the need to bring in outside resources

- Describe what interventions will be used with students

- Note how interactions and referrals to outside agencies will be managed

- Describe the process for decision-making regarding disclosures to the media

- Detail what follow-up is needed after each event

The plan should also include information from the Center for Disease Control and Prevention regarding health and natural disaster–related crises. Notes about local contacts with the Red Cross and other disaster response teams as well as the local police can be incorporated into the plan.

Further, it helps to have handouts about traumatic stress reactions available for teachers and parents, sample letters to parents and guardians, sample press releases, and other useful documents ready prior to any event.

The need for information

Everyone who experiences a traumatic event needs to be aware of the normal reactions and common feelings of survivors, as well as receive accurate information about the event itself (when this is not known publicly). They also need to know what the school is doing in response. This means that the district needs to make clear decisions about the actions the school is taking, including what parents and guardians need to know and do, and communicate these plans succinctly and in a timely manner to all in the school community. Information also needs to flow to the larger community. Specific, to-the-point information is valuable; avoid all rumors.

Intervention for students

Most commonly, school counselors, teachers, and other school personnel will be available for crisis counseling and support in a designated room for a day or two after a traumatic event. Some districts will invite local experts in traumatic stress response or grief counseling to come to the school to aid school personnel. Interventions include listening, normalizing the reactions of students, offering to call parents and guardians, and making arrangements for the student to go home early when needed. Referrals to outside professionals may also be made.

Self-care during and after the event

Part of a school crisis plan should spell out how responders and other school personnel will receive and give support during the implementation of the crisis management plan. Further, crisis team members need to get rest and support after doing crisis response work. This work is very demanding, and the effects on responders may not be immediately apparent. Secondary post-traumatic stress is a concern, particularly when the crisis response team has multiple or ongoing situations to manage. Adequate administrative and personal support, time off, and sufficient training and debriefing are essential.

Follow-up planning

After events that compromise safety or involve crisis, school leaders must do a few things. Reporting to district administrators, local police, parents, students, and sometimes media should be spelled out as part of the crisis management plan. Sometimes this reporting happens during the course of the event; other times it occurs after the fact. Regardless, reporting needs to happen as soon as possible. Once the situation is stabilized but before too much time has passed, the team and school administrators must sit down with other staff members and discuss the performance of the school community in responding to the crisis. From that discussion, the team can then make informed modifications to the plans. New plans, of course, must then be communicated to all school community members.

The following Web sites have information about emergency response, school crisis management, traumatic stress reactions, and related topics:

www.nctsnet.org/nccts/nav.do?pid=ctr_aud_schlmeans that part of the crisis response

www.cdc.gov/niosh/unp-trinstrs.html

www.aaets.org/trresp.htm

www.apa.org/practice/traumaticstress.html

www.ed.gov/admins/lead/safety/training/responding/crisis_pg11.html?exp=2.

For information on assessing your school's risk during a crisis event see the Web site of the National Clearinghouse for Educational Facilities:

http://www.ncef.org/pubs/mitigating_hazards.pdf.

ASSESSMENT OF TEACHING SKILLS— PERFORMANCE (ATS-P)

What Is the ATS-P?

Developed as part of the New York State Teacher Certification Examinations (NYSTCE®), the Assessment of Teaching Skills—Performance (ATS-P) was developed by the New York State Education Department and Pearson's Evaluation Systems division to demonstrate teacher candidates' instruction aptitude in an actual classroom setting. Teacher candidates are encouraged to produce their 20 to 30 minute video-recorded sample once they have completed one or two years of experience to ensure they have the knowledge and ability to apply their teaching skills effectively. However, they should turn in the submission no later than one year before their provisional certificate expiration date. Once a candidate has registered for the ATS-P, he or she should ensure the video is submitted by the final submission deadline or risk having to reregister without a refund or credit.

The session must be filmed in a public or nonpublic Pre-K, elementary, middle, or secondary school where the candidate currently teaches. Those working in a team-teaching environment should record a lesson they primarily conduct. If he or she does not have a teaching engagement, a lesson can be arranged; however, the classroom must not be the candidate's student teaching assignment and should be within the teaching area in which the candidate seeks permanent certification. The candidate's lesson plan and submission must be his or her own original work. Submissions comparable to another candidate's will result in the validity of both being questioned.

What Should the Recorded Lesson Include?

The recorded session must demonstrate the candidate's knowledge and skills with regard to the established ATS-P objectives:

1. Comprehension of the principles and procedures involved with arranging and implementing lessons in a way that enables learners to construct meaning and obtain intended outcomes

2. Comprehension of multiple instruction methods to assist learning in a variety of situations

3. Comprehension of motivational principles and procedures implemented to increase student achievement and active engagement

4. Demonstrated ability to implement various communication modes to increase student learning and create trust and support within the classroom setting

5. Demonstrated ability to structure and manage a classroom to create a safe and productive learning environment

It is important to plan the lesson objectives and content to ensure it easily conveys the teaching skills described above. The session should have a planned beginning and end. For lessons longer than the allotted time, the recording should focus on the portion that best demonstrates the candidate's active, effective teaching and that provides students with direct, explicit instruction. While other teaching personnel or educational support staff may be present, they should not provide substantial instruction (no more than a minute). Candidates are also encouraged to limit administrative tasks such as taking attendance and collecting homework, as well as the use of instructional media (film, slide, audiotape presentation) to less than five minutes.

Essentially, the video should demonstrate actively engaged and motivated students; a structured environment that allows all students to communicate and excel; and various teaching methods that enable learner mastery and desired instructional outcomes. **Candidates are strongly encouraged to visit the official NYSTCE Web site at** *www.nystce.nesinc.com* **for further information on the ATS-P objectives and submission requirements and to ensure they have the most up-to-date information as requirements sometimes change.**

Additional requirements

In addition to meeting the required objectives, the recorded session must adhere to a minimum of 20 minutes and maximum of 30 minutes of continuous recording and include at least 10 minutes of non-whole-group instruction. Non-whole-group instruction requires the teacher to provide a framework and learning conditions to individual learners or small groups of learners, then oversee and monitor the experience as the learners actively participate in their learning. This instruction format, which is considered not primarily teacher-directed, allows the teacher to answer any questions or concerns as students create their own educational experience. Some examples of non-whole-group lessons include small-group projects, discussions or presentations, peer tutoring, or cooperative learning activities. As most effective teachers integrate various instructional strategies into their lessons, the non-whole-group instruction can be broken down into segments within the 30 minutes of video recording.

Recording the session

Most schools have the video equipment required to complete the ATS-P, but candidates are encouraged to purchase a new videotape or DVD to ensure the highest recording quality and that there is no additional material on the tape. Only the following formats are acceptable:

- Standard ½-inch VHS videotape

- DVD or mini DVD

Candidates can either prepare a self-recorded video or have someone in the school (teacher, teaching intern, paraprofessional, or student) serve as the camera operator. While the self-recorded session limits the field of view, the camera can be moved to a new position during the lesson; however, extreme care should be taken to avoid turning the camera off as that will automatically disqualify the taping. The recording should have no interruptions, even accidental ones, or it will receive a Requirements Not Met (RNM) designation. Please note that no modifications can be made to the tape—it must be continuous without any breaks or edits including removing audio, adding subtitles, freeze-frames, or other special effects. With camera-operated taping, the teacher can move about the classroom as the person recording can track movement and zoom in and out to capture the lesson and teaching. The recorder should be encouraged not to interact with the students or influence their behavior.

Tips for recording

Regardless of which method is used, the filming equipment should be stabilized on a tripod or other device and the electronic stabilization function should be turned on if available. As the quality of the battery life can impact the video recording quality, ensure the camera is connected to either an AC power source or a fully charged battery. Be sure to enunciate words, speak up, and encourage students to speak up to ensure the audio is adequately captured. Given that video microphones frequently amplify ambient sounds, such as air conditioners and street noises, try to record in a quiet location so that instruction and students' interactions and responses can be clearly heard. To capture the highest quality filming, the camera lens should be directed away from windows or other sources of light. Candidates are also encouraged to turn on the autofocus function and turn off the date/time stamp.

Lessons should be planned and camera positioning situated in a way that predominantly captures the candidate, making his or her instruction clearly visible and audible. If the audio and video production or the playback quality prevents the scorers from assessing the candidate, the tape will be deemed RNM. Any chalkboards, flipcharts, or overhead projectors essential to the lesson should be captured as well. To ensure the recording meets the timing requirements, including the 10 minutes of non-whole-group instruction, candidates are encouraged to use a stop watch or ask the camera operator to track recording time.

While candidates are encouraged to inform students in advance and conduct a few practice recorded sessions to test the equipment and help students adjust to being filmed, recording for the purpose of the ATS-P does not require parent/guardian permission as the tape is considered a confidential classroom assessment record. Recording a few lessons before creating the submission video may make the teacher, students, and camera operator more comfortable. In addition, candidates are strongly encouraged to show their video to multiple permanently certified teachers for feedback on whether their submission aligns with the ATS-P objectives.

Finalizing the submission video
When submitting a ½-inch VHS videotape, candidates should remove the record-enabling tab found on the tape's spine and completely rewind the tape. Those submitting a DVD or mini DVD must finalize the disc before it can be played on a standard DVD player. Refer to the instruction manual or technology support personnel for specific procedures. DVD finalization is crucial because DVDs that do not play are considered RNM. Comprehensive finalization details will be mailed to the candidate within the ATS-P Procedures Manual once he or she has registered for the ATS-P. As the submitted video will not be returned, candidates are advised to make a copy for their records.

Accompanying paperwork
In addition to the actual video recording, teachers will need to submit the Context of Instruction Form. While the form is not scored, care should be taken in completing it because it helps the scorers review the submission. Be sure to fill out the classroom level, as omitting that information results in returned materials. Candidates are also advised against submitting any additional sheets that are not requested. Another mandatory form is the Candidate Identification Form, which requires a witness to view a portion of the candidate's video and verify that the video recording and Candidate Identification Form accurately reflect the candidate's identity. The witness must either provide his or her own social security number or provide the Candidate Identification Form and identification to a notary who will complete the Notary Acknowledgment portion and provide an official notary seal. Additionally, the witness must meet the following criteria:

- Hold a permanent New York State teaching certificate and work in the same public or nonpublic school or school district to which the candidate is employed;

- Hold a permanent certificate in another state and work as a certified professional in the same public or nonpublic school or school district to which the candidate is employed; or

- Serve as a school administrator in the same public or nonpublic school to which the candidate is employed, but which is not a New York State school.

Receipt of submission and results

If the candidate's materials are deemed complete, he or she will be mailed a receipt acknowledgment. The ATS-P video will be assessed independently by qualified New York State educators based on a holistic rating scale (an overall judgment). While the teaching quality—not the audio or video quality—will be scored, the scorers must be able to hear and view the instructor's lesson and implementation.

To pass the ATS-P, teachers must meet all five established objectives, demonstrating a structured lesson that achieves acceptable application of principles and procedures and which helps students create meaning and attain desired goals. The various teaching methods must assist student learning, motivate, and engage. The candidate should use questioning and other communication practices to advance student learning and support respect—in both the students themselves and for others. Structured and adequately managed, the classroom environment should prove the teacher's ability to produce a suitable learning climate in which rules and proper behavior are upheld.

Submission checklist

- Approved format (VHS videotape, DVD, or mini DVD)

- Camera is secured on tripod or other stabilization device

- Camera is connected to power source or has fully charged battery

- Autofocus and electronic stabilization are turn on and date/time stamp is turned off

- Practice sessions have been conducted to adjust teacher and students to filming and ensure that equipment is properly functioning

- Permanently certified educators have been asked for input on previously recorded sessions

- Timer is in place to ensure teacher captures minimum of 20 minutes, maximum of 30 minutes

- Video includes 10 minutes of non-whole-group instruction

- Lesson and filming provide ample evidence of teaching skills according to ATS-P objectives

- Lesson reflects the candidate's original work in an actual teaching situation (not simulated or staged)

- Student actions and responses have not been scripted

- Teacher is predominantly on-screen as are any essential visual elements (chalkboards, flipcharts, etc.)

- Recording has no breaks, interruptions, or edits (including special effects)

- Quality of audio and visual production as well as playback are adequate for scoring purposes

- Videotape has only the candidate's recorded session on the first 30 minutes

- Session focuses on candidate's teaching not administrative duties or presentations by others or media

- Copy of submission has been made for candidate's files

- Videotape has been rewound all the way or DVD has been finalized

- Properly completed Context of Instruction Form is included

- Properly completed (including witness and notary, if applicable) Candidate Identification Form is included

BONUS
SAMPLE TEST

To provide you with even more value, we're including a free BONUS sample test with this guide.

The extra NYSTCE LAST Liberal Arts and Sciences Test 001 will help you practice for the real exam with state-aligned questions. **XAMonline: dedicated to helping you succeed the first time.**

SAMPLE TEST

Scientific, Mathematical, and Technological Processes

(Easy) (Skill 1.4)

1. When is a hypothesis formed?

   A. Before the data is taken

   B. After the data is taken

   C. After the data is analyzed

   D. Concurrent with graphing the data

(Average) (Skill 2.1)

2. In an experiment measuring the growth of bacteria at different temperatures, what is the independent variable?

   A. Number of bacteria

   B. Growth rate of bacteria

   C. Temperature

   D. Size of bacteria

(Rigorous) (Skill 2.1)

3. A scientist exposes mice to cigarette smoke and notes that their lungs develop tumors. Mice that were not exposed to the smoke do not develop as many tumors. Which of the following conclusions may be drawn from these results?

   I. Cigarette smoke causes lung tumors

   II. Cigarette smoke exposure has a positive correlation with lung tumors in mice

   III. Some mice are predisposed to develop lung tumors

   IV. Mice are often a good model for

humans in scientific research.

   A. I and II only

   B. II only

   C. I , II, and III only

   D. II and IV only

(Easy) (Skill 2.1)

4. The following chart shows the yearly average number of international tourists visiting Palm Beach for 1990-1994. How many more international tourists visited Palm Beach in 1994 than in 1991?

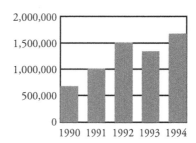

   A. 100,000

   B. 600,000

   C. 1,600,000

   D. 8,000,000

(Average) (Skill 2.1)

5. What is the mode of the data in the following sample?

   9, 10, 11, 9, 10, 11, 9, 13

   A. 9

   B. 9.5

   C. 10

   D. 11

(Average) (Skill 2.1)

6. Consider the graph of the distribution of the length of time it took individuals to complete an employment form.

Minutes

Approximately how many individuals took less than 15 minutes to complete the employment form?

A. 35

B. 28

C. 7

D. 4

(Easy) (Skill 3.1)

7. $0.74 =$

A. $\frac{74}{100}$

B. 7.4%

C. $\frac{33}{50}$

D. $\frac{74}{10}$

(Average) (Skill 3.1)

8. 303 is what percent of 600?

A. 0.505%

B. 5.05%

C. 505%

D. 50.5%

(Average) (Skill 3.1)

9. Select the rule of logical equivalence that directly (in one step) transforms the statement (I) into statement (II),

I. Not all the students have books.

II. Some students do not have books.

A. "If p, then q" is equivalent to "if not q, then b"

B. "Not all are p" is equivalent to "some are not p"

C. "Not q" is equivalent to "p"

D. "All are not p" is equivalent to "none are p"

(Rigorous) (Skill 3.1)

10. Given that:

I. No athletes are weak

II. All football players are athletes

determine which conclusion can be logically deduced.

A. Some football players are weak

B. All football players are weak

C. No football player is weak

D. None of the above is true

(Rigorous) (Skill 3.2)

11. $(\frac{-4}{9}) + (\frac{-7}{10}) =$

A. $\frac{23}{90}$

B. $\frac{-23}{90}$

C. $\frac{103}{90}$

D. $\frac{-103}{90}$

(Average) (Skill 3.2)

12. $(5.6) \times (-0.11) =$

    A. -0.616

    B. 0.616

    C. -6.110

    D. 6.110

(Average) (Skill 3.2)

13. $\frac{7}{9} + \frac{1}{3} \div \frac{2}{3} =$

    A. $\frac{5}{3}$

    B. $\frac{3}{2}$

    C. 2

    D. $\frac{23}{18}$

(Rigorous) (Skill 3.2)

14. Choose the statement that is true for all real numbers.

    A. $a = 0$, $b \neq 0$, then $\frac{b}{a} =$ undefined

    B. $-(a + (-a)) = 2a$

    C. $2(ab) = -(2a)b$

    D. $-a(b + 1) = ab - a$

(Rigorous) (Skill 3.4)

15. The owner of a rectangular piece of land 40 yards in length and 30 yards in width wants to divide it into two parts. She plans to join two opposite corners with a fence as shown in the diagram below. The cost of the fence will be approximately $25 per linear foot. What is the estimated cost for the fence needed by the owner?

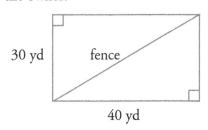

30 yd   fence

40 yd

A. $1,250

B. $62,500

C. $5,250

D. $3,750

(Easy) (Skill 3.4)

16. What is the area of a square whose side is 13 feet?

    A. 169 feet

    B. 169 square feet

    C. 52 feet

    D. 52 square feet

(Easy) (Skill 3.4)

17. The trunk of a tree has a 2.1 meter radius. What is its circumference?

    A. 2.1π square meters

    B. 4.2π meters

    C. 2.1π meters

    D. 4.2π square meters

(Easy) (Skill 3.4)

18. What is the area of this triangle?

10"

8"

A. 80 square inches

B. 20 square inches

C. 40 square inches

D. 30 square inches

(Average) (Skill 3.5)

19. A car gets 25.36 miles per gallon. The car has been driven 83,310 miles. What is a reasonable estimate for the number of gallons of gas used?

    A. 2,087 gallons

    B. 3,000 gallons

    C. 1,800 gallons

    D. 164 gallons

(Rigorous) (Skill 3.5)

20. If $4x - (3 - x) = 7(x - 3) + 10$, then:

    A. $x = 8$

    B. $x = -8$

    C. $x = 4$

    D. $x = -4$

(Average) (Skill 3.5)

21. Given the formula $d = rt$, (where $d =$ distance, $r =$ rate, and $t =$ time), calculate the time required for a vehicle to travel 585 miles at a rate of 65 miles per hour.

    A. 8.5 hours

    B. 6.5 hours

    C. 9.5 hours

    D. 9 hours

(Rigorous) (Skill 3.5)

22. $3x - \frac{2}{3} = \frac{5x}{2} + 2$ Solve for x.

    A. $5\frac{1}{3}$

    B. $\frac{17}{3}$

    C. 2

    D. $\frac{16}{2}$

(Average) (Skill 3.6)

23. An item that sells for $375 is put on sale at $120. What is the percent of decrease?

    A. 25%

    B. 28%

    C. 68%

    D. 34%

(Rigorous) (Skill 3.6)

24. It takes five equally skilled people 9 hours to shingle Mr. Joe's roof. Let t be the time required for only 3 of these men to do the same job. Select the correct statement of the given condition.

    A. $\frac{3}{5} = \frac{9}{t}$

    B. $\frac{9}{5} = \frac{3}{t}$

    C. $\frac{5}{9} = \frac{3}{t}$

    D. $\frac{14}{9} = \frac{t}{5}$

(Rigorous) (Skill 3.6)

25. In a sample of 40 full-time employees at a particular company, 35 were also holding down a part-time job requiring at least 10 hours/week. If this proportion holds for the entire company of 25,000 employees, how many full-time employees at this company are actually holding down a part-time job of at least 10 hours per week.

    A. 714

    B. 625

    C. 21,875

    D. 28,571

Answer Key

1. A	11. D	21. D
2. C	12. A	22. A
3. B	13. D	23. C
4. B	14. A	24. B
5. A	15. D	25. C
6. C	16. B	
7. A	17. B	
8. D	18. C	
9. B	19. B	
10. C	20. C	

Rigor Table

RIGOR TABLE	
Rigor level	**Questions**
Easy 20%	1, 4, 7, 16, 17, 18
Average 40%	2, 5, 6, 8, 9, 12, 13, 19, 21, 23
Rigorous 40%	3, 10, 11, 14, 15, 20, 22, 24, 25

Sample Test with Rationales: Scientific, Mathematical, and Technological Processes

(Easy) (Skill 1.4)

1. When is a hypothesis formed?

   A. Before the data is taken

   B. After the data is taken

   C. After the data is analyzed

   D. Concurrent with graphing the data

   Answer: A.

   A hypothesis is an educated guess made before undertaking an experiment. The hypothesis is then evaluated based on the observed data. Therefore, the hypothesis must be formed before the data is taken, not during or after the experiment.

(Average) (Skill 2.1)

2. In an experiment measuring the growth of bacteria at different temperatures, what is the independent variable?

   A. Number of bacteria

   B. Growth rate of bacteria

   C. Temperature

   D. Size of bacteria

   Answer: C.

   To answer this question, recall that the independent variable in an experiment is the entity that is changed by the scientist in order to observe the effects (the dependent variable(s)). In this experiment, temperature is changed in order to measure growth of bacteria.

(Rigorous) (Skill 2.1)

3. A scientist exposes mice to cigarette smoke and notes that their lungs develop tumors. Mice that were not exposed to the smoke do not develop as many tumors. Which of the following conclusions may be drawn from these results?

   I. Cigarette smoke causes lung tumors

   II. Cigarette smoke exposure has a positive correlation with lung tumors in mice

   III. Some mice are predisposed to develop lung tumors

   IV. Mice are often a good model for humans in scientific research

   A. I and II only

   B. II only

   C. I, II, and III only

   D. II and IV only

   Answer: B.

   Although cigarette smoke has been found to cause lung tumors (and many other problems), this particular experiment shows only that there is a positive correlation between smoke exposure and tumor development in these mice. It may be true that some mice are more likely to develop tumors than others, which is why a control group of identical mice should have been used for comparison. Mice are often used to model human reactions, but this is as much due to their low financial and emotional cost as it is due to their being a "good model" for humans.

(Easy) (Skill 2.1)

4. The following chart shows the yearly average number of international tourists visiting Palm Beach for 1990-1994. How many more international tourists visited Palm Beach in 1994 than in 1991?

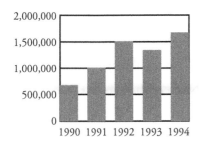

A. 100,000

B. 600,000

C. 1,600,000

D. 8,000,000

Answer: B.

The number of tourists in 1991 was 1,000,000 and the number in 1994 was 1,600,000. Subtract to get a difference of 600,000.

(Average) (Skill 2.1)

5. What is the mode of the data in the following sample?

9, 10, 11, 9, 10, 11, 9, 13

A. 9

B. 9.5

C. 10

D. 11

Answer: A.

The mode is the number that appears most frequently. 9 appears 3 times, which is more than the other numbers.

(Average) (Skill 2.1)

6. Consider the graph of the distribution of the length of time it took individuals to complete an employment form.

Approximately how many individuals took less than 15 minutes to complete the employment form?

A. 35

B. 28

C. 7

D. 4

Answer: C.

According to the chart, the number of people who took under 15 minutes is 7.

(Easy) (Skill 3.1)

7. $0.74 =$

A. $\frac{74}{100}$

B. 7.4%

C. $\frac{33}{50}$

D. $\frac{74}{10}$

Answer: A.

$0.74 \rightarrow 4$ is in the hundredths place, so the answer is $\frac{74}{100}$.

(Average) (Skill 3.1)

8. **303 is what percent of 600?**

   A. 0.505%

   B. 5.05%

   C. 505%

   D. 50.5%

   Answer: D.

   Use x for the percent. $600x = 303$.
   $\frac{600x}{600} = \frac{303}{600} \rightarrow x = 0.505 = 50.5\%$.

(Average) (Skill 3.1)

9. **Select the rule of logical equivalence that directly (in one step) transforms the statement (I) into statement (II),**

   I. Not all the students have books.

   II. Some students do not have books.

   A. "If p, then q" is equivalent to "if not q, then b"

   B. "Not all are p" is equivalent to "some are not p"

   C. "Not q" is equivalent to "p"

   D. "All are not p" is equivalent to "none are p"

   Answer: B.

   If we assume that the statement p is "students have books," then "not p" is "students do not have books." It is clear that statements (I) and (II) are equivalent to choice B.

(Rigorous) (Skill 3.1)

10. **Given that:**

    I. No athletes are weak

    II. All football players are athletes

    determine which conclusion can be logically deduced.

    A. Some football players are weak

    B. All football players are weak

    C. No football player is weak

    D. None of the above is true

    Answer: C.

    According to the law of syllogism, "if p then q and if q then r" implies "if p then r." We can rephrase the statements above to read:

    I. If a person is a football player, he or she is an athlete

    II. If a person is an athlete, he or she is not weak

    Then, using the law of syllogism, we can conclude: If a person is a football player, he or she is not weak. This statement is equivalent to the one in choice C.

(Rigorous) (Skill 3.2)

11. $\left(\frac{-4}{9}\right) + \left(\frac{-7}{10}\right) =$

    A. $\frac{23}{90}$

    B. $\frac{-23}{90}$

    C. $\frac{103}{90}$

    D. $\frac{-103}{90}$

    Answer: D.

    Find the LCD of $\frac{-4}{9}$ and $\frac{-7}{10}$. The LCD is 90, so you get $\frac{-40}{90} + \frac{-63}{90} = \frac{-103}{90}$.

(Average) (Skill 3.2)

12. $(5.6) \times (-0.11) =$

    A. -0.616

    B. 0.616

    C. -6.110

    D. 6.110

Answer: A. -0.616

This problem involves simple multiplication. The answer will be negative because a positive number times a negative number is a negative number. $5.6 \times -0.11 = -0.616$.

(Average) (Skill 3.2)

13. $\frac{7}{9} + \frac{1}{3} \div \frac{2}{3} =$

    A. $\frac{5}{3}$

    B. $\frac{3}{2}$

    C. 2

    D. $\frac{23}{18}$

Answer: D.

First, do the division.
$\frac{1}{3} \div \frac{2}{3} = \frac{1}{3} \times \frac{3}{2} = \frac{1}{2}$

Then add.
$\frac{7}{9} + \frac{1}{2} = \frac{14}{18} + \frac{9}{18} = \frac{23}{18}$.

(Rigorous) (Skill 3.2)

14. **Choose the statement that is true for all real numbers.**

    A. $a = 0, b \neq 0$, then $\frac{b}{a}$ = undefined

    B. $-(a + (-a)) = 2a$

    C. $2(ab) = -(2a)b$

    D. $-a(b + 1) = ab - a$

Answer: A.

A is the correct answer because any number divided by 0 is undefined.

(Rigorous) (Skill 3.4)

15. **The owner of a rectangular piece of land 40 yards in length and 30 yards in width wants to divide it into two parts. She plans to join two opposite corners with a fence as shown in the diagram below. The cost of the fence will be approximately $25 per linear foot. What is the estimated cost for the fence needed by the owner?**

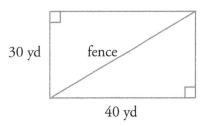

    A. $1,250

    B. $62,500

    C. $5,250

    D. $3,750

Answer: D.

Find the length of the diagonal by using the Pythagorean theorem. Let x be the length of the diagonal.

$30^2 + 40^2 = x^2 \rightarrow 900 + 1600 = x^2$
$2500 = x^2 \rightarrow \sqrt{2500} = \sqrt{x^2}$
$x = 50$ yards

Convert to feet:

$\frac{50 \text{ yards}}{x \text{ feet}} = \frac{1 \text{ yard}}{3 \text{ feet}} \rightarrow 1500$ feet

It cost $25 per linear foot, so the cost is $(1500 \text{ ft})(\$25) = \$3,750$.

(Easy) (Skill 3.4)

16. **What is the area of a square whose side is 13 feet?**

    A. 169 feet

    B. 169 square feet

    C. 52 feet

    D. 52 square feet

    Answer: B.

    Area = length times width (*lw*).
    Length = 13 feet.
    Width = 13 feet (in square, length and width are the same)
    Area = 13 × 13 = 169 square feet.
    Area is measured in square feet.

(Easy) (Skill 3.4)

17. **The trunk of a tree has a 2.1 meter radius. What is its circumference?**

    A. 2.1π square meters

    B. 4.2π meters

    C. 2.1π meters

    D. 4.2π square meters

    Answer: B.

    Circumference is 2π*r*, where r is the radius. The circumference is 2π2.1 = 4.2π meters (not square meters because we are not measuring area).

(Easy) (Skill 3.4)

18. **What is the area of this triangle?**

    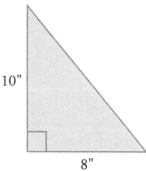

    A. 80 square inches

    B. 20 square inches

    C. 40 square inches

    D. 30 square inches

    Answer: C.

    The area of a triangle is $\frac{1}{2}bh$.
    $\frac{1}{2} \times 8 \times 10 = 40$ square inches.

(Average) (Skill 3.5)

19. **A car gets 25.36 miles per gallon. The car has been driven 83,310 miles. What is a reasonable estimate for the number of gallons of gas used?**

    A. 2,087 gallons

    B. 3,000 gallons

    C. 1,800 gallons

    D. 164 gallons

    Answer: B.

    Divide the number of miles by the miles per gallon to determine the approximate number of gallons of gas used. $\frac{83310 \text{ miles}}{25.36 \text{ miles per gallon}} = 3285$ gallons. This is approximately 3,000 gallons.

(Rigorous) (Skill 3.5)

20. If $4x - (3 - x) = 7(x - 3) + 10$, then:

    A. $x = 8$

    B. $x = -8$

    C. $x = 4$

    D. $x = -4$

    Answer: C.

    Solve for x.
    $4x - (3 - x) = 7(x - 3) + 10$
    $4x - 3 + x = 7x - 21 + 10$
    $5x - 3 = 7x - 11$
    $5x = 7x - 11 + 3$
    $5x - 7x = -8$
    $-2x = -8$
    $x = 4$

(Average) (Skill 3.5)

21. Given the formula $d = rt$, (where $d =$ distance, $r =$ rate, and $t =$ time), calculate the time required for a vehicle to travel 585 miles at a rate of 65 miles per hour.

    A. 8.5 hours

    B. 6.5 hours

    C. 9.5 hours

    D. 9 hours

    Answer: D.

    We are given $d = 585$ miles and $r = 65$ miles per hour and $d = rt$. Solve for t.
    $585 = 65t \rightarrow t = 9$ hours.

(Rigorous) (Skill 3.5)

22. $3x - \frac{2}{3} = \frac{5x}{2} + 2$ Solve for x.

    A. $5\frac{1}{3}$

    B. $\frac{17}{3}$

    C. 2

    D. $\frac{16}{2}$

    Answer: A.

    $3x(6) - \frac{2}{3}(6) = \frac{5x}{2}(6) + 2(6)$
    6 is the LCD of 2 and 3
    $18x - 4 = 15x + 12$
    $18x = 15x + 16$
    $3x = 16$
    $x = \frac{16}{3} = 5\frac{1}{3}$

(Average) (Skill 3.6)

23. An item that sells for $375 is put on sale at $120. What is the percent of decrease?

    A. 25%

    B. 28%

    C. 68%

    D. 34%

    Answer: C.

    Use $(1 - x)$ as the discount. $375x = 120$.
    $375(1 - x) = 120 \rightarrow 375 - 375x = 120 \rightarrow 375x = 255 \rightarrow x = 0.68 = 68\%$

(Rigorous) (Skill 3.6)

24. It takes five equally skilled people 9 hours to shingle Mr. Joe's roof. Let t be the time required for only 3 of these men to do the same job. Select the correct statement of the given condition.

A. $\frac{3}{5} = \frac{9}{t}$

B. $\frac{9}{5} = \frac{3}{t}$

C. $\frac{5}{9} = \frac{3}{t}$

D. $\frac{14}{9} = \frac{t}{5}$

Answer: B.

$$\frac{9 \text{ hours}}{5 \text{ people}} = \frac{3 \text{ people}}{t \text{ hours}}$$

(Rigorous) (Skill 3.6)

25. In a sample of 40 full-time employees at a particular company, 35 were also holding down a part-time job requiring at least 10 hours/week. If this proportion holds for the entire company of 25,000 employees, how many full-time employees at this company are actually holding down a part-time job of at least 10 hours per week.

A. 714

B. 625

C. 21,875

D. 28,571

Answer: C.

$\frac{35}{40}$ full time employees have a part time job also. Out of 25,000 full time employees, the number that also have a part time job is $\frac{35}{40} = \frac{x}{25000} \rightarrow 40x = 875000 \rightarrow x = 21875$, so 21,875 full time employees also have a part time job.

SAMPLE TEST

Historical and Social Scientific Awareness

(Average) (Skill 7.2)

1. The major force in eighteenth- and nineteenth-century politics was:

    A. Nationalism

    B. Revolution

    C. War

    D. Diplomacy

(Average) (Skill 7.2)

2. The end to hunting, gathering, and fishing of prehistoric people was due to:

    A. Domestication of animals

    B. Building crude huts and houses

    C. Development of agriculture

    D. Organized government in villages

(Rigorous) (Skill 7.2)

3. Which of these is NOT a true statement about Roman civilization?

    A. Its period of *Pax Romana* provided long periods of peace during which travel and trade increased, enabling the spread of culture, goods, and ideas over the known world

    B. It borrowed the concept of democracy from the Greeks and developed it into a complex representative government

    C. It flourished in the arts with realistic approach to art and a dramatic use of architecture

    D. It developed agricultural innovations such as crop rotation and terrace farming

(Rigorous) (Skill 7.2)

4. How did the ideology of John Locke influence Thomas Jefferson in writing the Declaration of Independence?

    A. Locke emphasized human rights and believed that people should rebel against governments who violated those rights

    B. Locke emphasized the rights of government to protect its people and to levy taxes

    C. Locke believed in the British system of monarchy and the rights of Parliament to make laws

    D. Locke advocated individual rights over the collective whole

(Rigorous) (Skill 7.4)

5. As a sociologist, you would be most likely to observe:

    A. The effects of an earthquake on farmland

    B. The behavior of rats in sensory-deprivation experiments

    C. The change over time in Babylonian obelisk styles

    D. The behavior of human beings in television focus groups

(Easy) (Skill 8.1)

6. The U.S. Constitution:

    A. Is an unwritten constitution

    B. Is a precise, formal, written document

    C. Does not allow states to be sovereign in their own affairs

    D. Can be amended on the vote of two-thirds of the states

(Rigorous) (Skill 8.1)

7. In 2002, then-president George W. Bush briefly transferred his presidential power to Vice President Dick Cheney for about an hour while undergoing a colonoscopy. Under what amendment was this covered?

   A. The Nineteenth Amendment

   B. The Twentieth Amendment

   C. The Twenty-second Amendment

   D. The Twenty-fifth Amendment

(Easy) (Skill 8.2)

8. Populism arises out of a feeling:

   A. Of intense happiness

   B. Of satisfaction with the activities of large corporations

   C. That women should not be allowed to vote

   D. Perceived oppression

(Easy) (Skill 8.5)

9. Economics is best described as:

   A. The study of how money is used in different societies

   B. The study of how different political systems produce goods and services

   C. The study of how human beings use limited resources to supply their necessities and wants

   D. The study of how human beings have developed trading practices through the years

(Average) (Skill 8.5)

10. Capitalism and Communism are alike in that they are both:

    A. Organic systems

    B. Political systems

    C. Centrally planned systems

    D. Economic systems

(Rigorous) (Skill 8.5)

11. Which of the following countries has historically operated in a market economy?

    A. Great Britain

    B. Cuba

    C. Yugoslavia

    D. India

(Rigorous) (Skill 8.5)

12. In the fictional country of Nacirema the government controls the means of production and directs resources. It alone decides what will be produced. As a result, there is an abundance of capital and military goods but a scarcity of consumer goods. What type of economy is this?

    A. Market economy

    B. Centrally planned economy

    C. Market socialism

    D. Capitalism

(Average) (Skill 9.2)

13. The international organization established to work for world peace at the end of the Second World War is the:

    A. League of Nations

    B. United Federation of Nations

    C. United Nations

    D. United World League

(Average) (Skill 9.2)

14. How did the labor force change after 1830?

    A. Employers began using children

    B. Employers began hiring immigrants

    C. Employers began hiring women

    D. Employers began hiring nonimmigrant men

(Rigorous) (Skill 9.2)

15. One of the political parties that developed in the early 1790s was led by:

    A. Thomas Jefferson

    B. George Washington

    C. Aaron Burr

    D. John Quincy Adams

(Rigorous) (Skill 9.2)

16. The post–Civil War years were a time of low public morality, and a time of greed, graft, and dishonesty. Which one of the reasons listed would not be accurate?

    A. The war itself, because of the money and materials needed to carry on the war

    B. The very rapid growth of industry and big business after the war

    C. The personal example set by President Grant

    D. Unscrupulous heads of large impersonal corporations

(Average) (Skill 10.4)

17. A political scientist might use all of the following EXCEPT:

    A. Investigation of government documents

    B. A geological timeline

    C. Voting patterns

    D. Polling data

(Rigorous) (Skill 10.4)

18. A geographer wishes to study the effects of a flood on subsequent settlement patterns. Which might he or she find most useful?

    A. A film clip of the floodwaters

    B. Aerial photograph of the river's source

    C. Census data taken after the flood

    D. A soil map of the A and B horizons beneath the flood area

(Average) (Skill 10.5)

19. For the historian studying ancient Egypt, which of the following would be least useful?

  A. The record of an ancient Greek historian on Greek–Egyptian interaction

  B. Letters from an Egyptian ruler to his/her regional governors

  C. Inscriptions on stele of the Fourteenth Egyptian Dynasty

  D. Letters from a nineteenth-century Egyptologist to his wife

(Rigorous) (Skill 11.2)

20. An economist investigates the spending patterns of low-income individuals. Which of the following would yield the most pertinent information?

  A. Prime lending rates of neighborhood banks

  B. The federal discount rate

  C. Citywide wholesale distribution figures

  D. Census data and retail sales figures

Answer Key

1. A	11. A
2. C	12. B
3. D	13. C
4. A	14. B
5. D	15. A
6. B	16. C
7. D	17. B
8. D	18. C
9. C	19. D
10. D	20. D

Rigor Table

RIGOR TABLE	
Rigor level	**Questions**
Easy 20%	6, 8, 9
Average 40%	1, 2, 10, 13, 14, 17, 19
Rigorous 40%	3, 4, 5, 7, 11, 12, 15, 16, 18, 20

Sample Test with Rationales: Historical and Social Scientific Awareness

(Average) (Skill 7.2)

1. **The major force in eighteenth- and nineteenth-century politics was:**

   A. Nationalism

   B. Revolution

   C. War

   D. Diplomacy

   Answer: A.

   Nationalism was the driving force in politics in the eighteenth and nineteenth century. Groups of people that shared common traits and characteristics wanted their own government and countries. This often led to revolution, war, and the failure of diplomacy.

(Average) (Skill 7.2)

2. **The end to hunting, gathering, and fishing of prehistoric people was due to:**

   A. Domestication of animals

   B. Building crude huts and houses

   C. Development of agriculture

   D. Organized government in villages

   Answer: C.

   Although the domestication of animals, the building of huts and houses, and the first organized governments were all very important steps made by early civilizations, it was the development of agriculture that ended the once dominant practices of hunting, gathering, and fishing among prehistoric people. The development of agriculture provided a more efficient use of time and for the first time a surplus of food. This greatly improved the quality of life and contributed to early population growth.

(Rigorous) (Skill 7.2)

3. **Which of these is NOT a true statement about Roman civilization?**

   A. Its period of *Pax Romana* provided long periods of peace during which travel and trade increased, enabling the spread of culture, goods, and ideas over the known world

   B. It borrowed the concept of democracy from the Greeks and developed it into a complex representative government

   C. It flourished in the arts with realistic approach to art and a dramatic use of architecture

   D. It developed agricultural innovations such as crop rotation and terrace farming

   Answer: D.

   China developed crop rotation and terrace farming.

(Rigorous) (Skill 7.2)

4. **How did the ideology of John Locke influence Thomas Jefferson in writing the Declaration of Independence?**

    A. Locke emphasized human rights and believed that people should rebel against governments who violated those rights

    B. Locke emphasized the rights of government to protect its people and to levy taxes

    C. Locke believed in the British system of monarchy and the rights of Parliament to make laws

    D. Locke advocated individual rights over the collective whole

Answer: A.

The Declaration of Independence is an outgrowth of both ancient Greek ideas of democracy and individual rights and the ideas of the European Enlightenment and the Renaissance, especially the ideology of the political thinker John Locke. Thomas Jefferson was the author of the Declaration and borrowed much from Locke's theories and writings. John Locke was one of the most influential political writers of the seventeenth century, and he put great emphasis on human rights and put forth the belief that when governments violate those rights people should rebel. He wrote the book *Two Treatises of Government* in 1690, which had tremendous influence on political thought in the American colonies and helped shape the U.S. Constitution and Declaration of Independence.

(Rigorous) (Skill 7.4)

5. **As a sociologist, you would be most likely to observe:**

    A. The effects of an earthquake on farmland

    B. The behavior of rats in sensory-deprivation experiments

    C. The change over time in Babylonian obelisk styles

    D. The behavior of human beings in television focus groups

Answer: D.

Predominant beliefs and attitudes within human society are studied in the field of sociology. The effects of an earthquake on farmland might be studied by a geographer. The behavior of rats in an experiment falls under the field of behavioral psychology. Changes in Babylonian obelisk styles might interest a historian. None of these answers fit easily within the definition of sociology. A focus group, where people are asked to discuss their reactions to a certain product or topic, would be the most likely method for a sociologist of observing and discovering attitudes among a selected group.

(Easy) (Skill 8.1)

6. **The U.S. Constitution:**

    A. Is an unwritten constitution

    B. Is a precise, formal, written document

    C. Does not allow states to be sovereign in their own affairs

    D. Can be amended on the vote of two-thirds of the states

Answer: B.

The U.S. Constitution is not an unwritten constitution. It is not true that the U.S. Constitution fails to allow states to be sovereign in their own affairs. It requires three-fourths of the states, not two-thirds, to amend the U.S. Constitution.

(Rigorous) (Skill 8.1)

7. **In 2002, then-president George W. Bush briefly transferred his presidential power to Vice President Dick Cheney for about an hour while undergoing a colonoscopy. Under what amendment was this covered?**

    A. The Nineteenth Amendment

    B. The Twentieth Amendment

    C. The Twenty-second Amendment

    D. The Twenty-fifth Amendment

Answer: D.

Presidential succession is the focus of the Twenty-fifth Amendment, which provides a blueprint of what to do if the president is incapacitated or killed. The long battle for voting rights for women ended in success with the passage of the Nineteenth Amendment. The date for the beginning of terms for the president and the Congress was changed from March to January by the Twentieth Amendment. The Twenty-second Amendment limited the number of terms that a president could serve to two.

(Easy) (Skill 8.2)

8. **Populism arises out of a feeling:**

    A. Of intense happiness

    B. Of satisfaction with the activities of large corporations

    C. That women should not be allowed to vote

    D. Perceived oppression

Answer: D.

Perceived oppression felt by average people toward the wealthy elite gave rise to Populism. Populists do not become prominent when people are happy, or when people are satisfied with the activities of large corporations. Populists and other progressives fought for, not against, voting rights for women.

(Easy) (Skill 8.5)

9. **Economics is best described as:**

    A. The study of how money is used in different societies

    B. The study of how different political systems produce goods and services

    C. The study of how human beings use limited resources to supply their necessities and wants

    D. The study of how human beings have developed trading practices through the years

Answer: C.

How money is used in different societies might be of interest to a sociologist or anthropologist. The study of how different political systems produce goods and services is a topic of study that could be included under the field of political science. The study of historical trading practices could fall under the study of history. Only is the best general description of the social science of economics as a whole.

(Average) (Skill 8.5)

10. **Capitalism and Communism are alike in that they are both:**

    A. Organic systems

    B. Political systems

    C. Centrally planned systems

    D. Economic systems

Answer: D.

While economic and political systems are often closely connected, capitalism and Communism are primarily economic systems. Capitalism is a system of economics that allows the open market to determine the relative value of goods and services. Communism is an economic system where the market is planned by a central state. Communism is a centrally planned system; this is not true of capitalism. Organic systems are studied in biology, a natural science.

(Rigorous) (Skill 8.5)

11. **Which of the following countries has historically operated in a market economy?**

    A. Great Britain

    B. Cuba

    C. Yugoslavia

    D. India

Answer: A.

A market economy is based on supply and demand and the use of markets. Although Great Britain may have socialized medicine, it operates a market economy. Cuba, with its ties to Communism, has a centrally planned economy. Historically, China has had a centrally planned economy but is now moving toward a market economy. Yugoslavia was a market socialist economy, but the country no longer exists—it has been split into Montenegro and Serbia.

(Rigorous) (Skill 8.5)

12. **In the fictional country of Nacirema the government controls the means of production and directs resources. It alone decides what will be produced. As a result, there is an abundance of capital and military goods but a scarcity of consumer goods. What type of economy is this?**

    A. Market economy

    B. Centrally planned economy

    C. Market socialism

    D. Capitalism

Answer: B.

In a planned economy, the means of production are publicly owned, with little, if any, private ownership. Instead of the "three questions" being solved by markets, there is a planning authority that makes the decisions. The planning authority decides what will be produced and how. Since most planned economies direct resources into the production of capital and military goods, there is little remaining for consumer goods; the result is often chronic shortages.

(Average) (Skill 9.2)

13. **The international organization established to work for world peace at the end of the Second World War is the:**

    A. League of Nations

    B. United Federation of Nations

    C. United Nations

    D. United World League

Answer: C.

The international organization established to work for world peace at the end of the Second World War was the United Nations. From the ashes of the failed League of Nations, established following the First World War, the United Nations continues to be a major player in world affairs today.

(Average) (Skill 9.2)

14. **How did the labor force change after 1830?**

    A. Employers began using children

    B. Employers began hiring immigrants

    C. Employers began hiring women

    D. Employers began hiring nonimmigrant men

Answer: B.

Employers began hiring immigrants who were arriving in large numbers. Children and women began entering the labor force prior to 1830. Employers had always used nonimmigrant men.

(Rigorous) (Skill 9.2)

15. **One of the political parties that developed in the early 1790s was led by:**

    A. Thomas Jefferson

    B. George Washington

    C. Aaron Burr

    D. John Quincy Adams

Answer: A.

George Washington warned against the creation of "factions." Aaron Burr is the man who killed Alexander Hamilton in a duel. John Quincy Adams was still a young man at that time.

(Rigorous) (Skill 9.2)

16. The post–Civil War years were a time of low public morality, and a time of greed, graft, and dishonesty. Which one of the reasons listed would not be accurate?

   A. The war itself, because of the money and materials needed to carry on the war

   B. The very rapid growth of industry and big business after the war

   C. The personal example set by President Grant

   D. Unscrupulous heads of large impersonal corporations

Answer: C.

The post–Civil War years were a particularly difficult time for the nation and public morale was especially low. The war had plunged the country into debt and ultimately into a recession by the 1890s. Racism was rampant throughout the South and the North where freed blacks were taking jobs for low wages. The rapid growth of industry and big business caused a polarization of rich and poor, workers and owners. Many people moved into the urban centers to find work in the new industrial sector, jobs were typically low-wage, long hours, and poor working conditions. The heads of large impersonal corporations were arrogant in treating their workers inhumanely and letting morale drop to a record low. The heads of corporations showed their greed and malice toward the workingman by trying to prevent and disband labor unions.

(Average) (Skill 10.4)

17. A political scientist might use all of the following EXCEPT:

   A. Investigation of government documents

   B. A geological timeline

   C. Voting patterns

   D. Polling data

Answer: B.

Political science is primarily concerned with the political and governmental activities of societies. Government documents can provide information about the organization and activities of a government. Voting patterns reveal the political behavior of individuals and groups. Polling data can provide insight into the predominant political views of a group of people. A geological timeline describes the changes in the physical features of the Earth over time and would not be useful to a political scientist.

(Rigorous) (Skill 10.4)

18. A geographer wishes to study the effects of a flood on subsequent settlement patterns. Which might he or she find most useful?

   A. A film clip of the floodwaters

   B. Aerial photograph of the river's source

   C. Census data taken after the flood

   D. A soil map of the A and B horizons beneath the flood area

Answer: C.

A film clip of the flood waters may be of most interest to a historian; an aerial photograph of the river's source, and soil maps tell little about the behavior of the individuals affected by the flood. Census surveys record the population for certain areas on a regular basis, allowing a geographer to tell if more or fewer people are living in an area over time. These would be of most use to a geographer undertaking this study.

(Average) (Skill 10.5)

19. **For the historian studying ancient Egypt, which of the following would be least useful?**

    A. The record of an ancient Greek historian on Greek–Egyptian interaction

    B. Letters from an Egyptian ruler to his/her regional governors

    C. Inscriptions on stele of the Fourteenth Egyptian Dynasty

    D. Letters from a nineteenth-century Egyptologist to his wife

Answer: D.

Historians use primary sources from the actual time they are studying whenever possible. Ancient Greek records of interaction with Egypt, letters from an Egyptian ruler to regional governors, and inscriptions from the Fourteenth Egyptian Dynasty are all primary sources created at or near the actual time being studied. Letters from a nineteenth century Egyptologist would not be considered primary sources, as they were created thousands of years after the fact and may not actually be about the subject being studied.

(Rigorous) (Skill 11.2)

20. **An economist investigates the spending patterns of low-income individuals. Which of the following would yield the most pertinent information?**

    A. Prime lending rates of neighborhood banks

    B. The federal discount rate

    C. Citywide wholesale distribution figures

    D. Census data and retail sales figures

Answer: D.

Local lending rates and the federal discount rate might provide information on borrowing habits, but not necessarily spending habits, and they give no information on income levels. Citywide wholesale distribution figures would provide information on the business activity of a city, but tell nothing about consumer activities. Census data records the income levels of households within a certain area and retail sales figures for that area would give an economist data on spending, which can be compared to income levels, making this the most pertinent source.

SAMPLE TEST

Artistic Expression and the Humanities

(Easy) (Skill 12.1)

1. The term for rhythm that is measured and divided into equal parts is:

    A. Harmony

    B. Consonance

    C. Meter

    D. Dissonance

(Easy) (Skill 12.1)

2. A series of single tones that add up to a recognizable pattern is called a:

    A. Cadence

    B. Rhythm

    C. Melody

    D. Sequence

(Average) (Skill 12.1)

3. Creating movements in response to music helps students to connect music and dance in which of the following ways?

    A. Rhythm

    B. Costuming

    C. Harmony

    D. Vocabulary skills

(Average) (Skill 12.3)

4. Universal themes are those that:

    A. Explain how the universe was created

    B. Explain the nature of the universe

    C. Can be experienced by all people

    D. Belong to specific groups of people

(Average) (Skill 13.1)

5. The history of theater is important to describe how theater has evolved over time. In which of the following theatrical traditions were the two main forms of theater, tragedy and comedy, developed?

    A. Roman drama

    B. Greek theater

    C. Medieval drama

    D. Renaissance theater

(Average) (Skill 13.1)

6. In the visual arts, the terms *fauvism* and *surrealism* relate to which of the following periods?

    A. Roman art

    B. Baroque art

    C. Ancient Greek art

    D. Twentieth-century art

(Average) (Skill 13.1)

7. In the Middle Ages, the overwhelming majority of the art created had to do with:

    A. Neoclassicism

    B. Individual expression

    C. Religious themes

    D. Social realism

(Average) (Skill 13.1)

8. **Impressionism in art and music was an attempt to:**

   A. Capture the transitory aspects of the world

   B. Impress the audience with a photo-graphic view of the world

   C. Express heart-felt emotions about nature

   D. Portray the common people in a heroic light

(Rigorous) (Skills 13.1, 13.3, and 15.6)

9. **Twentieth-century themes in art and literature are marked by:**

   A. Practicality and utilitarianism

   B. Idealized figures and exotic destinations

   C. Harmony and balance

   D. Diversity of views and individualism

(Average) (Skill 13.4)

10. **Renaissance artists and writers highly valued the forms and ideas of:**

    A. Ancient China and India

    B. Medieval France

    C. Northern Europe

    D. Classical Greece and Ancient Rome

(Rigorous) (Skill 15.3)

11. **A fiction reader's enjoyment of a work usually involves:**

    A. Disputing the author's claims

    B. Reading the author's biography

    C. Suspension of belief

    D. Attention to facts

(Easy) (Skill 15.3)

12. **The following type of writing is NOT a form of nonfiction:**

    A. Newspaper

    B. Diary

    C. Bildungsroman

    D. Biography

(Rigorous) (Skill 15.3)

13. **Some literature of the Renaissance period:**

    A. Could be vulgar and appealed to the masses

    B. Was created solely for use in monasteries

    C. Was based on linear perspective

    D. Was formal, quiet, and restrained

(Average) (Skill 16.1)

14. **In the religion of Hinduism, the three aspects of the universal spirit are:**

    A. Brahma, Vishnu, and Shiva

    B. Nirvana, Vishnu, and the Buddha

    C. Veda, Ramayana, and the Buddha

    D. Rig-Veda, Rama, and Shiva

(Average) (Skill 16.1)

15. **Buddhism emphasizes:**

    A. Preoccupation with the supernatural

    B. Strict adherence to the caste system

    C. Ancestor worship

    D. Spiritual peace through righteous living

(Easy) (Skill 16.1)

16. **Judaism was the first of the world's great religions to:**

    A. Emphasize belief in an afterlife

    B. Evolve from folk traditions

    C. Practice belief in one God

    D. Promote worship of many deities

(Rigorous) (Skill 16.1)

17. **The schism within the Christian religion resulted in the creation of the following parts:**

    A. Saints and sinners

    B. The Roman Catholic Church and the Orthodox Church

    C. Protestants and Jesuits

    D. The Roman Catholic Church and the Irish Catholic Church

(Average) (Skill 16.1)

18. **The philosophy best associated with Lao-tse is:**

    A. Government should be a strong force in society

    B. Mankind should live in fear of the gods

    C. Mankind should live in harmony with nature

    D. Mankind should strive toward intellectual perfection

(Easy) (Skills 16.1 and 16.3)

19. **The world religion associated with the caste system is:**

    A. Buddhism

    B. Hinduism

    C. Sikhism

    D. Jainism

Answer Key

1. C	11. C
2. C	12. C
3. A	13. A
4. C	14. A
5. B	15. D
6. D	16. C
7. C	17. B
8. A	18. C
9. D	19. B
10. D	

Rigor Table

RIGOR TABLE	
Rigor level	**Questions**
Easy 20%	1, 2, 12, 16, 19
Average 40%	3, 4, 5, 6, 7, 8, 10, 14, 15, 18
Rigorous 40%	9, 11, 13, 17

Sample Test with Rationales: Artistic Expression and the Humanities

(Easy) (Skill 12.1)

1. The term for rhythm that is measured and divided into equal parts is:

   A. Harmony

   B. Consonance

   C. Meter

   D. Dissonance

Answer: C.

When rhythm is measured and divided into parts of equal time value, it is called meter.

(Easy) (Skill 12.1)

2. A series of single tones that add up to a recognizable pattern is called a:

   A. Cadence

   B. Rhythm

   C. Melody

   D. Sequence

Answer: C.

The melody of a musical piece refers to the pattern of single tones in a composition that does more than simply reinforce rhythm or provide harmony. The melody of a musical piece is often considered the "horizontal" aspect of the piece that flows from start to finish.

(Average) (Skill 12.1)

3. Creating movements in response to music helps students to connect music and dance in which of the following ways?

   A. Rhythm

   B. Costuming

   C. Harmony

   D. Vocabulary skills

Answer: A.

Rhythm refers to the pattern of regular or irregular pulses in music that result from the melodic beats of the music. Simple techniques to teach and practice rhythm include clapping hands and tapping feet to the beat of the music. Teachers can also incorporate the use of percussion instruments to examine rhythmic patterns, which also increases students' awareness of rhythm.

(Average) (Skill 12.3)

4. Universal themes are those that:

   A. Explain how the universe was created

   B. Explain the nature of the universe

   C. Can be experienced by all people

   D. Belong to specific groups of people

Answer: C.

Universal themes are themes that reflect the human experience regardless of time period, location, social standing, economic considerations, or religious or cultural beliefs.

5. The history of theater is important to describe how theater has evolved over time. In which of the following theatrical traditions were the two main forms of theater, tragedy and comedy, developed?

   A. Roman drama

   B. Greek theater

   C. Medieval drama

   D. Renaissance theater

Answer: B.

The history of theater can be dated back to early sixth century in Greece. From the Greek dramatic tradition the two main forms of drama developed: tragedy typically involved conflict between characters, and comedy involved paradoxical relationships between humans and the gods.

6. In the visual arts, the terms *fauvism* and *surrealism* relate to which of the following periods?

   A. Roman art

   B. Baroque art

   C. Ancient Greek art

   D. Twentieth-century art

Answer: D.

Major artistic movements of the twentieth century include symbolism, art nouveau, fauvism, expressionism, cubism (both analytical and synthetic), futurism, nonobjective art, abstract art, surrealism, social realism, constructivism, pop and op art, and conceptual art.

7. In the Middle Ages, the overwhelming majority of the art created had to do with:

   A. Neoclassicism

   B. Individual expression

   C. Religious themes

   D. Social realism

Answer: C.

Although the time span is expansive, the major themes remain relatively constant. Since the Roman Catholic Church was the primary patron of the arts, most work was religious in nature. Specific themes varied from the illustration of Bible stories to interpretations of theological allegory, to lives of the saints, and to consequences of good and evil.

8. Impressionism in art and music was an attempt to:

   A. Capture the transitory aspects of the world

   B. Impress the audience with a photographic view of the world

   C. Express heart-felt emotions about nature

   D. Portray the common people in a heroic light

Answer: A.

The themes behind Impressionism were the constant flux of the universe and the immediacy of the moment.

(Rigorous) (Skills 13.1, 13.3, and 15.6)

9. **Twentieth-century themes in art and literature are marked by:**

    A. Practicality and utilitarianism

    B. Idealized figures and exotic destinations

    C. Harmony and balance

    D. Diversity of views and individualism

Answer: D.

Artists and writers explored expression of a multitude of themes through a wide variety of forms. There were so many disparate artistic movements in the twentieth century—the audience for art became increasingly diverse, and artists felt liberated.

(Average) (Skill 13.4)

10. **Renaissance artists and writers highly valued the forms and ideas of:**

    A. Ancient China and India

    B. Medieval France

    C. Northern Europe

    D. Classical Greece and Ancient Rome

Answer: D.

The Renaissance period was concerned with the rediscovery of the works of classical Greece and Rome. The art, literature, and architecture were inspired by classical orders, which tended to be formal, simple, and concerned with the ideal human proportions.

(Rigorous) (Skill 15.3)

11. **A fiction reader's enjoyment of a work usually involves:**

    A. Disputing the author's claims

    B. Reading the author's biography

    C. Suspension of belief

    D. Attention to facts

Answer: C.

Enjoying fiction depends upon the ability of readers to suspend disbelief. Readers make a deal with writers that for the time it takes to read the story, their own belief will be put aside and be replaced by the convictions and reality that the writer has presented in the story. This is not true in nonfiction.

(Easy) (Skill 15.3)

12. **The following type of writing is NOT a form of nonfiction:**

    A. Newspaper

    B. Diary

    C. Bildungsroman

    D. Biography

Answer: C.

A bildungsroman (from the German meaning "novel of formation") is a novel that traces the spiritual, moral, psychological, or social development and growth of the main character from childhood to maturity.

(Rigorous) (Skill 15.3)

13. **Some literature of the Renaissance period:**

    A. Could be vulgar and appealed to the masses

    B. Was created solely for use in monasteries

    C. Was based on linear perspective

    D. Was formal, quiet, and restrained

    Answer: A.

    The Renaissance saw the introduction of the inexpensive chapbooks, which were condensed versions of mythology and fairy tales. Designed for the common people, chapbooks could be vulgar and grammatically imperfect, but were immensely popular because of their adventurous contents.

(Average) (Skill 16.1)

14. **In the religion of Hinduism, the three aspects of the universal spirit are:**

    A. Brahma, Vishnu, and Shiva

    B. Nirvana, Vishnu, and the Buddha

    C. Veda, Ramayana, and the Buddha

    D. Rig-Veda, Rama, and Shiva

    Answer: A.

    In Hinduism, the universal soul assumes the three forms of Brahma (the creator), Vishnu (the preserver), and Shiva (the destroyer).

(Average) (Skill 16.1)

15. **Buddhism emphasizes:**

    A. Preoccupation with the supernatural

    B. Strict adherence to the caste system

    C. Ancestor worship

    D. Spiritual peace through righteous living

    Answer: D.

    Buddhists follow the "eightfold path" toward spiritual living. Nirvana (spiritual peace), may be reached even in one lifetime by righteous living. Buddhism opposes the worship of numerous deities, the Hindu caste system, and preoccupation with the supernatural.

(Easy) (Skill 16.1)

16. **Judaism was the first of the world's great religions to:**

    A. Emphasize belief in an afterlife

    B. Evolve from folk traditions

    C. Practice belief in one God

    D. Promote worship of many deities

    Answer: C.

    Judaism is the oldest of the eight great world religions and it was the first to teach and practice the belief in one God.

(Rigorous) (Skill 16.1)

17. **The schism within the Christian religion resulted in the creation of the following parts:**

    A. Saints and sinners

    B. The Roman Catholic Church and the Orthodox Church

    C. Protestants and Jesuits

    D. The Roman Catholic Church and the Irish Catholic Church

    Answer: B.

    A schism resulted in the Western (Roman Catholic) and Eastern (Orthodox) parts.

(Average) (Skill 16.1)

18. **The philosophy best associated with Lao-tse is:**

    A. Government should be a strong force in society

    B. Mankind should live in fear of the gods

    C. Mankind should live in harmony with nature

    D. Mankind should strive toward intellectual perfection

    Answer: C.

    Philosopher Lao-tse taught that because laws cannot improve man's lot, government should be a minimal force in man's life. Man should live passively in harmony with Tao (nature).

(Easy) (Skills 16.1 and 16.3)

19. **The world religion associated with the caste system is:**

    A. Buddhism

    B. Hinduism

    C. Sikhism

    D. Jainism

    Answer: B.

    Though forbidden today by law, a prominent feature of Hinduism in the past was a rigid adherence to, and practice of, the infamous caste system. The caste system, which is incredibly complicated and nuanced, prevailed as the social system of India until modern times. In 1000 BCE four principal castes existed: priests and scholars, rulers and warriors, artisans and merchants, and unskilled workers.

SAMPLE TEST

Written Analysis and Expression

DIRECTIONS: The passage below contains several errors. Read the passage. Then answer each test item by choosing the option that corrects an error in the underlined portion(s). No more than one underlined error will appear in each item. If no error exists, choose "No change is necessary."

Every job places different kinds of demands on their employees. For example, whereas such jobs as accounting and bookkeeping require mathematical ability; graphic design requires creative/artistic ability.

Doing good at one job does not usually guarantee success at another. However, one of the elements crucial to all jobs are especially notable: the chance to accomplish a goal.

The accomplishment of the employees varies according to the job. In many jobs the employees become accustom to the accomplishment provided by the work they do every day.

In medicine, for example, every doctor tests him self by treating badly injured or critically ill people. In the operating room, a team of Surgeons is responsible for operating on many of these patients. In addition to the feeling of accomplishment that the workers achieve, some jobs also give a sense of identity to the employees'. Professions like law, education, and sales offer huge financial and emotional rewards. Politicians are public servants: who work for the federal and state governments.

President Obama is basically employed by the American people to make laws and run the country.

Finally; the contributions that employees make to their companies and to the world cannot be taken for granted. Through their work, employees are performing a service for their employers and are contributing something to the world.

(Rigorous) (Competency 22)

1. Every job <u>places</u> different kinds of demands on <u>their</u> <u>employees</u>.

   A. place

   B. its

   C. employes

   D. No change is necessary

(Average) (Competency 22)

2. <u>For example,</u> <u>whereas</u> such jobs as accounting and bookkeeping require mathematical <u>ability;</u> graphic design requires creative/artistic ability.

   A. For example

   B. whereas,

   C. ability,

   D. No change is necessary

(Rigorous) (Competency 22)

3. Doing <u>good</u> at one job does not <u>usually</u> guarantee <u>success</u> at another.

   A. well

   B. usualy

   C. succeeding

   D. No change is necessary

(Average) (Competency 22)

4. <u>However,</u> one of the elements crucial to all jobs <u>are</u> especially <u>notable:</u> the accomplishment of a goal.

   A. However

   B. is

   C. notable;

   D. No change is necessary

(Rigorous) (Competency 22)

5. The <u>accomplishment</u> of the <u>employees</u> <u>varies</u> according to the job.

   A. accomplishment,

   B. employee's

   C. vary

   D. No change is necessary

(Average) (Competency 22)

6. In many jobs the employees <u>become</u> <u>accustom</u> to the accomplishment <u>pro-</u> <u>vided</u> by the work they do every day.

   A. became

   B. accustomed

   C. provides

   D. No change is necessary

(Average) (Competency 22)

7. In addition to the feeling of accomplish-ment that the workers <u>achieve</u>, some jobs also <u>give</u> a sense of self-identity to the <u>employees'</u>.

   A. acheive

   B. gave

   C. employees

   D. No change is necessary

(Easy) (Competency 22)

8. Politicians <u>are</u> public <u>servants: who</u> <u>work</u> for the federal and state governments.

   A. were

   B. servants who

   C. worked

   D. No change is necessary

Read the following passage and answer questions 9 to 17.

One of the most difficult problems plagu-ing American education is the assessment of teachers. No one denies that teachers ought to be answerable for what they do, but what exactly does that mean? The *Oxford American Dictionary* defines accountability as: the obligation to give a reckoning or explanation for one's actions.

Does a student have to learn for teaching to have taken place? Historically, teaching has not been defined in this restrictive manner; the teacher was thought to be responsible for the quantity and quality of material covered and the way in which it was presented. However, some definitions of teaching now imply that students must learn in order for teaching to have taken place.

As a teacher who tries my best to keep current on all the latest teaching strategies, I believe that those teachers who do not bother even to pick up an educational journal every once in a while should be kept under close watch. There are many teachers out there who have been teaching for decades and refuse to change their ways even if research has proven that their methods are outdated and ineffective. There is no place in the profession of teaching for these types of individuals. It is time that the American educational system clean house, for the sake of our children.

(Rigorous) (Competency 22)

9. **What is the organizational pattern of the second paragraph?**

   A. Cause and effect

   B. Classification

   C. Addition

   D. Explanation

(Average) (Competency 22)

10. **What is the main idea of the passage?**

    A. Teachers should not be answerable for what they do

    B. Teachers who do not do their job should be fired

    C. The author is a good teacher

    D. Assessment of teachers is a serious problem in society today

(Rigorous) (Competency 22)

11. **From the passage, one can infer that:**

    A. The author considers herself a good teacher

    B. Poor teachers will be fired

    C. Students have to learn for teaching to take place

    D. The author will be fired

(Average) (Competency 22)

12. **Teachers who do not keep current on educational trends should be fired. Is this a fact or an opinion?**

    A. Fact

    B. Opinion

(Average) (Competency 22)

13. **What is the author's purpose in writing this?**

    A. To entertain

    B. To narrate

    C. To describe

    D. To persuade

(Rigorous) (Competency 22)

14. **Is there evidence of bias in this passage?**

    A. Yes

    B. No

(Average) (Competency 22)

15. **The author's tone is one of:**

    A. Disbelief

    B. Excitement

    C. Support

    D. Concern

(Easy) (Competency 22)

16. **What is meant by the word "plaguing" in the first sentence?**

    A. Causing problems

    B. Causing illness

    C. Causing anger

    D. Causing failure

(Easy) (Competency 22)

17. **Where does the author get her definition of "accountability?"**

    A. *Webster's Dictionary*

    B. *Encyclopedia Brittanica*

    C. *Oxford American Dictionary*

    D. *World Book Encyclopedia*

(Rigorous) (Competency 22)

18. A figure of speech in which someone absent or something inhuman is addressed as though present and able to respond describes:

    A. Personification

    B. Synechdoche

    C. Metonymy

    D. Apostrophe

(Average) (Competency 22)

19. A sixth-grade science teacher has given her class a paper to read on the relationship between food and weight gain. The writing contains signal words such as "because," "consequently," "this is how," and "due to." This paper has which text structure?

    A. Cause and effect

    B. Compare and contrast

    C. Description

    D. Sequencing

(Average) (Competency 22)

20. Which of the following is not a figure of speech (figurative language)?

    A. Simile

    B. Euphemism

    C. Onomatopoeia

    D. Allusion

Answer Key

1. B	11. A
2. C	12. B
3. A	13. D
4. B	14. A
5. C	15. D
6. B	16. A
7. C	17. C
8. B	18. A
9. D	19. A
10. D	20. D

Rigor Table

RIGOR TABLE	
Rigor level	**Questions**
Easy 20%	8, 16, 17
Average 40%	2, 4, 6, 7, 10, 12, 13, 15, 19, 20
Rigorous 40%	1, 3, 5, 9, 11, 14, 18

Sample Test with Rationales: Written Analysis and Expression

DIRECTIONS: The passage below contains several errors. Read the passage. Then answer each test item by choosing the option that corrects an error in the underlined portion(s). No more than one underlined error will appear in each item. If no error exists, choose "No change is necessary."

Every job places different kinds of demands on their employees. For example, whereas such jobs as accounting and bookkeeping require mathematical ability; graphic design requires creative/artistic ability.

Doing good at one job does not usually guarantee success at another. However, one of the elements crucial to all jobs are especially notable: the chance to accomplish a goal.

The accomplishment of the employees varies according to the job. In many jobs the employees become accustom to the accomplishment provided by the work they do every day.

In medicine, for example, every doctor tests him self by treating badly injured or critically ill people. In the operating room, a team of Surgeons is responsible for operating on many of these patients. In addition to the feeling of accomplishment that the workers achieve, some jobs also give a sense of identity to the employees'. Professions like law, education, and sales offer huge financial and emotional rewards. Politicians are public servants: who work for the federal and state governments. President Obama is basically employed by the American people to make laws and run the country.

Finally; the contributions that employees make to their companies and to the world cannot be taken for granted. Through their work, employees are performing a service for their employers and are contributing something to the world.

(Rigorous) (Competency 22)

1. Every job <u>places</u> different kinds of demands on <u>their</u> <u>employees</u>.

   A. place

   B. its

   C. employes

   D. No change is necessary

   Answer: B.

   The singular possessive pronoun *its* must agree with its antecedent *job*, which is singular also. Option A is incorrect because *place* is a plural form and the subject, *job*, is singular. Option C is incorrect because the correct spelling of *employees* is given in the sentence.

(Average) (Competency 22)

2. <u>For example,</u> <u>whereas</u> such jobs as accounting and bookkeeping require mathematical <u>ability;</u> graphic design requires creative/artistic ability.

   A. For example

   B. whereas,

   C. ability,

   D. No change is necessary

Answer: C.

An introductory dependent clause is set off with a comma, not a semicolon. Option A is incorrect because the transitional phrase *for example* should be set off with a comma. Option B is incorrect because the adverb *whereas* functions like *while* and does not take a comma after it.

(Rigorous) (Competency 22)

3. Doing <u>good</u> at one job does not <u>usually</u> guarantee <u>success</u> at another.

    A. well

    B. usualy

    C. succeeding

    D. No change is necessary

Answer: A.

The adverb *well* modifies the word *doing*. Option B is incorrect because *usually* is spelled correctly in the sentence. Option C is incorrect because *succeeding* is in the wrong tense.

(Average) (Competency 22)

4. <u>However,</u> one of the elements crucial to all jobs <u>are</u> especially <u>notable:</u> the accomplishment of a goal.

    A. However

    B. is

    C. notable;

    D. No change is necessary

Answer: B.

The singular verb is is needed to agree with the singular subject *one*. Option A is incorrect because a comma is needed to set off the transitional word *however*. Option C is incorrect because a colon, not a semicolon, is needed to set off an item.

(Rigorous) (Competency 22)

5. The <u>accomplishment</u> of the <u>employees</u> <u>varies</u> according to the job.

    A. accomplishment,

    B. employee's

    C. vary

    D. No change is necessary

Answer: C.

The singular verb *vary* is needed to agree with the singular subject *accomplishment*. Option A is incorrect because a comma after *accomplishment* would suggest that the modifying phrase *of the employees* is additional instead of essential. Option B is incorrect because *employees* is not possessive.

(Average) (Competency 22)

6. In many jobs the employees <u>become</u> <u>accustom</u> to the accomplishment <u>provided</u> by the work they do every day.

    A. became

    B. accustomed

    C. provides

    D. No change is necessary

Answer: B.

The past participle *accustomed* is needed with the verb *become*. Option A is incorrect because the verb tense does not need to change to the past *became*. Option C is incorrect because *provides* is the wrong tense.

(Average) (Competency 22)

7. In addition to the feeling of accomplishment that the workers <u>achieve</u>, some jobs also <u>give</u> a sense of self-identity to the <u>employees'</u>.

   A. acheive

   B. gave

   C. employees

   D. No change is necessary

Answer: C.

Option C is correct because *employees* is not possessive. Option A is incorrect because *achieve* is spelled correctly in the sentence. Option B is incorrect because *gave* is the wrong tense.

(Easy) (Competency 22)

8. Politicians <u>are</u> public <u>servants: who work</u> for the federal and state governments.

   A. were

   B. servants who

   C. worked

   D. No change is necessary

Answer: B.

A colon is not needed to set off the introduction of the sentence. In Option A, *were*, is the incorrect tense of the verb. In Option C, *worked*, is in the wrong tense.

Read the following passage and answer questions 9 to 17.

One of the most difficult problems plaguing American education is the assessment of teachers. No one denies that teachers ought to be answerable for what they do, but what exactly does that mean? The *Oxford American Dictionary* defines accountability as: the obligation to give a reckoning or explanation for one's actions.

Does a student have to learn for teaching to have taken place? Historically, teaching has not been defined in this restrictive manner; the teacher was thought to be responsible for the quantity and quality of material covered and the way in which it was presented. However, some definitions of teaching now imply that students must learn in order for teaching to have taken place.

As a teacher who tries my best to keep current on all the latest teaching strategies, I believe that those teachers who do not bother even to pick up an educational journal every once in a while should be kept under close watch. There are many teachers out there who have been teaching for decades and refuse to change their ways even if research has proven that their methods are outdated and ineffective. There is no place in the profession of teaching for these types of individuals. It is time that the American educational system clean house, for the sake of our children.

(Rigorous) (Competency 22)

9. What is the organizational pattern of the second paragraph?

   A. Cause and effect

   B. Classification

   C. Addition

   D. Explanation

Answer: D.

The meaning of this word is directly stated in the same sentence.

(Average) (Competency 22)

10. **What is the main idea of the passage?**

    A. Teachers should not be answerable for what they do

    B. Teachers who do not do their job should be fired

    C. The author is a good teacher

    D. Assessment of teachers is a serious problem in society today

Answer: D.

Most of the passage is dedicated to elaborating on why teacher assessment is such a problem.

(Rigorous) (Competency 22)

11. **From the passage, one can infer that:**

    A. The author considers herself a good teacher

    B. Poor teachers will be fired

    C. Students have to learn for teaching to take place

    D. The author will be fired

Answer: A.

The first sentence of the third paragraph alludes to this.

(Average) (Competency 22)

12. **Teachers who do not keep current on educational trends should be fired. Is this a fact or an opinion?**

    A. Fact

    B. Opinion

Answer: B.

There may be those who feel they can be good teachers by using old methods.

(Average) (Competency 22)

13. **What is the author's purpose in writing this?**

    A. To entertain

    B. To narrate

    C. To describe

    D. To persuade

Answer: D.

The author does some describing, but the majority of her statements seemed geared toward convincing the reader that teachers who are lazy or who do not keep current should be fired.

(Rigorous) (Competency 22)

14. **Is there evidence of bias in this passage?**

    A. Yes

    B. No

Answer: A.

The entire third paragraph is the author's opinion on the matter.

(Average) (Competency 22)

15. **The author's tone is one of:**

    A. Disbelief

    B. Excitement

    C. Support

    D. Concern

Answer: D.

The author appears concerned with the future of education.

(Easy) (Competency 22)

16. **What is meant by the word "plaguing" in the first sentence?**

    A. Causing problems

    B. Causing illness

    C. Causing anger

    D. Causing failure

Answer: A.

The first paragraph makes this definition clear.

(Easy) (Competency 22)

17. **Where does the author get her definition of "accountability?"**

    A. *Webster's Dictionary*

    B. *Encyclopedia Brittanica*

    C. *Oxford American Dictionary*

    D. *World Book Encyclopedia*

Answer: C.

This is directly stated in the third sentence of the first paragraph.

(Rigorous) (Competency 22)

18. **A figure of speech in which someone absent or something inhuman is addressed as though present and able to respond describes:**

    A. Personification

    B. Synechdoche

    C. Metonymy

    D. Apostrophe

Answer: A.

Personification gives human reactions and thoughts to animals, things, and abstract ideas alike. This figure of speech is often present in allegory: for instance, the Giant Despair in John Bunyon's *Pilgrim's Progress*. Also, fables use personification to make animals able to speak.

(Average) (Competency 22)

19. **A sixth-grade science teacher has given her class a paper to read on the relationship between food and weight gain. The writing contains signal words such as "because," "consequently," "this is how," and "due to." This paper has which text structure?**

    A. Cause and effect

    B. Compare and contrast

    C. Description

    D. Sequencing

Answer: A.

Cause and effect is the relationship between two things when one thing makes something else happen. Writers use this text structure to show order, inform, speculate, and change behavior. This text structure uses the process of identifying potential causes of a problem or issue in an orderly way. It is often used to teach social studies and science concepts. It is characterized by signal words such as because, so, so that, if… then, consequently, thus, since, for, for this reason, as a result of, therefore, due to, this is how, nevertheless, and accordingly.

(Average) (Competency 22)

20. **Which of the following is not a figure of speech (figurative language)?**

    A. Simile

    B. Euphemism

    C. Onomatopoeia

    D. Allusion

Answer: D.

Allusion is an implied reference to a person, event, thing, or a part of another text. A simile is an indirect comparison between two things. Euphemism is the substitution of an agreeable or inoffensive term for one that might offend. Onomatopoeia is a word that vocally imitates the meaning it denotes, some sound.

Teaching in another state? XAMonline carries 14 other state-specific series including the MTEL, MTTC and ICTS. Also check out our 30+ Praxis titles!

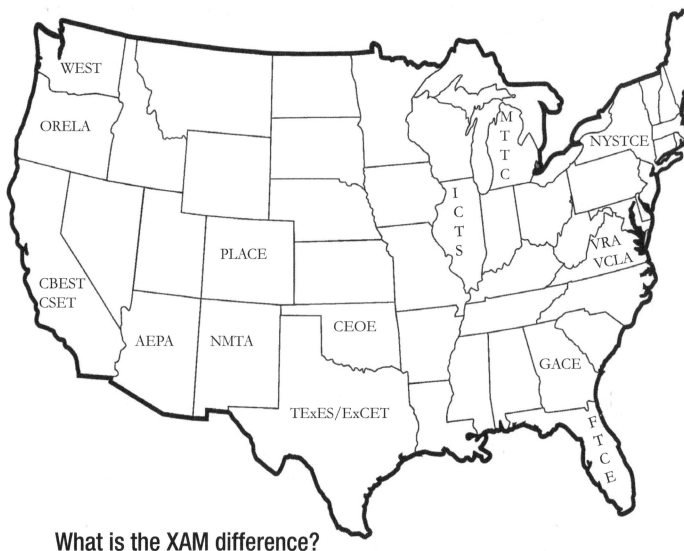

What is the XAM difference?

- State-aligned, current and comprehensive content
- Reviews all required competencies and skills
- Practice test questions aligned to actual test in both number and rigor level
- Questions include full answer rationale and skill reference for easy, efficient study
- Additional resources available online: diagnostic tests, flashcards, timed and scored practice tests and study/test tips

CPSIA information can be obtained at www.ICGtesting.com
Printed in the USA
LVOW02s1728160713

343162LV00005B/251/P

9 781607 871552